TEXTUALITY AND KNOWLEDGE

TEXTUALITY AND KNOWLEDGE

ESSAYS

PETER L. SHILLINGSBURG

THE PENNSYLVANIA STATE UNIVERSITY PRESS | UNIVERSITY PARK, PENNSYLVANIA

Essay 2 first appeared as "Textual Criticism, the Humanities, and J. M. Coetzee," *English Studies in Africa* 49, no. 2 (2006).

Essay 8 includes materials first published in Willard McCarty, ed., *Text and Genre in Reconstruction: Effects of Digitalization on Ideas, Behaviours, Products and Institutions* (Cambridge: OpenBook, 2010), doi:10.11647/OBP.0008. Essay 9 includes material first published in "How Literary Works Exist: Convenient Scholarly Editions," *Digital Humanities Quarterly* 2, no. 2 (2009).

Grateful acknowledgment is made to The Society of Authors as the Literary Representative of the Estate of Virginia Woolf for permission to photo-quote from Woolf's original documents.

Library of Congress Cataloging-in-Publication Data

Names: Shillingsburg, Peter L., author.
Title: Textuality and knowledge : essays / Peter L. Shillingsburg.
Other titles: Penn State series in the history of the book.
Description: University Park, Pennsylvania : The Pennsylvania State University Press, [2017] | Series: The Penn State series in the history of the book | Includes bibliographical references and index.
Summary: "A collection of essays exploring the role of textual studies in understanding and editing texts, and in understanding the historical developments and cultural differences in editorial and archival systems"—Provided by publisher.
Identifiers: LCCN 2017000666 | ISBN 9780271078502 (cloth : alk. paper)
Subjects: LCSH: Criticism, Textual. | Editing.
Classification: LCC P47 .S35 2017 | DDC 801/.959—dc23
LC record available at https://lccn.loc.gov/2017000666

CONTENTS

Sound evidence undergirds knowledge; unsound evidence cannot lead to or support knowledge—except by accident. That maxim distinguishes knowledge from speculation, belief, hope, superstition, and demonstrable falsehood. In literary studies, all evidence is textual. It depends on documents, document preservation, and textual replication. Interpretive strategies are for understanding the evidence. Of any proposition in literary history, one asks first, "How do you know?" "What is the evidence?" Once evidence is produced, the first question to ask is "Where did that come from?" Only when one knows what one is examining does it make sense to explore the associated questions about contexts of writing and publication, effects on readers, and probable or plausible intentions for the purposes, meanings, or significance of texts.

To address these questions, one needs not only original documents but a discipline for understanding them. That discipline is textual criticism. Textual criticism investigates what passes for knowledge of the past and what passes for sound interpretive opinions about the past. Textual criticism is fundamental to literary criticism and literary history. Together, these fields mark the boundaries of book history, including investigations of manuscripts and digital materials, which together constitute the history of documents and texts and of the means of their production, dissemination, consumption, and preservation.

As I suggest in the essay on the novelist J. M. Coetzee, later in this volume: "Textual criticism, focusing on the material, semiotic, communicative, and provocative elements of text, provides a fundamental act of self-examination and cannot be skipped over in studia humanitatis. Texts are the material and substance that condition all knowledge and all beliefs. The critical investigation of texts as text, operating in a textual condition and thus affecting human interaction, is the fundamental studia humanitatis."

Lest one think that the discipline of textual criticism and a burning interest in ferreting out and verifying sources can solve the riddle of the connection between textuality and knowledge, it should be noted that no one ever read the original of any literary work; one can only read a copy—manuscript, proof, or print—each is a copy or a copy of a copy. None, not even the first copy, is the original. We work at an unbridgeable distance from the object of our attention. Is it a book? Is it a text? Is it a work? What are the consequences of that gap? Does it give us freedom to think and say anything we want? Or, does it impose a responsibility to be met thoughtfully?

The Plan

The essays in this collection are about the relationship between textuality and knowledge. Though written over a period of time for a variety of venues, they all contribute to that central idea. Textual awareness, or lack thereof, affects teaching, reading, and research. The first essay lays out the general functions of textual criticism for nonspecialist students and critics, emphasizing the interpretive consequences of textual variation and the value of textual awareness. The second essay explores further the role of textual criticism in the history of humanistic study, demonstrating the interpretive consequences of major revisions in a sample work (J. M. Coetzee's *Elizabeth Costello*). Essay 3 takes up a contentious debate of the last quarter century in textual studies: the meaning of the bibliographical condition (the physicality) of literary texts. Although this essay argues the issues technically and explores what some might consider scholarly internecine warfare, its primary point is that students and literary critics are affected both overtly and subliminally by the physicality of texts. The next essay exposes the role of editors in shaping the works that readers encounter. Readers are at the mercy of editors, who frequently intervene to disambiguate and to correct apparent errors, often enough without due regard to the original text's potential. Essay 5 consists of two case studies demonstrating the ambiguities and uncertainties that prevent editors from knowing exactly what to do, showing that knowledge of a text's genesis often reveals nuances and richness not available from the well-edited single text presented as a finished product. The sixth essay follows from the case study, developing the idea that literary texts, at some level, are communicative, and that editors (and indeed readers, generally) frequently rely on their sense of coherence in language use to detect errors and substitute corrections that provide a more satisfying communicative experience. That fact reveals as much as anything the distinction between the book (material document) and the work (the verbal, conceptual art). Essay 7 examines the capacity of texts to be communicative by exploring the old conundrum of authorial intentions, adding the intentions of editors, publishers, and readers to the mix. Having explored a number of areas of difficulty, uncertainty, and the impossibility of correctness, the next essay attempts to define and describe the ways in which literary works exist, developing earlier notions of the work as a conceptual entity, as material objects, and as experienced events. Each aspect of textual existence has editorial consequences and, hence, reader consequences. And yet, editors, publishers, and readers need and desire "convenient" editions, paperbacks, books (with margins wide enough to accommodate annotations), or digital texts. The desire for convenience often entails a temptation to treat books as infinitely malleable in form but stable in content. Despite the interpretive value of genetic textual study, students, critics, and readers seldom demand the full picture, preferring convenience over comprehensiveness. The next two essays, 10 and 11, take up the fact that textual studies, as practiced in different countries and in disciplines other than literature, has followed trajectories different from that of Anglo-American textual studies. These essays attempt to show how multinational and multidisciplinary theory and practice in editing is informative and can influence the work of any single tradition. Essay 12 digs a bit deeper into the relationship between authoring and book production, illustrating the role of bibliographical and book history investigations in identifying as precisely as possible the text one is examining. It illustrates the lengths to which one can go to answer this book's fundamental questions about knowledge: Where did that come from? How do you know? The final chapter reverts to the subject of the relations between textual studies and cultural studies, focusing attention on the ethical issue of social justice with regard to the generation and dissemination of textual knowledge. My aim in the whole is to explain the role of textual studies in literary studies. Any old text will not do, unless one does not care what it does.

The Gender and Politics of Knowledge

In the last quarter of the twentieth century, the study of literature explored with great enthusiasm and intellectual profit the proposition that disinterested knowledge—knowledge that purported to be unassailable because of its comprehensive grounding in verifiable evidence and because it rejected overt political biases and agendas—was, in fact, deeply committed to biases and political agendas related to the "mainstream" sense of self. Unacknowledged political agendas of disinterested pursuits of knowledge were, it became widely thought, designed to protect the status quo power structures in academe and in society. One result of the rebellion against disinterested (but actually self-interested) scholarship was to pursue openly a vast array of interests and agendas, both in the original literary texts and in the scholarship purporting to elucidate such works. Among the most valuable ensuing developments were women's studies, postcolonial studies, gay and lesbian studies, and ethnic studies. In this book, it might have been good to illustrate the relationship between textuality and knowledge and these overtly political approaches to literature; however, I have not done that. The central concern of this book is not the writings by men or women or minorities. Instead, my central concern is the value, indeed necessity, of determining the relationship between the texts one is using and the knowledge one purports to support by reference to them. The principles I am exploring are, I believe, the same regardless of the gender, geography, ethnicity, or temporal placement of a writer. The relation between documents as evidence and criticism as argument is without gender, nationality, time, or place. In order to keep my illustrations from being a litany of "he said, she said" hearsay evidence, I had to confine my illustrations to textual histories that I had examined firsthand. Case studies in this book include: extended illustrations from the works of a twentieth-century English woman, Virginia Woolf; a living South African, J. M. Coetzee; and a nineteenth-century Englishman, William Makepeace Thackeray. There are many other references to smaller points in the textual histories of other writers, many more of them men than women. But my concern is with the relationships between evidence and knowledge, and that is not, per se, a gendered or political issue, though the criticism that is based on that knowledge probably is. I do not know how to illustrate one relationship between document and knowledge that holds true only for the writings of women and a different one that holds true only for the writings of men. I do, however, show the consequences of ignoring, or of being aware of, the importance of documentary evidence in critical arguments.

Dedication and Acknowledgments

I dedicate this book to those scholars who introduced me to international textual studies: H. T. M. (Dick) Van Vliet led me to historical critical editing, which has such sway in the Netherlands and Germany—road trips with Dick to Amsterdam, The Hague, Lingen, Aachen, Leuven, and Munster extended opportunities to dispute textual issues; Sukanta Chaudhuri opened for me Bengali editorial issues and goals—particularly in a weeklong seminar in Santiniketan to plan an edition of Rabindranath Tagore's works;[1] Harry Heseltine and Paul Eggert encouraged my thinking about editing in Australia—particularly the recovery and editing of Colonial Australian literary works; John Gouws exposed me to the very difficult range of issues facing South African textual criticism in multiple languages—an unforgettable four-day trip with Gouws and Eggert on Australia's Great Ocean Road focused attention on the ethics of editing; and Kiyoko Myojo and Christian Wittern initiated my acquaintance with Japanese and Chinese textual problems—and demonstrated the compatibility between peripatetic textual seminars and Japan's exquisite museum of printing, a bullet train, ancient architecture and gardens, and good eating. Having drawn so much from these very generous scholars, I am happy to claim deep friendship with them as well.

Other scholars have contributed significantly to my thinking about texts and criticism. My major professor James B. Meriwether put me on the career track that has brought me to this point. James L. W. West III, editor of this series, has given valuable editorial advice. Peter Robinson is an inspiration in the area of digital textuality and was responsible for moving me to England in 2003, thus enabling my participation in the European Society for Textual Scholarship, where I encountered a refreshing and challenging range of new textual problems and rationales for textual criticism. George Bornstein and David Greetham have influenced my thinking over the years, though I see Paul Eggert's hand and ideas in most of what I write. G. Thomas Tanselle and

---

1. Sukanta Chaudhuri, *The Metaphysics of Text* (Cambridge: Cambridge University Press, 2010), esp. chapter 10.

James Thorpe, serving on the Modern Language Association's Committee on Scholarly Editions while I was its coordinator in 1976–77, set for me a standard in the art of civil disagreement and persuasion. All of textual criticism and scholarly editing owes incomparable debts to Fredson Bowers and Jerome McGann for making us think, rethink, and push forward our ideas about texts and textuality.

I began this book as a collection of lectures and essays, thinking it would be a relatively simple act of gathering mementos of the occasions that stimulated them. Jim West and Paul Eggert commented on the original copy; serious cutting and reworking followed. I no longer care much for the origins of each chapter, except to cite them as starting points.

I am grateful for permission to reuse previously published works: essay 8 incorporates materials first published in *Text and Genre in Reconstruction* (Open Book 2010), essay 9 incorporates material first published in *Digital Humanities Quarterly*, essay 2 first appeared in *English Studies in Africa*, and essay 12 is based in part on work published by University of Virginia Press and Palgrave. Thanks to The Society of Authors as the Literary Representative of the Estate of Virginia Woolf for permission to photo-quote, in essay 5, passages from the proofs and early editions of *To the Lighthouse*.

A special note of thanks goes to Nicholas Hayward for partnering with me to create the Woolf Online project and preparing the photo-quotes for this book. I wish also to thank Laura Reed-Morrisson, from Penn State University Press, and Nicole Wayland for very good copy-editing, saving me from errors, inconsistencies, and omissions in the details.

My deepest debt is, however, to my friend, colleague, and wife, Miriam C. Jones Shillingsburg, who among other things learned how to apply computing to text collation and pushed development of CASE (Computer Assisted Scholarly Editing) programs, which I, and a significant number of other editors, have used for more than thirty years to investigate textual histories and to prepare scholarly editions.

The Evidence for Literary Knowledge

The answer to the question "Does textual criticism matter?" must emerge from an understanding of what textual criticism is. Assertions about it have already failed to convince most members of literature departments, which for the most part do not require that graduate students get training in the subject. To me (full disclosure) that is like a dairy science department that does not require bovine anatomy of its graduates. There are reasons, I admit. "Textual criticism" has had a deadly ring for many scholars, critics, and teachers. By those who do not understand it, it is considered pedantic, boring, insignificant, and mired in critical dogmas long since abandoned by literary critics who find more fertile ground in epistemological uncertainty, aesthetic appreciation, cultural relevance, and, because it relates more particularly to how we live now, the rhetorical constructs of power evident in political engagements, gender issues, environmental conditions, and numerous other life matters that literature explores. Nevertheless, recent worldwide critical and scholarly trends are challenging the notion that textual criticism is a harmless sideline to literary criticism. Why did textual criticism suffer a bad press? Why it is emerging once again as a fundamental and exciting mode of investigating the texts we find significant for literary criticism?

Textual criticism may seem unappetizing to those who know little about it. It is a perception more than a reality, but a thing is what one thinks it is as long as one thinks it—so perceptions matter. The most frequent advocates of textual criticism, university and college teachers of Bibliography and Methods of Research, can make textual criticism look like a mountain made of a mole hill. Proofreading is more drudgery. Textual apparatuses seem too small and too coded to read. Negative perceptions of textual criticism often arise from direct encounters with scholarly editions, of which there are several types. One provides textual information at the foot of the pages, some of which have a few lines of text at the top held in place there by many more lines of fine print about variant forms that one cannot understand without referring repeatedly to the list of symbols.[1] Another type offers a textual introduction, which one can skip easily enough, followed by a clear text of the work with no compositional, revisional, or transmissional complications, because all of that business is relegated to textual apparatuses at the back. Casual acquaintance with the textual introduction and lists of variants suffice to show the wisdom of getting straight into the text of the work.[2] The critical significance of the textual apparatus seems hidden like a needle in a haystack.

The first point is a defense of pedantry: as R. B. McKerrow once remarked, *pedant* is a name given to anyone whose standard of accuracy is higher than your own. The rate at which literary critics and students of literature create or perpetuate factual errors is astonishing. Were emergency ward doctors to be as careless of the facts, they would kill enough people to put their jobs at risk. If pedantry can raise our standard of accuracy, we could use a little more pedantry.

Although lack of concern for accuracy makes a bad doctor, accuracy alone does not make a good one. Some scholars seem to think it is enough to get the facts right—the dates, the sequence, the variants, and the sources. Somehow, then, the accumulation of accurate facts will produce of their own accord excitement, understanding, wisdom, and other forms of significance. It does not. As a consequence some persons, probably not known for their thoughtfulness, conclude that accuracy is not so important and can be left to the pedants while they (we) focus on that which does lead to excitement, understanding, wisdom, and so forth, unmindful that if the facts are wrong the conclusions will be wrong, no matter how attractive and exciting the misprisions are.

To be fair, much in our experience of school and college, and what passes for investigative behavior in the sources of our general information about the world, to wit, the news and infotainment, conspire to promote the notion that texts are stable, identical, and accurate (at least accurate enough for pedagogy and criticism). Teachers allow multiple editions of the same book to stand for the work they are teaching—perhaps because college bookstores routinely stock cheap editions as well as, or instead of, the ones ordered.

1. For example, the magnificent but difficult John Clare edition, *Poems of the Middle Period, 1822–1837*, ed. Eric Robinson et al. (Oxford: Clarendon Press, 1996).

2. For example, almost any edition with the Modern Language Association's CEAA seal of approval from the 1960s and 1970s.

Likewise some librarians do not order a new or different edition because the same title is already on the shelf; some even "weed" the "extra copies." In their essays, some critics even cite paperbacks with texts of unknown origin or cite an "authoritative" text even if they did not actually use it in their research. Copies of texts are not identical (not ever). Often the differences have interpretive consequences. The basic questions are: Which text is that? How does it differ from other copies? and Where did that come from? If one does not know the answers, then how does one know what one is talking about?

On Being Textually Aware

This section title refers to Dirk Van Hulle's book *Textual Awareness*, a book that grew out of his University of Antwerp PhD thesis, a genetic study written primarily in English and exploring the manuscripts of James Joyce's *Finnegans Wake*, Marcel Proust's *Remembrance of Things Past*, and Thomas Mann's *Doctor Faustus*, each examined in its own language. He also uses letters, proofs, and revised editions to ferret out the implications of these materials to an understanding of what the authors were doing and how that might relate to interpretive strategies that could be applied to their works.[3] For many of us, myself included, awareness of the text is just what we avoid when we treat the text as a transparent window into stories or poems, or into the cultural conditions implied by them. In contrast to common reading practice, attention to the elements that constitute any given material text is basic to book history, and fairly widely acknowledged in reader response theory and textual studies alike. They agree that the format and material manifestations of a text significantly influence reading experiences. If one begins with the texts commonly used in classrooms—which might at first seem evidence to the contrary—and asks, for example, how an anthology, by its material form, might affect one's reading experience, it becomes hard to ignore that merely *being* an anthology suggests strongly that the works contained are of literary significance.This evaluative presumption was not, in most cases, signaled in the work's original published form, which could have been a newspaper, magazine, pamphlet, or book out there competing for attention with an undifferentiated range of texts. The fact that the works

---

3. Subsequently published as *Textual Awareness: A Genetic Study of Late Manuscripts by Joyce, Proust, and Mann* (Ann Arbor: University of Michigan Press, 2004).

included in the anthology are all printed in the same type font suggests that there is an equality of value, or at least that some minimum standard of literariness is represented by each work. More than that, homogenized font signals to all of us that type font has no significance. The footnotes and biographical introductions send similar messages about the importance of the works included: the texts are worthy of our studied attention. Despite the dates attached to each work, sometimes distinguishing and sometimes confusing the date of composition and date of first publication, anthologies convey a sense of timelessness for each included work, reminding us, perhaps, of E. M. Forster's fantasy, in *Aspects of the Novel*, of the old British Museum rotunda reading room with authors from all times sitting together in one place writing their timeless works.

There are interpretive strategies and interpretive communities that thrive in an ambiance of timeless texts, untethered from the contexts of their origination and existing in our time for our uses (I won't say abuses). There are good reasons to treat literary works in a variety of ways. As I have acknowledged elsewhere, meaning or significance is constructed not just from words in a text but from real or imagined notions of time, place, speaker, and occasion, which readers use to identify the meanings they believe to be appropriate to the text, eliminating irrelevant and misleading possibilities.[4] So long as one is willing to imagine contextual elements for a communicative enterprise, or so long as one is convinced that attempts to construct historically accurate accounts of the real contexts of text origination are doomed to failure and distortion, then it follows that an anthology's homogenizing effect on its collection of literary works is of small importance.

In the absence of original documents, and lacking much historical context for the writing and original publication of texts, the chief skills that a reader must cultivate are an aesthetic sensibility, a sensitivity to language, and the ability to detect subtle evidence of gender, politics, class, and religion. When that is the case, bringing to bear on the work the concerns of our own time trumps by default any effort to understand the work as representative of its own time or of its author's or publishers' particular concerns. When we do find an author's or a publisher's concerns of interest, do we always (do we ever) look directly at a material object that they produced, or is our material

4. Peter Shillingsburg, *Resisting Texts: Authority and Submission in Constructions of Meaning* (Ann Arbor: University of Michigan Press, 1997), and *From Gutenberg to Google: Electronic Representations of Literary Texts* (Cambridge: Cambridge University Press, 2006), particularly chapter 3, "Script Act Theory."

text always the latest cheapest modern reprint, anthology, or electronic text? If so, how do we know that the repackaged material form of the work is not obscuring significant evidence or deceiving us in a significant way?

Interpretive Difficulties

What I have been writing about tends to posit a divide between what might be called presentism and historicism, as if the two were mutually exclusive or as if either were a definite, knowable thing that could be used as a bargaining chip in an argument. Literary study would lose some vitality if that kind of oversimplification were allowed to go unquestioned, just as it loses vitality when no effort is made to see literary works as they were seen by their authors or by the succession of audiences through the ages, each with its own biases.

Having imagined the reader with an anthology, let's imagine a reader confronting a manuscript or a first edition or a work in its original periodical or pamphlet appearance. A range of unfamiliar evidence accompanies a lexical text thus encountered. If one reads the 1848 *Communist Manifesto*, it will be in German, in a text not published in England and not available in English until 1850. It is more likely that one will, nowadays, encounter the *Communist Manifesto* in a modern edition. The first item in the Google search engine, when I tested this theory, was the Penguin paperback edition, of which it is said: "Originally published on the eve of the 1848 European revolutions, *The Communist Manifesto* is a condensed and incisive account of the worldview Marx and Engels developed during their hectic intellectual and political. . . ." My attention was caught by the phrase "published on the eve of the 1848 European revolutions." The locution suggests that perhaps a causal relation existed between the publication and the revolutions. There is more than just a hint of a suggestion that the Penguin text represents that 1848 text. I wonder how much it matters to a modern American or English reader that the text reproduced in the Penguin edition (the English text) was *not* available anywhere on earth on the eve of the 1848 European revolutions? Suppose we said that it did matter, would we not have an obligation to ourselves and our students to say how those revolutions and the writing and publishing of the *Communist Manifesto* were related? Of course there are other ways to encounter that work. It is now no longer in print in soft red leather covers, printed on thin India paper, with gilt edges and a red ribbon place marker. In the 1990s, at the fall of the Soviet Union, however, it was available in that form and might have been ironically appropriate as a coffee table book in the home of a rich capitalist.

Without having touched yet on the text itself, it seems clear that the material form of the texts we read and teach send messages of their own, supplanting the messages indexed by original publications. That might be worth noting and discussing, even if for no other reason than to show the pitfalls of taking too literal an approach to historical information.

Next let us look at the lexical text—at the edition and the version of the work it represents. Does it matter that W. E. B. Du Bois's 1915 *The Negro*, when revised thirty-some years later in the wake of World War II and when the atrocities of the German death camps had become known, omitted the pejorative references to Jews as complicit in the suppression of the rights and opportunities of Negroes?[5] Do the reprints now available actually say which version is being presented or point out that such changes were made? Or, does it matter if John Keats put a comma after the word "still" in the first line of "Ode on a Grecian Urn"? Is it supposed to be

Thou still unravished bride of quietness

Or

Thou still, unravished bride of quietness

Can we know who either put the comma in or took it out? Unfortunately, no; but if we could know who did it, would that affect how we react to the differences? Is the urn a "motionless" unravished bride or an "as yet" unravished bride?[6]

Are there supposed to be quotation marks around the words "Beauty is truth, truth beauty" in the last but one line of Keats's ode, or does the urn speak the whole of the last two lines, as indicated by quotation marks in some editions, or are there no quotation marks at all, as in other editions? Actually, at the moment, we cannot know the answers to the questions about the "Ode on a Grecian Urn" because the four surviving manuscripts and two lifetime editions of the poem, which offer all of these options, are none of them in

5. See George Bornstein, "W. E. B. Du Bois and the Jews: Ethics, Editing, and The Souls of Black Folk," *Textual Cultures* 1, no. 1 (2006): 64–74.

6. For details on Keats's poem, see Jack Stillinger, ed., *John Keats: Complete Poems* (Cambridge, Mass.: Harvard Belknap Press, 1982).

John Keats's hand or known to have been proofread by him. The questions remain, nevertheless, about what the textual variants do to the reading and teaching experiences of that poem.

Editorial Functions

Most people would know that the primary functions of editing are to (1) preserve our cultural heritage (to use a fund-raising phrase) and (2) to detect and correct errors. Some people might think that proofreading is all that textual criticism is about. That is, in fact, an important aspect of it, for sometimes typos or miscopyings have important effects. These two functions of textual criticism are activities we usually want someone else to take care of. In showing our approval—even when we don't ourselves want to do the work—we call it preserving or restoring the integrity of texts. "Integrity of texts" is a phrase that has rhetorical force; few would say they do not care if texts have integrity. How often, however, do we care enough to check? Perhaps we consider that to be an editorial task, and many of us do not consider ourselves editors.

Can we trust editors? Some editors use the terms of textual criticism more as a tool of persuasion than as a method of clarifying the issues and exploring the significance of the facts. The Modern Library edition of George Meredith's *The Ordeal of Richard Feverel*, introduced by Lionel Stevenson, claims to reprint the first edition (1859) because, in Stevenson's opinion, the revisions Meredith made for subsequent editions were "so roughly handled as to suggest haste and impatience" and "wrought positive harm upon the story."[7] Thirty-three years later, the Dover Publications edition of the same novel claims to have reprinted a revised edition (Boston, 1888) that "incorporates further emendations by the author."[8] The Dover text, clearly not seriously "edited," gives no analysis of the nature or effects of the revisions, nor does it mention what else might have been incorporated in the late US edition chosen as copy-text. Readers are at the mercy of the thoroughness and perspicuity of the editor's research and decisions in these matters. The Meredith example comes from books produced at a time when it was generally assumed

7. Lionel Stevenson, intro. to George Meredith, *The Ordeal of Richard Feverel* (New York: Random House, 1950), xxv.
8. Copyright notice in George Meredith, *The Ordeal of Richard Feverel* (New York: Dover Publications, 1983).

that everyone should be reading the same established standard edition of the work. It was thought to be an editor's task to provide such a text. There are, however, more fruitful questions to ask of editions. Textual and literary critics find value in contemplating for themselves the revisions. Texts and their meanings and implications are fluid and develop over time. Texts are changed as editors and publishers react to historical events. Even unaltered texts undergo transformations simply by existing into a time when values are different. That which went without saying and determined the intended or expected meanings at the time of writing and publication no longer goes without saying. Old works are interpreted in the light of recent or present events and conditions that are deemed effective even though unknown to the texts' originators.

Error

Scholarly editing does not guarantee that history has been nailed down and forced to serve faithfully as the contextual determinant of meaning. If we look to Fredson Bowers's Wesleyan Edition of Henry Fielding's *Tom Jones* for information about what to do with the "Man in the Hill" section, we might conclude that poor Sheridan Baker, bless his heart, in his practical edition of the novel, was just plain wrong to reprint the text of the fourth edition, which omits that section. Bowers contradicted Baker's reasoning.[9] Later, however, Bowers reversed himself, admitting that he had misinterpreted the evidence. The point is that, instead of an edited text claiming to be the right text, we might want to know both the early version and the revised version for the light the comparison casts on each version. Which is the right text for all time no longer seems the right question to ask.

Viewing alternative versions of texts can put each text in a new light. It is not just that each version can prompt a different reading experience. It is that seeing two or more versions in contrast can provoke reactions not likely to occur to a reader who does not know the alternative. As we learn the probable motives for the changes, and as we place the changes in the context

9. Henry Fielding, *Tom Jones*, ed. Fredson Bowers (Oxford: Clarendon Press, 1974); Fielding, *Tom Jones*, ed. Sheridan Baker (New York: W. W. Norton, 1973). Bowers's correction was first made public in a paper delivered at the biennial convention of the Society for Textual Scholarship, New York City, April 1985. Bowers's correction is incorporated in the paperback version of the Wesleyan edition of *Tom Jones*.

of events and circumstances that triggered them, our understanding can be further clarified or nuanced about what the text was meant to mean or what the text was taken to mean in its original form. We can carry this kind of inquiry into the work's significant historical iterations.

These are not new ideas. Gordon Ray gave wonderful instances of how the materiality of books convey information otherwise lost. In an essay titled "The Importance of Original Editions," published in 1952, he argued for having libraries purchase and retain multiple editions so that histories of their effects on readers and the evidence of reputations would be possible. One example he gave was of the works of Émile Zola, whose original publications were not very popular, whose subsequent reputation was gained through cheap editions with lurid illustrations on the covers and who finally achieved literary status in a drab but imposing edition of the collected works. Ray's notion of the importance of preserving books that are never checked out is that they form the physical evidence needed for understanding the history of books. If the value of a book in the library is to be gauged by the number of times it is used or the number of people to use it, he wrote, then the phone book is the most important book in the library.[10] Phone books are now more commonly consulted online. So too are the texts of many literary works. Will digital transcriptions or images suffice to answer our fundamental questions about literary evidence: Where did that come from? Can I see the original document? Is not a digitized text different from its source just as a new print edition, completely reclothed in new forms, new mediums, and in a new context, erasing the evidence one is seeking when looking at an "original document"? Attending to the material contents of our libraries is a central concern of textual criticism, too.

For, suppose we accept the challenge of introducing our students to the issues, problems, opportunities, and interpretive consequences of seeing the texts we teach and read as physical objects with histories of composition, revision, production, and reproduction in new designs for new purposes including the designs and purposes of anthologies. In order to do that, do we not need a library that contains these physical objects? Can we address the

10. Gordon N. Ray, "The Importance of Original Editions," in *Nineteenth-Century English Books: Some Problems in Bibliography*, ed. Gordon N. Ray, Carl J. Weber, and John Carter (Urbana: University of Illinois Press, 1952), 1–24. He added what is too often still true: "Our state of contented ignorance has generated a culpable carelessness about the versions of nineteenth-century books that we read. We do not even demand that publishers of reprints state the sources of their texts" (9).

questions fundamental to the history of texts and books and literary works without having a library possessing the materials about which we profess to be experts?[11] Do we have such a library? Do we have such libraries within reasonable reach to justify our emphasis on the textual condition of the works we teach?

A Note on Digital Textuality

Since the advent of the Internet, the greatest amount of new energy devoted to textual criticism has focused on the use of digital technologies. Electronic media has the potential to minimize the drudgery, to increase the ability to process details, and to enhance access to sound textual evidence through the Web, that is, not in the presence of physical texts. I do not address these concerns in detail in this volume, having devoted two books to the subject.[12] Nevertheless, because technology advances so rapidly and because in applying new technology to old problems one learns new things about textuality itself, there is always room for more consideration of this topic. Textual and literary critics often resist computing until they see advantages in the form of useful results. They are not usually inclined to explore digital capabilities out of curiosity. When they do come to believe in computing as an aid to their work, they are inclined to see computer scientists as aides, people who can help the literary scholar with his or her work. That is a big, all too common, mistake. Computer scientists are not aides; they are co-investigators on an equal footing with the literary scholar, exploring the possibilities together. There is no money in "literary computing," but there can be sheer joy in meeting a challenge and creating new and better solutions to problems—both in criticism and in computing. Literary scholarship offers very complex problems not normally encountered in computer science departments. Computer scholarship offers to literary studies a way of thinking not normally encountered there. Hierarchies do not work well in this partnership.

---

11. "Work and Document," edited by Barbara Bordalejo, is a discussion of the terms and concepts of *document, text,* and *work,* and of reader/student access to them, published in *Ecdotica* 10 (2013), with contributions by Barbara Bordalejo, Hans Walter Gabler, Paul Eggert, Peter Robinson, and Peter Shillingsburg.

12. Peter Shillingsburg, *Scholarly Editing in the Computer Age: Theory and Practice* (Ann Arbor: University of Michigan Press, 1996), and *From Gutenberg to Google.*

The intellectual exchange between humanities scholarship and computer science has not been without problems on both sides.[13] The humanities prides itself on its complexities and ambiguities and even its mysteries; so, "computing the humanities" seems reductive. Computer science prides itself on its precision and the comprehensive organization of all research questions into sequences that a computer can use or "understand." Its watchword is control. It would seem then that humanities scholars and computer scientists might have difficulty communicating and mapping shared goals. Despite the challenges, both disciplines have contributed significantly to the intellectual growth of the other. The variables in literary study challenge the precise ways of computing, just as the precision of computing challenges the vagaries of literature. Textual critics and computer scientists explore digital enhancements in dealing with textual complexity as a joint venture. Scholarship in both fields distinguishes itself from polemics and idle curiosity by its adherence to the rules of evidence. That requires comprehensiveness, verification of facts, and carefully articulated analysis of inferences before the announcement of conclusions.

I discovered for myself the intellectual value of an embrace between textual studies and technology in 1978. I thought I had been unusually careful and comprehensive in my approach to textual evidence and use of the logical deployment of analysis and representation. In developing Computer Assisted Scholarly Editing (CASE), a series of nine interrelated programs for manuscript transcription and collation, I was required to reduce my processes to questions that can be answered *yes* or *no* and into sequences defined by *if* or *else*.[14] I learned that if one fails to be absolutely clear, the program fails, entering an endless loop or jamming. Humanists tend to skip the bits they don't understand. Rhetorical dexterity allows it. Little fudges and mistakes do not automatically send up a red flag. We may not even realize we are not

13. The following is revised from a presentation at the Fifth Symposium on Textual Scholarship (2008) at the Centre for Textual Scholarship, De Montfort University (the word *Scholarship* in the Centre's name was subsequently changed to *Studies*), http://cts.dmu.ac.uk/repository/shillingsburg-2008.html.

14. To produce CASE, Miriam Shillingsburg worked with Susan Follet, and I worked with Russell Kegley, Michele Cotell, Charles Layton, and Boyd Nation. For precursors of CASE, see Penny Gilbert, "Automatic Collation: A Technique for Medieval Texts," *Computers and the Humanities* 7 (1973): 139–47; and George R. Petty Jr. and William M. Gibson, *Project OCCULT: The Ordered Computer Collation of Unprepared Literary Text* (New York: New York University Press, 1970; reissued by Oak Knoll, http://www.oakknoll.com/pages/books/114955/george-r-petty-jr-william-m-gibson).

being clear. Reducing my work to the unforgiving demands of a "stupid" computer exposed my own gaps and leaps of logic and thoroughness. I developed real respect for the potential of computer technology to make humanities research better.

Technology cannot, however, substitute for scholarship. The computer is not a scholar, though it takes a scholar to teach the computer. The "market" does not design tools for textual scholarship. Humanists normally do not (cannot?) know enough or spend enough time to learn the full capabilities of computers *and* be committed textual scholars and scholarly editors at the same time. Trust me. Technology and literary scholarship both work better when a humanities scholar and computer scientist join forces to develop a technical tool—not when a scholar simply uses a computer program or treats the computer scientist as a programming assistant. As equal partners, each forces thinking upon the other that sharpens the analytical skills of both. The truth of this view can be seen in Woolf Online, designed by a computer scientist, Nicholas Hayward, and a textual scholar, me, to fulfill a literary critic's, Julia Briggs, project for a digital virtual archive or "sandbox" of Virginia Woolf's *To the Lighthouse.*[15]

---

15. See http://www.woolfonline.com. Chief contributors to this project are Professors Mark Hussey and Pamela Caughie, but see also the full listing of participants on the site. The content management system (CMS), called Mojulem, is the first ever designed specifically for literary archives. It is designed so that the system, the tools, and the content are all replaceable and extendible components, giving the impression of an integrated whole, but able to be repaired or replaced, one bit at a time. See a description of the technical side of the project in the HRIT NEH White Paper: http://hritwiki.ctsdh.luc.edu/neh-white-paper.

Textual Criticism, the Humanities, and J. M. Coetzee

In "The Humanities in Africa," lesson five of *Elizabeth Costello*, humanities studies are explored as intellectual, social, and ethical goods—a commodity—used and abused by diverse, ideologically coherent groups; but in the end, it appears, the lesson leaves each individual with a responsibility that cannot be institutionalized or codified without stripping the humanities and humanitarianism of human value. I focus on Coetzee's "The Humanities in Africa" because one of its own subjects is the role of hermeneutics, and more fundamentally, textual criticism, in identifying humanities studies and humanism. Coetzee's story presents and analyzes the very subject that it illustrates by its publication and reception. I begin by acknowledging the problem of meaning generally, and then I focus on the special difficulties in knowing what Coetzee means with regard to a particular part of this short story. Finally, I use textual criticism as an aid to interpretive criticism to try to understand what the story has to say, and what it fails to say, about its subject: the humanities in Africa.[1]

Originally published in *English Studies in Africa* 49, no. 4 (2006): 13–27.

1. The two most important versions of this essay/narrative/lesson/chapter are: John M. Coetzee's *The Humanities in Africa / Die Geisteswissenschaften in Afrika* (Munich: Carl Friedrich von Siemens Stiftung, 2001) and J. M. Coetzee, *Elizabeth Costello* (London: Secker and Warburg, 2003). The first is referred to as *HA*; the second, much revised, version is referred to as *EC*. The American edition of *Elizabeth Costello* (New York: Viking, 2003) and the London Vintage paperback (2004) are photographically identical to the London (Secker and Warburg) edition—the same typesetting. (I determined this by comparing the publications with a Lindstrand Comparator.) This revised version (*EC*) of Coetzee's story has twice been editorially truncated and printed in Australia: *The Best Australian Stories 2002*, ed. Peter Craven (Melbourne: Black, 2002), 101–99, and *Resistance and Reconciliation: Writing in the Commonwealth*, ed. Bruce Bennett et al. (Canberra: ACLALS, 2003), 16–28. Neither of those publications appears to have involved guiding action by Coetzee. I give a full account of those versions in "Publications of Coetzee's 'The Humanities in Africa,'" *Script and Print* (*BSANZ*)

Allegorical auras in J. M. Coetzee's fictions invite applications that cannot be quite unambiguously pinned down. Rather than evasion or misdirection on his part, he seems to be exploring critical conventions about the interpretive uncertainty that is fundamental to all reading experiences. By consciously employing a strategy that undermines explicit clarity, his fiction forces readers to adjust and then readjust ideas that previously might have settled into the fabric of enlightened thinking. While one can bring ideological differences to bear on any story and use any story to illustrate interpretive complexities, Coetzee seems to make his own (the author's own) positions complex and nuanced yet deliberately hidden. This gives his readers greater freedom, or places on them a greater responsibility, to engage the ethical consequences of the issues under discussion. Readers unable to pin ideas onto a stable "author figure" may find it difficult to sit back and contemplate the ideas in the abstract. They have to sort out the ethics for themselves—whether about animal rights or ways to extend charity to suffering humanity. In *Elizabeth Costello*, Coetzee gives us eight lessons without spelling out whether they are lessons Elizabeth learned, or lessons we are to learn, or lessons the author was figuring out as he wrote. The conscious ambiguities of writing reflect the palpable ambiguities of moral life in a socially interdependent world. He leaves each reader individually to recognize or apply whatever lesson there is.

This element of uncertainty, as an integral part of the writing and reading process, may distinguish "serious" works of fiction from other kinds (e.g., didactic, escape, entertainment). In volume 2 of her autobiography, Doris Lessing writes that each new novel and story involved working out what she thought as she wrote. Each was a serious quest or journey of discovery. That would be one way to understand, in *Elizabeth Costello*, why Elizabeth, both as person and as writer, seems frequently ill at ease. She is often at a loss for words to say exactly how she feels or what she thinks. This aspect has been noted by reviewers and critics, who usually point particularly to Elizabeth's difficulties in making a statement of beliefs in lesson eight. Andrew Reimer wrote, "For Elizabeth Costello, there are no certainties; she does not know whether she believes what she thinks she believes. Everything is provisional, constantly challenged by doubt, by gnawing skepticism."[2] One attractive way

---

28, no. 4 (2004): 105–12. My thanks to Paul Eggert, who reacted to an earlier version and who is the source of some of the better lines in this one.

2. Andrew Reimer, "Elizabeth Costello," *Sydney Morning Herald*, September 13, 2003, http://www.smh.com.au/articles/2003/09/12/1063341766203.html.

to understand Coetzee's method is to say he is groping for answers rather than hiding his answers or teasing us. Uncertainty seems also to undermine or threaten realism and realistic fiction. The temptation is to cover it up, as discussed in lesson one, titled "Realism." That lesson contains Elizabeth's own lecture, titled "What is Realism?"—essays on realism nested like Russian dolls. In the frame essay, Coetzee (or his third-person narrator) compares the writer's task to building a bridge from "where we are, which is, as yet, nowhere, to the far bank" (*EC* 1). He sets up Elizabeth's lecture with comments about realism's reliance on "details, signs of a moderate realism" (*EC* 4), and about realism's difficulties with ideas and debate. "[R]ealism is premised on the idea that ideas have no autonomous existence, can exist only in things," writes the narrative voice. (Is it Coetzee in his own person?) "So when realism needs to debate ideas, as here, it is driven to invent situations" (*EC* 9). The circular notion of ideas premised on ideas and the insight that realism is invention have already set up conundrums even before Elizabeth takes the stage.

Furthermore, on the third time the narrator interrupts the narrative to explicitly and "unrealistically" skip a scene for the sake of time and space, he pauses to note that "[i]t is not a good idea to interrupt the narrative too often, since storytelling works by lulling the reader or listener into a dreamlike state in which the time and space of the real world fade away, superseded by the time and space of the fiction. Breaking into the dream draws attention to the constructedness of the story, and plays havoc with the realist illusion. However, unless certain scenes are skipped over we will be here all afternoon" (*EC* 16). Breaking in to explain that breaking in is not good, using locutions such as "realist illusion" and invoking the commonsense notion that we can't "be here all afternoon"—in other words, cannot be in an illusion forever—puts the strategies of realism on display by the ultimate realistic move of admitting that the story is a story, made up. It "isn't autobiography. It is a work of fiction. I made it up" (*EC* 12).

In her nested lecture, "What is Realism," Elizabeth says of the readers of Kafka's story about the lecturing ape: "We don't know. We don't know and will never know, with certainty, what is really going on in this story: whether it is about a man speaking to men or an ape speaking to apes or an ape speaking to men or a man speaking to apes (though the last is, I think, unlikely) or even just a parrot speaking to parrots" (*EC* 19). What we thought we knew "looks to us like an illusion now, one of those illusions sustained only by the concentrated gaze of everyone in the room" (*EC* 19–20). My point is simply that uncertainty, the constructedness of our "real worlds" and the "illusion of realism," is an integral aspect of Coetzee's writing method. It is also a substantive idea in this book, which I take, along with many of its reviewers, as a realistic fiction of ideas with epistemological and ethical consequences.

Lesson five's narrative point of view is third person with a center of consciousness limited to one character, Elizabeth Costello. Every sentence reflects her view, her sight lines, her hearing range, and her feelings. Nevertheless, the strongest speaker in the story is Elizabeth's sister, named Blanche by her parents but, on becoming a Catholic nun, renamed Sister Bridget—no doubt for St. Bridget, the Bride of Kildare, known in the sixth century for charity and justice. Sister Bridget gives a commencement address at a university that has honored her with a degree. Afterward, Bridget and Elizabeth argue over the subject of the address. In the early (Munich) version, Bridget gets the last word and declares that Elizabeth has lost. "You went for the wrong Greeks, Elizabeth," she said (*HA* 89/*EC* 145). The later book version has an additional ten pages, consisting primarily of a letter from Elizabeth to Bridget—a letter that is not sent—in which Elizabeth for the first time gets the last word and finally "wins" the argument—though Blanche/Bridget is never told.

The point of view from which the story is told infuses the whole with uncertainty about Coetzee's own position relative to the arguments because he does not say a single word in his own voice. That Coetzee is deliberate in this "distancing" might be inferred from Elizabeth's first lecture, where she remarks about Kafka's ape's monologue: "[I]t is cast in the form of a monologue, a monologue by the ape. Within this form there is no means for either speaker or audience to be inspected with an outsider's eye" (*EC* 18). Our understanding of any sentence is intimately connected to our perception or misconception of the person who is speaking. We have then a double vision, seen through a glass darkly, of ideas, arguments, and feelings limited to Elizabeth's consciousness but obviously authored by Coetzee. We can see clearly enough where Elizabeth stands, but her relation to the author is nowhere explicit. That uncertainty reflects also a crucial relationship between textual criticism and the humanities. That narratorial distance seems deliberate, central to Coetzee's own views. In the context of uncertainty, the story simply asserts human value. It does not rely on or accept external authority, as Bridget would like. Nor does it develop human value on the back of rational argument, as the story's academics would prefer.

Although not explicitly constructed as a three-part argument about the role of humanities not just in Africa but in the world, the essay's three strongest speakers appear to represent mutually exclusive positions: Sister Bridget's authoritarian morality ostensibly derived from God by way of the Catholic Church, an unnamed character's academically disciplined rationality, and Elizabeth Costello's individual aesthetics. Each position has a strong moral or ethical dimension, but the source or validation of right and wrong in each instance is very different. Such an analysis places Coetzee's essay in a tradition of debate about culture and the individual made famous by Matthew Arnold. However, unlike Arnold's writings, which promote an ideal balance, Coetzee's story/essay seems to call for a choice among these three—narrow authoritarian morality, disciplined ethical rationality, or individual compassionate aesthetics. Coetzee's essay suggests, I believe, that the moral authoritarian approach has too strong a tendency toward a dehumanizing regimentation fed by righteous certainty. The disciplined rational approach, by its cool distance and lack of engagement, tends toward a dehumanized overrationalization of the human condition. Elizabeth Costello, who possibly speaks for Coetzee, though that remains open to question, opts for a humanism of personal engagement and individual compassion, which is based on an aesthetic appreciation of human beauty and desire. Elizabeth, of course, and Coetzee, probably, reject the first two in favor of the third. The second is worth another look.

My first reading of "The Humanities in Africa" had a profound influence on my response both because it took place in isolation from any of the other essays/stories gathered in the book titled *Elizabeth Costello* and because it was in a different version, shorter and more ambiguous than the one more widely circulated in the book. From the early version, I speculated that Coetzee's own views were imbedded in the speech of one or another character. I could not say with confidence that my reaction to the essay/short story was a response to Coetzee's views; for it was not clear in that version that he was using the character of Elizabeth Costello to express his own views, as seems slightly more likely the case when one reads the revised version along with all the essays collected in the book *Elizabeth Costello*. In reading the early version, I aligned with the character who seemed to me to make the most sense. As it turned out, that character was not Elizabeth Costello, whose views are not elaborated in that version. On that first reading I chose to believe that Coetzee and I agreed with one of the academic speakers against both of the two main speakers, Sister Bridget and Elizabeth. I no longer believe that we agree.

The essay/story's support for Elizabeth Costello's individual aesthetic view of humanism is made inescapably clear in the revised, extended version. That view is achieved by a deliberate denigration of both the moral authoritarian view represented by Sister Bridget and the disciplined rational view of an unnamed academic in the story, both of which seemed more viable in the first version. The longer, later version differs from the earlier, shorter one in two striking ways. First, Coetzee made systematic textual revisions that alter the "spin" given to the arguments about rationality and textual criticism as central elements in the humanities. Second, he added ten new pages at the end, in which he, in the voice of Elizabeth, develops a compassionate, individualist argument, in parable form, about the humanities. Arguments, including my own, are never spin free, though rational people seem to prefer arguments that rely more on substance than style. I find Sister Bridget substantively unconvincing and possibly even dangerous, and so, perhaps, I do not see clearly how the substantive weakness of her views is achieved by a stylistic denigration of her position that might more accurately be attributed to Coetzee, who crafted her every word. Likewise, because I find the argument presented by an unnamed academic to be substantively strong, I perhaps see too clearly the denigrating spin put on rationality and discipline by Coetzee's revisions. While I have no objections to the third alternative, Elizabeth's plea for a compassionate individual and aesthetic humanism articulated in the final ten pages, I do not see it as an exclusive alternative to disciplined rationality, nor can I ignore the rhetorical strategy that gives it its dominant force in the final version.

In responding to Coetzee's arguments about the role of textual criticism in the humanities, I want also to demonstrate by the textual history of his essay that textual criticism holds a vital as well as foundational role in the humanities. That role is an intellectual and disciplined one, not to be brushed off in favor of a more emotional humanitarian one. The one is not incompatible with the other; a choice need not be made. Both, however, are antithetical to Sister Bridget's vision of religious authority.

Sister Bridget has the most to say about textual criticism and its relation to the humanities. Her voice is full of passionate certainty. Her view is that the humanities went wrong long ago and survives in universities in an etiolated form from which she distances herself even as she delivers a formal address within the precincts of humanities studies. She receives an honorary degree she does not honor and delivers a graduation address in which she criticizes her hosts. "[W]e must sometimes be cruel to be kind" [*HA* 25/*EC* 119],[3] she says. "I do not belong among you and have no message of comfort to bring you" [*HA* 33/*EC* 122]. She seems to offend in the hope of awakening some empty soul to the higher calling of the Catholic Church and of putting a public face on the "humanitarian" cause to which she is devoted—the children of Marianhill hospital.

I begin with the question of agency or voice. Who is speaking and what does it matter who is speaking?[4] We are familiar with that question from Samuel Beckett's asking of it, and from Michel Foucault and Jacques Derrida's invocations of it on the side of the answer that says it does *not* matter who was speaking. One of the reasons for this attitude toward voice is that interpretive despair and the absurdity of modern life have made the question uninteresting. Another is that when the text is read, it is the reader who is speaking, making up the tone and feeling about what is written. In textual critical circles, we are familiar with David Greetham's invocation of the question "What does it matter . . .?" in order to expose the soft spots in the thinking of scholarly editors pursuing an "author's final intentions."[5] I want to invoke the question in order to rehabilitate the answer that it *does* indeed matter who is speaking, though I try not to retreat to fortresses already abandoned.

Note in particular the change in the characterization of the unnamed academic man. In the early version, he is referred to simply as "a man who had not spoken before" (*HA* 49). In the book version, this is changed to "a young man seated next to Mrs Godwin" (*EC* 128). Five times the word

---

3. Page numbers in the form 25/119 indicate page 25 in the Munich version and page 119 in the book version.

4. The problem of voice is also taken up by Patrick Denman Flanery in "(Re-)Marking Coetzee and Costello: The (Textual) *Lives of Animals*," *English Studies in Africa* 47, no. 1 (2004): 61–84, where he points out Peter Singer's remarks on the same problem in the Princeton edition of *The Lives of Animals*. Singer, in what looks like the tables turned, invents a fictional philosopher whose own reaction has first to come to terms with the question "Are they Coetzee's arguments? That's just the point—that's why I don't know how to [respond] to this so-called lecture." The problem is doubly complex because of uncertainty about the footnotes. "Ownership is by no means clear."

5. D. C. Greetham, "'"""What Does It Matter Who Is Speaking," Someone Said, "What Does It Matter Who Is Speaking"?'" (Greetham Version), or '"What Does It Matter Who Is Speaking?": Editorial Recuperation of the Estranged Author' (Eggert Version)," in *The Editorial Gaze*, ed. Paul Eggert and Margaret Sankey (New York: Garland Publishing, 1998), 67–96.

"young" is added to references to him in the revision.[6] He was never referred to as young in the original. These changes are important for at least two reasons. The first is that they set up a later comment by Elizabeth, mocking him. ("So young, she thinks, and so sure of himself.") The second reason is that, in my first reading and writing on the early (2001) version of Coetzee's essay, not knowing of the revision, I praised this man's argument, assuming that the reticent author behind the voices of the story also approved his argument. Coetzee's 2003 revisions clearly rob this man of his dignity and thereby undermine his argument. Combined with the added ten pages of Elizabeth's response to Sister Bridget, the book version shifts the emphasis of the essay away from textual criticism, emphasizing instead Elizabeth's expanded Greek alternative to Bridget's religion. Elizabeth becomes more clearly Coetzee's spokesperson on behalf of compassion, beauty, sexuality, creativity, and personal responsibility as the chief counters offered by the humanities against the agony, suffering, ugliness, self-denial, and rigidity of the Catholic Church. Bridget's Catholic view is no longer the dominant voice, though what she says remains without significant change in both versions. More important than the mere development of Elizabeth's position is the fact that she sets her face clearly against the rational, disciplined academic, secular views raised at the graduation dinner, and particularly against the strongest articulation of those views by "the man who had not spoken before." In the whole 2003 book titled *Elizabeth Costello*, Elizabeth's views are also enhanced by her central role in the other essays, where we find other denigrations of rationality as inadequate to provide profoundly human answers to life's problems—such as the ethical treatment of animals and a properly horrified objection to abattoirs.

While Sister Bridget is a rigid and unlovely, though well-intentioned, representative of an authoritarian religious view, Coetzee has nevertheless allowed her at least one telling argument against academic humanism that seems to be shared by Elizabeth and by himself: that universities are the seat of an effete and ineffective form of intellectualism that is inadequate for the real business of living. This idea finds profound resonance in Coetzee's *Life*

---

6. In addition to the one cited: "says the young man" (*HA* 51/*EC* 129), "the young man pulls a face" (*HA* 51/*EC* 130), "So young, she thinks, and so sure of himself. He will remain with *studia*" (*HA* 51/*EC* 130), "The young man looks back at her uncomprehendingly" (*HA* 51/*EC* 130).

and Times of Michael K (1983) and *Age of Iron* (1990), both of which depict the helplessness of well-intentioned people to mitigate or stem an apartheidlike evil.

While agreeing with Coetzee about the importance of personal engagements, driven more by visceral than rational impulses, against evil in the world, I do not see why one must reject the power of rationality to undermine the foundations of authority and privilege.

The argument concerning textual criticism presented by the "man who had not spoken before" has a power Coetzee dismisses, possibly because he failed to see it. Yet it is worth noting that, when doing graduate work at the University of Texas at Austin, Coetzee was William Todd's student for a time. William Todd was at the time the editor of *Papers of the Bibliographical Society of America* and was already at work on his great project, providing a history and bibliography of the Bernhard Tauchnitz publishing firm of Leipzig, Germany. We can assume that Coetzee knows what textual criticism actually is, and that he has not picked on a narrow academic interest as a whipping boy for his general distrust of academics as moral activists. While it is not possible to say what Coetzee was thinking, his writings frequently express criticism of and disillusionment with humanities studies in the university. For example, in response to Professor Godwin's statement that the humanities "remain the core of any university," Elizabeth remarks wryly to herself, "its core enterprise . . . was the teaching of moneymaking" (*HA* 39). In the revised version, this remark is made even stronger by leaving out the phrase "the teaching of"; she thinks, "its core discipline . . . was moneymaking" (*EC* 125). At one level it matters whether Coetzee intended to mean what Elizabeth apparently means, though in practice most of us manage to get along fine without knowing for sure. We can, for example, say that the essay raises issues for contemplation and bats arguments around; and we find that useful because, at the end of the day, regardless of Coetzee's own views, we have clarified our own opinions, questions, and uncertainties on the subject.

It cannot be for nothing, however, that when Elizabeth Costello is awakened by a phone call, her first questions are "Where am I? . . . Who am I?," and her sister on the other end of the line seems to want to know the same thing. She says, "Elizabeth? Is that you?" The question of identity runs throughout, beginning with Blanche's name change to Sister Bridget and Peter Godwin's failure to recognize Elizabeth Costello's name, though his wife knows she is a writer. Elizabeth again raises the question when she identifies herself as Sister Bridget's blood sister as opposed to being a sister in spirit or order. Coetzee emphasizes identity when he introduces Bridget's graduation address with the words "Time for her to say her piece, Bridget, Blanche" (*HA* 23/*EC* 119), and as soon as she is done he refers to her as Blanche, though clearly she was speaking as Sister Bridget. Why individuation and identity matter to Coetzee does not actually become clear until the revised version, in which individual responsibility for decisions and actions becomes a central element of Elizabeth's final response to Bridget. It makes a difference who we think is speaking—who we are, who they are—and hence it matters. It may be that one's "sense of who is speaking" is wrong or an illusion or a way in which we fool ourselves, but it makes a difference to our understanding of ideas and our attitudes toward them, nonetheless.

Sister Bridget's statements about textual scholarship and the humanities are balanced against the statements of "the man who had not spoken before," though by the end of the chapter both positions are dismissed in favor of Elizabeth's individual aesthetic. Bridget says, "[T]he university embraced humane studies only in an arid, narrowed form. That narrowed form was textual scholarship: the history of humane studies in the university from the 15th century onwards is so tightly bound up with the history of textual scholarship that they may as well be called the same thing" (*HA* 27/*EC* 120). She adds, "Textual scholarship . . . was the living breath of humane studies. . . . But it did not take long for the living breath in textual scholarship to be snuffed out" (*HA* 27/*EC* 120). She then gives a succinct, if biased, view of textual scholarship, which is worth quoting:

> Textual scholarship meant, first, the recovery of the true text, then the true translation of that text; and true translation turned out to be inseparable from true interpretation, just as true interpretation turned out to be inseparable from true understanding of the cultural matrix from which the text had emerged. (*HA* 29/*EC* 121)

The sequence—text, translation, interpretation, understanding in relation to context—demarks the humanistic enterprise. That sequence of acts represents the only way we have of assessing and understanding the role of the humanities or any other subject that comes to us by way of texts, whether written or spoken. All texts are subject to editing, translating, interpreting, and understanding, and all are taken up in relation to some sense of context. Notably, Bridget's listing always emphasizes the word "true," which she clearly aligns with the Church's view of truth. She therefore seems to see both narrowness and a wrong turning in secular humanities. She believes humanities study lost itself in a futile endeavor to find a substitute religion in the secular "things of man." It could also be said that modern secular humanists sometimes have an even more narrowed view of textual scholarship as merely the pursuit of typo-free texts—a hyped-up copy-editing and proofreading activity. This view—not in fact mentioned by Coetzee—is as wrongheaded as Sister Bridget's. Neither view captures the dynamic vitality of textual scholarship.

A glimmer of rational intelligence emerges during the graduation dinner debate in the words of the unnamed "man who has not spoken before" (*HA* 49/ [revised to "young man seated next to Mrs Godwin," *EC* 128]). Before reading the expanded version, I guessed that this man, rather than Elizabeth, spoke for Coetzee. Now, I am confident that he does not, though he continues to give more humane answers than either of the Costello sisters. He focuses on the real flaws in Sister Bridget's argument by pointing to the Church's desire to control inquiry so that its only possible conclusion will be the dogma it began with—a strategy all too common in academe and politics, as well as the Church. This unnamed man expresses briefly a view that exactly parallels Sister Bridget's succinct summary of the methods and goals of *studia humanitatis*—text, translation, interpretation, and understanding in context. He says,

> If the Church had accepted the principle that Jerome's Vulgate was a human production, and therefore capable of being improved, rather than being the word of God itself, perhaps the whole history of the West would have been different.
>
> . . . If the Church as a whole had been able to acknowledge that its teachings, and its whole system of beliefs, were based on texts, and that those texts were [capable/susceptible] on the one hand [of/to] scribal corruption and so forth, on the other [of/to] flaws of translation, because translation is always an imperfect [business/process], and if the Church had also been able to concede that the interpretation of texts is a complex [business/matter], vastly complex, instead of claiming for

itself a monopoly of interpretation, then we [wouldn't/would not] be having this argument today. (*HA* 49/*EC* 129)[7]

What he says is applicable to all texts: one starts with text that can be flawed, or with inevitably flawed translation, and then there are the complexities of interpretation for which authority has not been irrefutably vested in any institution, neither Church nor university. The man does not explain why acknowledgment of potential flaws and complexity in interpretation would make "having this argument today" unnecessary, but I would like to venture an explanation.

The crucial idea, implicit but unspoken in Coetzee's text, is that acknowledgment of these textual conditions leads inevitably to an acknowledgment of uncertainty. We need to learn to live with uncertainty rather than invent illusions that will help us forget that what we think we know can be overturned by new knowledge. The Church and positivists in many secular "isms" decline to make that acknowledgment, starting instead with a declared truth, and then requiring inquiry to end in that predetermined truth.

The whole weight of honest studia humanitatis is contrary to that method. One starts in ignorance, asks questions, seeks evidence, and follows leads to the conclusions that seem inevitable regardless of how far from the status quo or preconceived end they might lead. Having found or formulated answers, studia humanitatis holds them tentatively and allows the light of new inquiry to alter or refute them, and then replaces them as needed. Sister Bridget has no use for this approach to truth. She accuses the unnamed man of painting "the humanist as a technician of textual interpretation" (*HA* 51/ *EC* 130). What he had said was, "The humanities begin . . . in textual scholarship, and develop as a body of disciplines devoted to interpretation" (*HA* 51/*EC* 129). "Discipline" for Bridget means something good when it refers to disciplining one's thinking to the dogmas of the Church, but it means something technical and dry as dust when it applies to the use of reason to, and a

---

7. The early version says, "capable . . . of scribal corruption," and the revision says, "susceptible . . . to corruption"—which makes more sense; texts are capable of nothing, being passive bits of paper and ink, but they are vulnerable to accidents and predations by active agents. Likewise, the changes from *business* first to *process* and in the next instance to *matter* remove the implication that translation and interpretation are commercial or interested undertakings. They probably are commercial and certainly are interested ones, but the revisions, in fact, give the man's articulation of the position a more neutral, less pejorative, tone.

request for accuracy in, the investigation of texts. She had concluded her graduation address with the idea that the imminent death of humanities "has been brought about by the monster enthroned by those very studies as animating principle of the universe: reason, mechanical reason" (*HA* 35/*EC* 123). The revised version drives home the point a bit more sharply: "the monster of reason, mechanical reason." Reason seems, for Bridget, always a monstrous mechanical enemy of truth—her truth. The results of reasoned inquiry are too unpredictable for those who prefer control.

This concept is worth pursuing, though it has no place in Coetzee's essay. When thinking persons come to the realization that objective, comprehensive truth cannot be determined finally by scientific or rational means and that every position statement begins with assumptions and cannot escape the biases inherent in one's own limited point of view—when thinking persons reach this intellectual impasse, they must make a choice about future thought, belief, and action. There are countless options, no doubt, but a few of the obvious and common ones are represented in Coetzee's essay. Sister Bridget opts to accept the authority of the Church and divine revelation, acknowledging her own human limitations but also giving her future actions irrefutable higher ground—a sort of humility with a purpose. Professor Peter Godwin, and the establishment academe he represents, may not really have come to grips with the limitations on knowledge, or, if he has, is taking refuge in a secular faith that intellectual progress is associated with the university of which the humanities is, somehow, the core.

Agreeing with the "young man" whom Elizabeth dismisses as "so sure of himself," I posit an alternative view of the humanities grounded in textual criticism, though not subservient to any preordained truth. The purpose of textual criticism is to pursue inquiry into the word of god or the word of any author, regardless of where the chips might fall. Though many of us, for many different reasons, are in a primary way interested in the meaning or teaching conveyed by the text, that goal is dependent upon the investigations of textual criticism, which assesses the nature and conditions of the text's conveyance of any meaning or teaching. It is not a mere, dry-as-dust search for error-free text. Textual criticism is in the first place the pursuit of evidence—of facts. It does not take a philosopher to sense the slipperiness of both the general concept of "facts" and of individual so-called facts. Facts are themselves neutral, but, because they cannot be held neutrally, even a back-to-basics statement such as "textual scholarship is the pursuit of evidence" comes out as a rhetorical flourish.

To acknowledge this condition of inquiry, not only that texts can be flawed but that facts and evidence do not provide bedrock certainty, is to acknowledge a great potential for deception in argument—both the deception of others and, more important, self-deception. The illusion of reality with which we began is now akin to the illusion of truth. Studia humanitatis encourages self-conscious examination of every form of self-deception and self-confidence. This does not mean we should throw up our hands and accept some ancient, supposedly revealed, truth as basic. If the humanities are to be conducted as disciplined study, and if the study of humanity is to have integrity, it must acknowledge its limitations and attend to its tools and methods. Humanity is fundamentally sexual, as Elizabeth's addendum to Coetzee's essay affirms, but it is also fundamentally textual, as seems to be hinted in an ancient text that claims, "In the beginning was the word." Textual criticism, focusing on the material, semiotic, communicative, and provocative elements of text, involves an act of self-examination that cannot be skipped over in studia humanitatis. Texts are the material and substance that condition all knowledge and all beliefs. The critical investigation of texts as text, operating in a textual condition and thus affecting every human interaction, is the fundamental studia humanitatis.

Textual criticism, understood broadly, is the study of how texts work or fail to work—which entails attempts to understand how language works or fails to work—which entails attempts to understand how cognition works or fails to work—which entails examinations of texts in active use (not just in laboratory conditions or language snippets offered by logicians and grammarians as examples). In short, textual criticism is the study of mankind using texts. That is what textual criticism involves, and that is why Sister Bridget is in a sense right when she identifies studia humanitatis with textual criticism. She is right to make that identification, not because textual criticism is intended to nail down the Truth but because its aim is to expose the truth about uncertainties and ambiguities even when to do so is inconvenient to the dogmas of the inquirer. Because the ambiguities and uncertainties that textual criticism exposes are endemic to the textual condition, and because texts, whether sacred or secular, are the basic medium of our intellectual discipline, it follows that the business of textual criticism is to bring the light of inquiry into the humanities, exposing, not obscuring, its uncertainties.

One hesitates to suggest that Coetzee did not see or understand that aspect of textuality or its relevance to humanities studies. In fact the way in which Coetzee has relied on narrative ambiguity to focus attention on the difficulties of identity and knowledge, particularly in works such as *Foe* and its extension in the Nobel Prize lecture, suggests that he has completely internalized the relation between uncertainty and individual responsibility. That insight entails what amounts to a leap of faith in one's own sense of humanity and compassion. Significantly, Elizabeth's description of her symbolic and actual acts of *caritas* with the dying artist, her mother's old friend, remain private—not communicated to her sister or anyone else in the world of the Costello fiction. As a further act of precision on Coetzee's part, he embedded Elizabeth's account of this secret act of compassion in a third-person limited omniscient narrative, which, though it reveals her secret to us as readers, is not an act of revelation on her part. *She* will not illustrate a graduation lecture on the humanities with this act of kindness.

The Semiotics of Bibliography

In *Bibliography and the Sociology of Texts*, the booklet based on his 1985 Panizzi Lectures, D. F. McKenzie takes to task W. W. Greg, Fredson Bowers, Ross Atkinson, and G. Thomas Tanselle for defining "bibliography" as scientific investigation divorced from the symbolic or semiotic meanings of the objects being examined and described. McKenzie accounts briefly but inadequately for why these bibliographers wished to isolate analytical bibliography from the critical uses of bibliographical information by comparing Greg's and Bowers's efforts and their times with the efforts of New Criticism to develop self-sufficiency (7). He concludes that their views of bibliography were insufficient to explain what bibliographers do or should be doing, and he accuses them of creating a notion about bibliography that rendered their work increasingly irrelevant. "Rare book rooms will simply become rarer," he remarked with more wit than logic (4).

We need a better understanding of why Greg and company thought it was necessary or useful to define the branches of bibliography strictly. What were they guarding against? We then should ask why McKenzie needed to limit the interests of these scholars to the confines of those precise definitions. What was he trying to accomplish?[1]

This essay, originally delivered as the presidential address to the Society for Textual Scholarship, March 2011, Pennsylvania State University, was revised and published in *Textual Cultures* 6, no. 1 (2011): 11–25 and is here further revised. D. F. McKenzie's observations on Greg et al. are in "The Book as an Expressive Form," in *Bibliography and the Sociology of Texts* (London: British Library, 1986), 1–2. (In the 1999 Cambridge edition of the lectures, the essay begins on page 9.)

1. For a more detailed analysis of the web of misquotations and misrepresentations of statements about bibliography, sociology of texts, editing, and book history, see Sarah Neville, "*Nihil biblicum a me alienum puto*: W. W. Greg, Bibliography, and the Sociology of Texts," *Variants* 11 (2014): 91–112.

That McKenzie was not giving these earlier scholars their full due is made clear by his own conclusion about the definitions—a clarity he either did not see or chose to ignore. Citing Atkinson, McKenzie pointed out that, in C. S. Peirce's terminology,[2] the definitions he quoted from Greg and others restricted attention to the "iconic" representation of printed material. He conceded that analytical bibliography rises to an "indexical" function but noted that this attention to "meaning" is confined to the indications that can be found in physical books about their modes of production. From this analysis of the definitions, McKenzie concluded: "If textual bibliography were merely iconic, it could produce only facsimiles of different versions." Anyone familiar with Greg's work, but more particularly with that of Bowers and Tanselle, knows that their interest was never confined to the production of facsimiles. They spent little time producing facsimiles, and they both wrote about the inadequacy of facsimiles as representations of original texts.[3]

Greg and other midcentury bibliographers had reason to worry about the methodology and focus of bibliography as it was practiced before their time. They sought to define its various branches strictly in order to avoid flaws they perceived in current practice. Bibliography before R. B. McKerrow and Greg—as practiced in the previous generation by book collectors such as T. J. Wise and Buxton Foreman, and scholar-critics such as Frederic George Kenyon, Geoffrey Keynes, George Saintsbury, and George Lyman Kittridge—reveals that reason. When one contrasts the 1890s to 1920s generation with their successors, John Carter, Graham Pollard, Simon Nowell-Smith, Dover Wilson, Michael Sadleir, and McKerrow and Greg, one sees immediately why this younger generation needed to establish something like a scientific basis for their work in order to counter the impressionistic and often sloppy use of

2. Peirce's triad of terms (*icon*, *index*, and *symbol*) is often used to expand the "expressive form of books" beyond the significance of the symbols or "lexical" text to include the way in which material objects *index* other things by standing as evidence of them, and to the *iconic* value of objects, where the thing both is what it is and stands for something else that is specific. The latter two semiotic dimensions are sometimes referred to as the bibliographic code, though it has been pointed out that the so-called code is not codified. See Paul Eggert, "Text as Algorithm and Process," in *Text and Genre in Reconstruction: Effects of Digitalization on Ideas, Behaviours, Products and Institutions*, ed. Willard McCarty (Cambridge: OpenBook, 2010), 183–202.

3. See, in particular, Fredson Bowers's "The Problem of the Variant Forme in a Facsimile Edition," *Library* 7, no. 4 (1952): 262–72 and "The Yale Folio Facsimile and Scholarship," *Modern Philology* 53 (1955): 50–57; and G. Thomas Tanselle's "Reproductions and Scholarship," *Studies in Bibliography* 42 (1989): 25–54.

bibliography to promote a priori religious convictions or aesthetic dogmas and to enhance financial interests (particularly by T. J. Wise and Buxton Foreman) in dodgy rare-book productions.

Nowell-Smith captures the problem faced by the post-1920s generation of bibliographers in his 1969 reminiscence of his youth at the opening of an address to the Bibliographical Society.[4] As an undergraduate Nowell-Smith had written an essay titled "A Plea for Standardized Bibliography," which was, he said, remarkable primarily for "the rebuffs it evoked." One éminence grise, Herbert Garland, "rejected my plea on the ground that bibliography was being 'increasingly recognized as a part of the critical apparatus of literary editorship and criticism', and that 'therefore' any 'limitation of method' tending to make it 'a mere technical code among certain specialists' was to be discouraged." Nowell-Smith then recalled Geoffrey Keynes's opinion: "'I have never concerned myself with the bibliography of the period discussed by Mr. Nowell-Smith, and am never likely to. . . . Bibliography is a pastime, *not* a formal science, so I am afraid I find myself in fundamental disagreement with Mr. Nowell-Smith.'"

McKenzie's objections to what he describes as the narrow, technical, scientific definitions proposed by Greg and company before midcentury seem, at first blush, to be cut from the same cloth as Garland's and Keynes's. The arguments of scholars for whom bibliography was not a mere pastime or a mere handmaiden to criticism stand with as much force against McKenzie's opening salvo as they did against Garland and Keynes.

Why, then, did McKenzie find it convenient or perhaps necessary to describe the scholarship of the generation preceding his own as ludicrously narrow? He must have known Nowell-Smith's account; he surely knew the battles McKerrow, Greg, and Bowers fought in order to establish standards in a world of casual bibliography. McKenzie knew that Bowers's own scholarship, though based on strict adherence to the rules of bibliographical evidence, was always used to expand a critical assessment of the semantic and semiotic meanings of historical bibliography for an understanding of literary works.[5] He also knew that McKerrow's *An Introduction to Bibliography* (Oxford, 1927), which had served as a textbook in bibliography from 1927 through the 1970s and beyond, had as its subtitle: *For Literary Students.* McKerrow's view

4. Simon Nowell-Smith, "T. J. Wise as Bibliographer," *The Library*, 5th ser., 24, no. 2 (1969): 129–41.

5. See, for example, his *Textual and Literary Criticism* (Cambridge: Cambridge University Press, 1959).

of bibliography for literary students was not dislodged by Philip Gaskell's *A New Introduction to Bibliography* (Oxford, 1972), which, justly, did not have that subtitle. Why should McKenzie have disparaged the views of bibliography put forth by Greg and Bowers before offering his very useful expansion of those definitions in ways that have been so influential in the adjacent fields of scholarly editing and book history—neither of which was considered, either before his lectures or afterward, to be, strictly speaking, bibliography?

One answer might be that the so-called scientific focus of bibliography did in fact narrow the attention of scholars. Believing that their primary purpose was to study an author, some scholars in their role as editors isolated and more or less repudiated the work of nonauthors in the production system. McKenzie's view brought a broader field of production personnel to scholarly attention. McKenzie's examination of Greg's definition of bibliography makes room for other definitions that point to the uses of bibliography as well as to the purview or subject matter of bibliography. In fact McKenzie's move is a strong indication of the success that bibliographers had had midcentury, both in bringing rigor to bibliographical investigations and in using the results to justify a major cultural phenomenon: their work had produced public support for scholarly editing. McKenzie, in claiming that "I am also convinced, however, that the premise informing Greg's classic statement, and therefore this refinement of it, is no longer adequate as a definition of what bibliography is and does" (2), prepares for his argument that bibliography, considered in a sociohistorical context, stimulates and underpins the superstructure of knowledge that explains not only what was said and thought historically but how it was said, distributed, maintained, understood, and preserved.

McKenzie, in the lectures as a whole, does more than anyone had before to convince us that in any aspect of intellectual history, the answer to the question "Where did that come from?" always follows a trail ending in a document beyond which it is impossible to go empirically, and that the meaning of documents lies not only in the significance of the lexical texts they preserve but also in the iconic significance of documents and in the socioeconomic contexts indexed by the material objects.

While McKenzie's opening salvo appears to be an attack on bibliography as practiced in the immediate past, the lectures as a whole justify the "scientific" and iconic attention that had been paid to documents by showing that the foundation of knowledge and the transmission of knowledge is in fact bibliographical. To me the rhetorical force of McKenzie's opening salvo on the narrowness of the bibliography of the past was a mistake. It is not uncommon for scholars with new insights and with the enthusiasm of initial discovery to think that the new view is contrary to, rather than supplementary to, prevailing wisdom. Thus, when McKenzie writes that "the vital interests of most of those known to me as bibliographers are no longer fully served by description, or even by editing, but by the historical study of the making and the use of books and other documents" (3), he is shifting his attention from a narrow understanding of the rules and methods of analytical and descriptive bibliography to the broader interests of the bibliographers who have followed those rules and methods. McKenzie is also acknowledging that their real interests outstrip the objectives of accurate description.

In my view, McKenzie did not enlarge the definition of bibliography; rather, he indicated that the human beings who wear bibliographical hats in their roles as bibliographers are also interested in the fields that are affected and illuminated by the investigations of bibliography. It is this larger interest that is the main topic of his lectures on bibliography and the sociology of texts. Greg, Bowers, and Tanselle were also readers, critics, and (at least the latter two) teachers of literature who were interested in the interpretive consequences of textual scholarship. Their rejection of a previous generation's sometimes sloppy use of impressionistic bibliography and their establishment of the discipline of bibliography as a precise, almost scientific, form of inquiry made them insist on the priority of those disciplinary claims. It did not, as McKenzie seems to suggest, cause them to reject or fail to develop their interest in the critical applications of bibliography. One measure of their commitment was the application of bibliography in the construction of critical editions—editions that had to incorporate critical judgment about the significance of bibliographical evidence without confusing the exercise of criticism with the duties of bibliographical investigation.

That does not mean that editorial practice under the influence of Greg and Bowers did not suffer from a problem. That problem was *not* that they chose a copy-text and emended it, as some editorial theorists have declared. It is, however, a problem that we can see more clearly now because of McKenzie's ideas about a sociology of texts. It is true that when the army of editors responsible for the Center for Editions of American Authors (CEAA) applied the fruits of their bibliographical research in the service of scholarly editing, they did not see in the bibliographical evidence what McKenzie has taught us to see. They did, however, see full well that a study of printing-house histories and practices, of paper making and distribution, of both the visual and chemical properties of book-making materials, and of the politics and economics, no less than the machinery, of book production provided information that was crucial for understanding how manuscript texts were transformed into distributable, salable products. They used this knowledge, however, in the service of authorial preferences and practices for the literary work, identifying and evaluating the work of other participants in the production process according to how well that labor served the purposes that their studies associated with the author.

McKenzie's insight into the sociology of texts required a different agenda, one might say a more democratic agenda, one that recognized not only the fact that each material text indexed a network of social, economic, and political forces, industries and purposes, but that this network of human interaction was interesting in its own right, deserving of our attention and respect. One of the early consequences of this shift in agenda was to see that bibliography and scholarly editing had, in the recent past, been used in an elitist and exclusionary manner, privileging what in the 1970s and 1980s were more and more frequently referred to as dead white males. The editorial community in America swiftly overreacted.

Following publication of McKenzie's lectures, there was something of a scramble to distance the purposes of scholarly editing from elitist rhetoric and the goals associated with that recent past in bibliography and textual studies. In those days, a growing awareness of the European principles of historical critical editing gave this tendency a boost. In European practice, the primary function of the bibliographer and scholarly editor was to identify, order, and reveal the historical record of textual existence. European editors looked askance at editions that were emended to represent more nearly the national cultural heritage or the desires of solitary geniuses. The results of historical critical editing looked a bit like condensed surrogate archives: an accurately reproduced text and an apparatus containing all the variants. Such editions could be used to study the history of text development, giving the textual details of what bibliography had identified. More positively, and more in keeping with the main arguments of McKenzie's lectures, was the development of book history as a cultural investigation of the interactions and influences of industries and crafts that affected the production of books. McKenzie directed his insights toward the history of the book far more than he did toward editorial policies.

My view of the semiotics of bibliography is based in part on the thought that, because we are human—rather than because we are bibliographers, textual critics, scholarly editors, or book historians—we can make the mistake of devaluing what our predecessors have done simply because they did not see what we, who are actually standing on their shoulders, are able to see. Sweeping away the bad old methods to make way for the new often has the unintended consequence of sweeping the good with it. I believe we have been reluctant to see or acknowledge how we have been guilty. The new argument went something like this: If we were to acknowledge and respect the network of humans involved in book production, it might seem logical to think that editing a work to reflect an author's intentions (i.e., excluding the participation of production personnel) would be an act of disrespect for the production team. In addition, emendation always creates a text that had not existed before (choice pejorative locutions are: neither flesh nor fowl nor ever seen on land or sea, and mongrel edition). Therefore, emended texts misrepresent historical documents, substituting a modern editor's judgment for the historical facts. To be fair to CEAA editors and others striving to fulfill an author's intentions, they never claimed to be "representing original documents" and hence cannot be charged with failure to do so. Theirs were critical editions; they strove to represent a "work," not a historical "document." Even those who did not edit well identified their base texts and listed their emendations.

In the rush to avoid elitism and adopt new rationales for editing, something was dropped from sight. By the logic of the sociology of texts and of the semiotics of bibliography, *any* reprint, even an accurate one with no emendations, is a new social act in a new sociological network producing new material (i.e., bibliographical) forms with new associations and meanings of their own. McKenzie knew that full well, writing, nearly twenty years later, in "What's Past Is Prologue" not only that

> [o]nce we accept the premise that the forms themselves encode the history of their production, it follows that to abstract what we're told is their "verbal information content" by transferring it to another medium is to contradict the very assumption that the artefact is the product of a distinctive complex of materials, labour, and mentality

but also that

> any simulation (including re-presentation in a database—a copy of a copy) is an impoverishment, a theft of evidence, a denial of more exact and immediate visual and tactile ways of knowing, a destruction of their

quiddity as collaborative products under the varying historical conditions of their successive realisations.[6]

I submit that *the sociology of texts*, as defined by McKenzie in his Panizzi Lectures, *has no editorial consequence*. If the sociology of texts is to be the guiding beacon, then editing must stop altogether, because it is the whole material product, not just the lexical text, that indexes (points to) the forces that created it. Only the first-edition indexes the forces that created it; only the second edition indexes its sociology. The scholarly edition, regardless of its editorial principles, indexes only the forces that produced it, not those that produced the source texts upon which it is based and/or which it claims to represent. McKenzie states flatly that facsimiles and virtual archives are also copies of copies and inevitably "an impoverishment, a theft of evidence, a denial of more exact and immediate visual and tactile ways of knowing, a destruction of their quiddity as collaborative products. . . ."

The genius of McKenzie's work is biobibliographical in a broad sense. He taught us to see how bibliographical investigation of individual books widens into book history, supporting a better understanding of manuscript and print culture. McKenzie's insights do nothing for scholarly editing. They do not even do anything for bibliography itself, except to broaden the range of materials upon which we might wish to exercise the tools and methods of bibliography. McKenzie's insights were not about editing or even about bibliography itself; instead, they were enormously important in bringing together bibliography and sociology in the new field of book history.

It can be argued that the phrase *sociology of texts* has confused as much as it has startled and energized bibliographers and textual critics. Books and their texts are the material objects that are catalogued and described by bibliography. These objects are the products of a variety of human activities operating in cultural and economic networks organized to produce books and texts as marketable objects. McKenzie has taught us to see the book object as the focal point of the network of human activity that produced it. More important, he has given us a way of seeing the semiotic force of these material objects, indexing or pointing to all who were involved in their production. We understand the book in relation to the contexts from which it

6. D. F. McKenzie, "'What's Past Is Prologue': The Bibliographical Society and History of the Book" (1993); repr. in *Making Meaning: "Printers of the Mind" and Other Essays*, ed. Peter D. McDonald and Michael F. Suarez, S.J. (Amherst: University of Massachusetts Press, 2002), 271.

emerged. The word *sociology*, as McKenzie uses it, lifts us from close scrutiny of the material object and above the semiotics of the texts inscribed in them in order to see the broader networks of human activities that produced both the text and the book.

McKenzie explained to us how meaning is affected not only by the words *from* a page but by the words *on* a page. The material form of the page, produced not only by the author but by those working in the production industries, has semiotic force beyond the lexical text, conveying and indicating meanings from and about authors *and* other book producers.

An editor cannot, however, apply the principles of sociology to editing. He or she may choose the historical critical principles of collecting, recording, and revealing the texts as found in all historical documents representing a work, rejecting all but the emendation of demonstrable errors and choosing to do that, perhaps, only in footnotes. But that is not sociology. Historical critical editing emerges from a respect for documents, not a respect for production personnel, and not from the sociology of texts. An editor can (and should) describe and explain the fruits of bibliographical, genetic, and book-historical investigations that analyze and explore the sociologies of source texts. No matter how the text is edited in a scholarly edition, it *cannot* reflect the principles or the insights of the sociology of texts, because the sociology of texts has no principles for editing or reproducing texts. Each new edition, including scholarly editions and virtual archives, *has* a sociology of its own, *is* the focus of a social network of industries and skills relative to itself. A scholarly edition can describe historical conditions and events; it cannot replicate them.

McKenzie's insights support other activities: the creation of material archives, the conduct of strong analytical bibliography, and the writing of investigative book history narratives. Collecting, cataloging, and describing books entails, for McKenzie, an extensive historical sociology. It is not an editing strategy. The flight from intentionalist editing in the late 1980s and 1990s is conceptually and logically unrelated to McKenzie's work. Comprehensive digital archives accompanied by explorations of networks of composition and book production are justifiable on the back of McKenzie's insights. Authorially oriented new editions are not in conflict with any of McKenzie's observations or conclusions.

McKenzie makes this point explicitly in the foreword, written when the Panizzi Lectures of the year before were published in 1986, noting that "[d]efinitive editions have come to seem an impossible ideal in face of so much evidence of authorial revision and, therefore, of textual instability. . . . [T]he variety of authorized forms has opened up editorial choice in new ways, even to the point of creating, through conflation, quite new versions thought more appropriate to the needs of newly defined markets" (x). Later, when McKenzie edited the works of William Congreve, he produced an eclectic edition, pursuing the author's intentions by selecting readings and formatting aspects from several editions to emend his copy-text.[7] McKenzie first acknowledges that "respect for historical form and content applies equally to the different textual structure of an *œuvre*" and that "lifting each item from the soil of its first growth . . . replants them in new relationships" (xviii). He was speaking of Congreve's own two editions of his collected works, but the principle applies equally to McKenzie's edition of Congreve's works. The fact that new editions replant old texts in new soil obviates the hope that the new edition will represent the original publications. Instead, it frees the editor to create a new iteration of the work. McKenzie selected a copy-text and emended it eclectically to fulfill the author's intention better than had the two lifetime collections. McKenzie's "respect for the historical form and content" of original editions influenced his careful exploration of the pros and cons of choosing a quarto or collected works edition as a starting point. As editor, McKenzie considered what he would have to do in each case to bring the chosen text into conformity with the author's intentions. He selected the 1710 *Works* as copy-text but adopted the format of the 1719–20 edition for speech prefixes. He surveyed the options for emending, concluding that "[t]he smaller compromise is to consider each reading on its merits and, if it seems to be justified in the interests of the play, to restore the earlier one" (xxix). In describing his edition, McKenzie says: "The text too is inescapably eclectic, 'critical' in the literal sense that its readings are chosen from a variety of witnesses besides the copy text" (xxxv).

——————

Jerome J. McGann was an early promoter, one might say appropriator, of McKenzie's insights. Though appearing to follow McKenzie's 1985–86 lead in expanding the scope of bibliography, McGann used McKenzie's ideas about bibliography and book history in order to further develop a "social theory of editing," which he had already initiated in *A Critique of Modern Textual Criticism* in 1983. McGann's theory has developed and changed over

7. *The Works of William Congreve*, ed. D. F. McKenzie, prepared for publication by C. Y. Ferdinand, 3 vols. (Oxford: Oxford University Press, 2011).

the past thirty years, but initially he claimed (illogically, I'm afraid) to find support in McKenzie's insights for his rejection of eclectic or "copy-text" editing. He was already repudiating his own Byron edition, conducted in the Bowers tradition, based on a copy-text to be emended. McGann used McKenzie's work to support a requirement that editors eschew emendation, except for the correction of demonstrable errors. To emend, McGann argued, disrespects the social dynamics of the sociology of texts. That appears to me to be the intent of McGann's writings on editing from 1983 (*A Critique of Modern Textual Criticism*) through at least to 1991 (*The Textual Condition*). This view is still palpable in 2005 in his "From Text to Work: Digital Tools and the Emergence of the Social Text."[8] Though McGann, in my opinion, misdirected McKenzie's work, his "editorial agenda" has logical support elsewhere. The logic is clear: if one is interested in either production history or reception history, one needs the texts that were actually produced and that prompted readers' responses in order to make sense of those aspects of literary history. Both of these rationales for study require historical texts, unemended texts, as basic evidence. Rather than saying that for understanding production and reception one must examine the actual historical texts, McGann argued that McKenzie's and his own views of production and reception should influence how scholarly editing is conducted. Neither of McGann's objectives for the study of texts (social dynamics of book production and the integrity of readers' interactions with texts) refutes in any way a separate interest in editions that "correct the errors of history" or that "aim to be better representations of authorial intentions" by means of emendation and eclectic editing. They are different, not antithetical, aims in the study of texts. Together they prove that no single edition of a work can do all of the work's work. Furthermore, neither of McGann's objectives is achieved satisfactorily through editions that reprint specific historical texts without emendation, because the "new soil" in which the historical text is planted subverts the historical social dynamics of the historical publication—obscuring both the original production and the stimulus for the history of readership.

An academic community that is hampered by ignorance of textual criticism allows—perhaps encourages—people to desire *the* standard or correct edition of a work. That makes it seem that one editorial method should

8. Jerome J. McGann, *A Critique of Modern Textual Criticism* (Chicago: University of Chicago Press, 1983), *The Textual Condition* (Princeton: Princeton University Press, 1991), and "From Text to Work: Digital Tools and the Emergence of the Social Text," *Variants* 4 (2005): 225–40.

be the right method. Understanding textual conditions (emphasis on the plural) makes one ask instead for each edition to declare its methods and aims, so that it can be used properly as the tool it was designed to be.

A weakness of McGann's so-called social editorial theory of editing as it was originally promoted in the 1990s and onward is that its positive agenda was presented as a refutation of, and replacement for, eclectic editions. Another weakness was its claim to be an editing strategy. It changed the meaning of "editing" from "the curation and improvement of texts" to "surrounding unedited texts with historical and critical commentary." If *editing* means "curating the text by correcting and emending," then *social editing*, as it appeared in McGann's writing in the 1980s and 1990, is a contradiction in terms. If editing means "to collect unemended historical texts of a work and surround them with commentary," there is no contradiction. It would have been a cleaner and less contentious proposition had McGann promoted "critical archiving" as a desirable publishing goal that was not being served by "scholarly critical editing." Where scholarly editing under the influence of Greg, Bowers, and Tanselle tended to promote the idea that a work could be best seen and understood in the text of a work of art extracted from the archive of historical manuscripts and editions, McGann's social view promoted a specificity about which particular text was being commented on or was being reproduced. But "reproduction" raised a new problem in McGann's appropriation of McKenzie's terminology from *Bibliography and the Sociology of Texts*.

A brief summary helps reveal this problem. Since every extant textual form of a work had a sociology of production, it follows that any text can be chosen as the copy-text for an edition, including the manuscript or any posthumous edition: each document indexes a social network. The problem is that every new edition, including facsimiles and new scholarly editions, indexes a new sociology of texts, supplanting the one indexed by the copy-text that was chosen. McKenzie, as a bibliographer, examined the physical object that is a document (manuscript or print) and found in it the work of several industries that were economically interdependent. He saw that exploring those dependencies could lead to a fuller understanding of book production and of the people involved in the various trades required by books. The result is a view in which documents become the center of a range of historical bibliographical investigations, spreading far beyond single-minded concerns about what an author did or wanted.

This broadened bibliographical interest suggests that emended texts create false representations of the social dynamics of book production and reception history. Examination demonstrates, however, that it fails to provide support for *any* editorial theory or practice. That is because every editorial act enacts a new sociological event with new materials, new industries, new personnel, new readers, and new outcomes that supplant the material witness or (C. S. Peircian) index to the sociology of the period during which the document in question (the copy-text) was created. It is impossible to *edit* according to sociological principles because the mere act of reprinting (even in photo-facsimile) displaces all the original sociological conditions on behalf of new ones.

McGann understood and got one part of that insight right. One cannot edit a text (in the sense of emending it) and still be faithful to the social dynamics that produced the work in each production process. I think McGann went seriously wrong when he thought one could represent or preserve a historical social dynamic in a new edition that rejected emendation. A social editor has to undertake mental sleight of hand to separate the *lexical* text from the material text, perhaps not realizing that in this initial act the logic of the sociology of text has already been irreparably violated. The significance of the sociological confluence of events is vested in, and indexed by, the whole *material* text—the tangible product of the forces at work at the time—not by the lexical text alone. Faithfully reproducing the lexical text in a new material form with a totally new sociology of text does not preserve either the sociological or the social significance of the document chosen as copy-text.

There is a more sympathetic way to describe the social editorial decision not to emend. It involves divorcing McKenzie's ideas about *bibliography* from McGann's ideas about *editing*—or, rather, not editing. The social reasoning begun by McGann in 1983 in *A Critique of Textual Criticism* seems to reflect the Marxist literary principles of determinism in the means of production of commodities. It elevates the agency of production personnel to an equal claim with the author on the attention of editors and readers. In this view, the social "editor" acknowledges the persons, actions, and intentions of publishers, compositors, and other production persons whose right to influence the text is now on an equal footing with the person, actions, and intentions of the author, who can be said to have been demoted to the role of just another one of the folks involved in creating a saleable commodity. The "editor" pays homage to production personnel by not "editing." It does not seem to make any difference if the motives for this decision involve a democratic respect for all production personnel or a socialist belief in the determining power of capitalism; the result is a refusal to emend or to prioritize the work of some over that of others in the process. Attempts to find support for this social approach in McKenzie's sociology of texts are unconvincing.

McKenzie brought many more facts into bibliography and book history, but it did not place a hierarchy of value or an equality of value on the players in the network of book production. McKenzie focused on the implications of that sociology for understanding the past in a broad spectrum of questions and evidence. The "social" theory of editing, by contrast, imposes a valuation on the evidence to support an editorial agenda: the work of all participants is given equal value.[9] One must admit that eclectic editors, pursuing an author's final intentions, also impose a valuation on the evidence: the work's author is served, well or ill, by production staff. Editing requires valuation because it is proactive; bibliography and sociology do not because they are descriptive.

McKenzie's insights brought attention to the fact that Greg, Bowers, and Tanselle valued the work of an author more than they valued the work of production personnel. McKenzie and especially McGann emphasize that without the ministrations of production personnel, authored texts would remain in the manuscript (except for self-publishers such as Blake). Although eclectic editors had always acknowledged that fact, it looked, from the social point of view, as if the editorial practices of Greg and company were elitist and exclusionary. McGann described the author as one of many involved in the production of reading materials. Social editorial theory and practice focused on the collaborative development of the text of a work. Because this view results in the wholesale acceptance of historical texts as integrated historical entities, it has seemed to some to also be a rejection of intentionalist editing. In fact social editing is equally intentionalist; it merely elevated the intentions of compositors, publisher's editors, censors, and everyone else to an equal level with authorial intentions. This is democratic and social, but it is not sociological in McKenzie's sense.

The result of "social" editing is that the reader is restricted to reading the literary work in a form that captures a rigid lexical text from a historical document, repackaged and, thus, indexing a totally new sociology of text mixed with a modern social collaboration. Appeals to the so-called bibliographic code are irrelevant to the results of *social editing* because all bibliographic codes are erased and supplanted by new ones in a new edition. To be fair, "eclectic" editing also restricts the reader to reading a text that has been emended to fulfill what an editor believes to be what the author wished the

9. McGann's arguments in *A Critique of Modern Textual Criticism* predate McKenzie's Panizzi Lectures (London: British Library, 1986), but McGann subsequently found support for his views in McKenzie's work, as did Jack Stillinger, particularly in *Multiple Authorship and the Myth of Solitary Genius* (New York: Oxford University Press, 1991).

text to be at some point in time. Both types of edition can provide readers with historical accounts of writing and revision, and provide textual apparatuses that show how other documents differ from the reading text. Social editions reproduce a historical *lexical* text in a new *bibliographical* form; eclectic editions create a new *lexical* text from historical evidence, but like all new editions, they are also packaged in a new *bibliographical* form. Both strategies produce editions that index a new sociology of texts. McKenzie's insights into bibliography do not support either approach because his work was on bibliography, not editing.

McGann's more recent writings have drifted from the Marxist rationales that informed his work in the 1980s and 1990s. He continues to use the word *editing* in a way that I find inappropriate or at least confusing. Early on McGann's writing emphasized the social networks of literary *production* more than the history of *reactions* to literary works through reading. He described "the book" as a combination of bibliographic and lexical codes. Printed books were at the center of a network of persons, businesses, and institutions who together made the work/book possible. Emphasizing the means of production loosened the "myth of genius" and fixations on authors. In a more recent work McGann focuses on the social experience of reading as events in which readers create the work anew in conjunction with a book (material) and a text (symbol).[10] This seems to me to shift the rationale for the "existence" of literature from a means of production on to a series of becomings in acts of reading. In this view, continually growing and changing senses of the work arise through a history of readership. That is not Marxian, but it does signal a duty for textual criticism. The social network of a work's composition, design, production, and dissemination still is vital, but it now appears just as important to see the book as that which provides readers with the grist for the creative experience of reading and influencing subsequent readings. In McGann's newer view neither an author's desires nor the historical production events wholly determine editorial method. Instead, the realities of the market and reading—the fact of literary reputations—is acknowledged. It is true that every edition of whatever quality has contributed to readers' interactions with the literary work—and vice versa. Scholarly editions can contribute to that history but cannot correct it or supplant it. That is the sense I draw from McGann's account of the textual condition in "Literary History and Editorial

10. Jerome J. McGann, "Literary History and Editorial Method," *New Literary History: A Journal of Theory and Interpretation* 40 (2009): 825–42.

Method" (especially pages 833–37). Literary documents are the sources for literary history. The continued renewal of literary works through the experience of readers (i.e., reception history) is the other half of the social condition of book production. Therefore, textual scholarship needs to focus its attention on the documents that have represented the work to readers through history, not just in the original manuscripts, proofs, and early editions. Textual studies embraces all the documents that influenced what the work became and continues to become through history. It is no longer enough to focus on production histories measured against authorial intentions. McGann's ideas support critical archiving, not editing.

McGann provides a logical, if difficult, justification for a social theory of textual archiving. It was impossible in the print era to think about editorial projects in the ways that digital "editing" has made possible. In the material world, the equivalent of the digital library McGann is talking about is a comprehensive library of manuscript and printed materials. Such libraries have served this goal, albeit in one place for a limited set of users (those with the means to seek out the particular archives that hold all forms of the work one wishes to study). McGann's basic principles for such a digital collection, articulated in the last three pages of "Literary History and Editorial Method," are exactly what is needed to fulfill this vision of the existence of literary works. However, it is not, strictly speaking, "editing"; it is "archiving" in the best sense of that word.

D. F. McKenzie focused on bibliography and book history (description of books and how they came to be), not on editions. His own editorial practice remained author-centered and eclectic. McKenzie's view of bibliography was not driven by political aims. McGann's social theory of textuality, particularly in the 1980s and early 1990s, had a political slant favoring a view of texts that emphasized the means of production in order to elevate production to the position previously held by authorship alone. His more recent approach elevates the history of reception as an equally necessary component of literary works, because without the reader the work lies inert.[11] He sees the relation

---

11. An early proponent of the idea that a work's afterlife is an integral part of a work was Paul Eggert, whose account of D. H. Lawrence's *The Boy in the Bush* argued that reception history made the book what it became: "The Literary Work of a Readership: *The Boy in the Bush* in Australia, 1924–1926," *Bibliographical Society of Australia and New Zealand Bulletin* 12 (1988): 149–66. Eggert theorized and expanded this view in *Biography of a Book: Henry Lawson's "While the Billy Boils"* (University Park: Pennsylvania State University Press, 2013).

between a material text and a reader as the double helix or DNA of the literary work. That metaphor seems to ignore or devalue the author and production personnel, once so important to his argument. Since no two readers will read the work into existence in the same way, one can no longer think reasonably about the work as a purely material thing. Nor can one think of the work as a purely symbolic thing. Nor can one think of the work as wholly encompassed by an author's intentions. The literary work, from authorial concept through multiple production processes, and in the experiences of countless readers, is endlessly becoming; the digital archive records and preserves the work's history. Can it do that? An archive, whether material or digital, is still an archive; it is not an edition. If one wants to read the text of lost documents or of intended texts thwarted by accident or unwanted interventions, one needs eclectically and critically edited approximations. I concur with McGann's support for digital archives full of images of historical editions, but we cannot forget that McKenzie's observation that digital copies are, despite all that can be said in their favor, still impoverished copies of copies.

My personal reaction to these arguments is to say I wear multiple disciplinary hats. As a *bibliographer*, I want to identify and collect and describe as precisely as possible all the relevant documents for a work. As a *book historian*, I want to understand each of those documents as the focal point of a network of industries and the persons who ran them and who produced the books. As an *archivist*, I want to create material archives, establishing the relationships among repositories of physical collections of documents. As a *digital archivist*, I want to create virtual archives that are anchored in images of historically extant documents and that are supported, first, by accurate transcriptions, second, by ways to identify and display textual variation, third, by explanations of the textual variation, and, fourth, by expansive narrative accounts of book history. As a *reader and critic*, I want to know which versions of the text gave rise to which critical receptions of the work. As an *editor*, I want to identify the agents of textual change that I value and the moments in the trajectory of textual development that I find interesting. I want then to produce new reading texts that benefit from the knowledge represented by the bibliography, the textual criticism, the book history, and the virtual archive's analysis and display of textual variation. Finally, I wish to encourage, not inhibit, other editors who prefer other ways of arranging the evidence and of extracting possible texts. The purpose of editing is not to replicate the past. That cannot be done, not even with facsimiles—and digital images are, sorry to say, facsimiles.

Documents and texts constitute the evidence upon which students of literature build knowledge, but a foundation of evidence is not itself knowledge. What constitutes knowledge is interpretive criticism, informed by textual criticism and enabled by editions of various kinds, each fully understood by the critic, with each view of the evidence placed in the historical and appropriative context of textuality.

Editing always foregrounds some aspect out of the many aspects that are buried in the mass of variant texts of a work. It is possible that a given historical text already foregrounds the aspects that a modern editor would like also to foreground, in which case reprinting that historical text, albeit in new clothing, makes sense. It is also possible that an aspect of the text, obscured by historical production processes, can be rescued from the variant mass only by strong critical analysis and emendation. Editors must have the option to produce such texts as well. The freedom I am advocating will lead to some new, previously unavailable, forms of the text that will have great appeal because of the scholarship and critical judgment that produced them. It will also lead to some eccentric, poorly prepared, abominable editions. It will *not* lead to supplanting any other edition, and it will *not* lead to the text that everyone should read and rely on to the exclusion of all others. Neither will any other editorial procedure.

———————

It is not necessary, when we have new insights, to kill off our fathers and reject their work. Authors had intentions. Evidence survives to indicate that those intentions were sometimes thwarted in production and to show that authors are sometimes influenced to accept changes made by others. Emendation is not an attack on history nor on documents. Emendation does not disrespect production personnel, who, like most people, were very likely doing the best they could with what they had to work with, and for reasons they believed to be appropriate. It is just that the surviving documents for any given work do not necessarily represent all the forms of a work that we might be interested in.

Texts emended in order to privilege one or a few agents of textual change over others should be created—not because they are correct or more nearly perfect texts, but because they foreground important aspects of the work that were obscured in previous productions. Most, if not all, historical documents reflect interventions and contain errors and sophistications introduced by persons with the *power* but not the *authority* to change the text. New texts, which correct errors and privilege the work of one or more agents over the work of others, will add to the ways in which readers can read and (re)create the work. Such editions take their places in the archive, and we can value them for filling, or deride them for failing to fill, perceived gaps in the textual development of a work. If it is a scholarly edition, it will report not only on the history of the lexical texts and describe the material forms those texts have taken but also describe the sociology of those texts—all without losing sight of the defamiliarization inevitable in the newly constructed edition.

McKenzie removed much of the sting of his criticism of older bibliographers when he remarked that if he were to

> describe what we severally do as bibliographers, we should note, rather, that it is the only discipline which has consistently studied the composition, formal design, and transmission of texts by writers, printers, and publishers; their distribution through different communities by wholesalers, retailers, and teachers; their collection and classification by librarians; their meaning for, and—I must add—their creative regeneration by, readers. However we define it, no part of that series of human and institutional interactions is alien to bibliography as we have, traditionally, practiced it. (4)

This describes what Bowers and Tanselle did as scholar-teachers. In the end, McKenzie's fundamental message is about the connections between bibliography and the wider interests of historical bibliography, broadly defined. He spurred acknowledgment that social and interpretive concerns were part of bibliographical studies. Unfortunately, to do that, he chose as a strategy first to disparage a strict definition of the discipline of bibliography espoused by his predecessors. There was a time when the term *philology* was broad enough to cover everything that McKenzie is asking us to pay attention to. The primary importance of McKenzie's work may be that it poured the light of fresh thinking on a field that had, in the hands of some practitioners, become ossified—not because of the thinking of its leading lights but because of its mechanical application in the hands of followers.

Bibliography, scholarly editing, book collecting, and book history occasionally exhibit narrow interests. Book collectors who single-mindedly pursue first printings in first states as distinguished by points, without regard to the social, economic, or intellectual significances of textual or bibliographical variation, might be faulted for not applying thought to their interests. Book historians intent on describing the number of books or newspapers found in colonial, urban, or working men's libraries might forget that the significance of their findings can go beyond the mere discovery of factual data. Scholarly editors rigorously recording textual variants, and following what they take to be the one true method of preparing an edition, might be faulted for giving a wrong impression of what they have achieved. In denying that they have edited in the one correct way, one does not necessarily imply that their achievement is unworthy. One could enumerate examples of scholars who did, or appear to have done, their work with blinkers on, but who, nevertheless, produced useful results.

In the end those who do the most damage to the cause of progress in knowledge are those with a cavalier attitude toward the accumulation of accurate facts and those so enthralled by the big picture that conclusions and generalizations seem more important than facts. One can almost trust the work of the mechanical sloggers in the field, but one must correct errors and mount careful arguments in order to counter generalizations extrapolated from too small a sample, to challenge conclusions based on selected bits of bibliographical evidence, or to refute arguments carried on the wings of rhetorical finesse.

As I look back on my own work in bibliography and scholarly editing, it seems to have a theme. It is that every choice has a consequence. Every decision to focus attention on some aspect of the history of books and texts entails a commitment to an array of evidence that slights other focuses and consequences. If one chooses to think that the text of a work is inevitably tied to the physical manifestation of that work, it follows that one cannot edit that work eclectically. If one chooses to think of every text in every manifestation as having been either detrimentally or beneficially altered (or both beneficially and detrimentally altered) in the production process, then one must choose either the responsibility of editing eclectically or to not be an editor. Scholarly editing entails understanding the consequences of every choice. There is no set of rules that will help anyone to produce the one true edition.

Some Functions of Textual Criticism

What do we do professionally that actually matters? Matthew Arnold defined *criticism* and *culture* in "The Function of Criticism at the Present Time" (1865) as "getting to know the best that is known and thought in the world." The function of education, he wrote, was to enable a "criticism of life" in which we "strive to see things as they really are." Arnold's formula for education, elaborated in *Culture and Anarchy* (1867–69) and defended in essays such as "Literature and Science" (1883), helped to shape all Anglo-American education, and especially humanities education in the twentieth century. In particular, he articulated the importance of the liberal arts as a form of study essential for developing a criticism of life—that is, a habit of facing the changing world with thoughtful resistance to the merely new and the merely practical, and an ability to expose and analyze disguised agendas.

In accepting Arnold's rationale for education, universities, particularly the liberal arts, infused their work with a mission to create better citizens—persons of wide cultural interests and knowledge whose behavior was governed by an internal center of authority that had been nurtured by reading the best that is "known and thought in the world and thus to establish a current of fresh and true ideas." In short, the label "higher education" served a double meaning, suggesting not only something beyond elementary and secondary education but something uplifting, something noble. It was an assertion that higher education, and in particular the liberal arts, mattered.

There is something self-congratulatory about this view, and the twentieth century presided, so to speak, over its deflation. We have come to think of Matthew Arnold as an elitist, perhaps forgetting that he warned against self-

Revised from my inaugural lecture as professor at De Montfort University, Leicester, January 26, 2005.

congratulations, quoting (and translating) Goethe: "the little that is done seems nothing when we look forward and see how much we have yet to do."[1] Some have come to think of Arnold as a little islander, guilty of Anglocentrism, forgetting that he could read seven languages and wrote: "as England is not all the world, much of the best that is known and thought in the world cannot be of English growth must be foreign. . . . The English critic of literature, therefore, must dwell much on foreign thought . . ." ("Function of Criticism," 282–83). "Higher education" has become more of a synonym for tertiary education than a mission statement about culture. Universities' mission statements have largely abandoned Arnold's rhetoric of noble intentions and the quasi-religious rhetoric of centers of authority, substituting more practical locutions, such as the creation of a better-educated workforce or, with even less self-pride, the creation of better taxpayers. As yet I have heard mentioned only in jest that the modern university sees its graduating classes as EETs (educationally enhanced throughputs), but the joke would strike no responsive chord in a world where "higher education" was not partly guilty. Perhaps the meanest proof of this about-face is to be found in a travel bureau brochure addressed to recent university graduates, suggesting, now that they have an academic degree, it is time to start learning how to live.

My purpose is not to take us back to good old days, which in all likelihood were just as bad as the present. Nor do we need to rehash the results of Arnold's views in the so-called two cultures of literature and science, or the multiple little fights between liberal and practical education, or between pure and applied sciences. For now, we can also leave aside the history of elitism in higher education, where, as it has been said repeatedly, the highbrow ideals of Arnold turned out to be reserved for the few who had either the brains or the money to take advantage of high culture, even in the idealized and socially beneficial forms Arnold mapped out.

Instead I ask, given the present state of higher education, what do I do that really matters? I ask not only as a university professor in the liberal arts or the humanities but much more specifically as a textual critic whose primary fields are nineteenth- and twentieth-century English and American literature. Arnold's ideals have not been entirely vitiated by time and progress. Students still respond with enthusiasm to Arnold's defense of rationality, which he

---

1. "Das wenige verschwindet leicht deln Blicke / Der vorwärts sieht, wie viel noch übrig bleibt—" ("The Function of Criticism at the Present Time" [1865], in *Lectures and Essays in Criticism*, ed. R. H. Super [Ann Arbor: University of Michigan Press, 1962], 272).

called the free play of mind, not restricted by party interests or the necessity of practical applications. Students also respond well to John Henry Newman's defense of the pursuit of knowledge for knowledge's sake, articulated so forcefully more than a century and a half ago in "The Idea of a University" (1852). He distinguished between philosophical and practical knowledge, each with an important role to play in education. For many of our students, however, pressing economic conditions make practical considerations more important than ideal ones. For many, the answer to the question "How is this done?" supersedes answers to the question "Why is this done?" Preparation for a career is more pressing than preparation for life.

A. E. Housman, the poet, Latin scholar, and textual critic, addressing this same concern in his 1892 inaugural lecture as professor of Latin, University College, London, rejected utility as a reason for education beyond minimum requirements, "because to pursue the classics further in the expectation of transforming and beautifying our inner natures is, for most of us, to ask from those studies what they cannot give; and because, if practical utility be our aim in studying Science, a very modest amount of Science will serve our turn."[2] He continues, "The acquisition of knowledge needs no such justification: its true sanction is a much simpler affair, and inherent in itself." And he quotes Aristotle: "All men possess by nature a craving for knowledge." And yet, from all directions come questions and skepticism about the value of what we do.

J. M. Coetzee, recipient of the Nobel Prize for Literature, won that distinction for *Elizabeth Costello* (2003). In that book, a professor of English claims that "faculties of humanities . . . remain the core of any university."[3] Not only do his words strike one as a platitude, but the main character, Elizabeth Costello, responds to herself disdainfully that the university's "core discipline . . . was moneymaking" (*EC* 125). Coetzee, a one-time professor of English himself, has questioned the power of rationality and criticized universities in almost every book for failing, in Matthew Arnold's terms, to produce either faculty members or an educated citizenry with the intellectual skills and the heart courage—the criticism of life—to do anything effective about evil in the world. Whether the university was designed to produce such

2. A. E. Housman, "Introductory Lecture," in Housman, *Selected Prose*, ed. John Carter (Cambridge: Cambridge University Press, 1961), 16. Lecture delivered before the Faculties of Arts and Laws and of Science in University College London, October 3, 1892.

3. J. M. Coetzee, *Elizabeth Costello* (New York: Viking, 2003), 125.

citizens is another question, but Coetzee is not alone in claiming that if one looks for the strength of mind and heart to combat evil, one does not look for it in the university.

And so the opening question stands: What do we do professionally in the university that matters? What do we do as textual critics and students of literature that matters? Let us review a few of the functions of textual criticism. We must be doing something right, since textual criticism is said to be the second-oldest profession in the world and to have been actively pursued in the library of Alexandria before fire destroyed its legendary achievements more than two thousand years ago.

I have claimed that all literary knowledge is textual. In common with some other fields, our basic materials are texts. In all fields, the results of examination and analysis are recorded textually. Unlike some other fields in which original works can be distinguished from copies, in our field all works exist only as copies. Because texts are multiplied for dissemination and because texts wear out and need to be replaced, an industry developed from the earliest times devoted to copying texts and increasing the number of texts of any work that seemed worthy of dissemination or preservation—copies of copies.

Anyone who has played the parlor game of pass the secret knows what happens when a text is copied or repeated. Corruptions by the inept and appropriations by the mischievous combine to produce entertaining end-texts. But in the case of knowledge, changes to the text by the inept and the mischievous are not entertaining. To accompany the industries of copying and preserving texts, there developed a discipline of textual criticism devoted in the first place, but not only, to the preservation of the integrity or accuracy of copied texts. Proofreading is the first function of textual criticism—a task at which many otherwise well-educated people are miserable practitioners, editors not excepted. On rereading George Eliot's *Middlemarch* (1871–72) in the most highly rated and expensive scholarly edition, published by the Clarendon Press at Oxford (1986) under the general editorship of one of the twentieth century's preeminent Eliot scholars, Gordon Haight, and edited by another eminent scholar, David Carroll, one finds in the first paragraph of chapter 2 the following sentence: "Now there some something singular." Puzzled, I picked up a cheap reprint of the novel and discovered that it should have been: "Now there was something singular." In chapter 4 of the same expensive scholarly edition, I found the following: "Mr. Brooke sat down in his arm-chair, stretched his legs towards the wood-fire, which had fallen into a wondrous mass of glowing dice between the dogs, and rubbed his hands gently, looking very mildly towards Dorothea, but with a neutral, leisurely air, as if he had she was aware of her uncle's presence, and rose as if to go."[4] Again the cheap reprint came to the rescue, supplying a whole missing line, so that I could read, "but with a neutral, leisurely air, as if he had nothing in particular to say. Dorothea closed her pamphlet, as soon as she was aware of her uncle's presence, and rose as if to go."

One does not resent much the errors in cheap reprints, though I recall with some amused anger my experience as a young man reading Sir Walter Scott's *Ivanhoe* and developing a fever pitch of anxiety about Rebecca imprisoned in the castle while the hero seemed to be failing to breach the walls. Raising my fevered eyes from the bottom of one page to the top of the next, I found myself reading from Scott's *The Black Dwarf* because a careless binder had included a gathering from that book in the middle of *Ivanhoe*, unfortunately at the same time leaving out the pages critical to the fate of Rebecca. By the time I found another copy of the book, the sharp edge of anxiety for that estimable young lady had been blunted by cruel time.

It is too easy to multiply stories of how the monitors of textual integrity have failed in ways that, if our profession were emergency ward medicine, would have us all up for malpractice suits. While working at De Montfort University, I team-taught a course with Peter Robinson, who one day was illustrating to a class the ease with which sound information about Shakespearean texts could be had from the premier textual site on the Internet, the British Library website, where in a portal labeled "Treasures" one could find, among other things, full facsimiles of the first and second Quartos of *King Lear* and expert commentary on the differences between the Quarto and Folio versions. Robinson then opened the commentary showing the differences in the endings, but lo and behold the transcriptions used to illustrate the differences did not come from either the Quarto or the Folio. The Quarto's prose was rendered as poetry. Both texts had added stage directions that do not exist in the originals.[5] Even if textual critics were always successful in preserving the integrity of copied and disseminated texts, which we are not, would that sufficiently answer the question "What do I do as a textual critic that matters?"

---

4. George Eliot, *Middlemarch*, ed. David Carroll (Oxford: Clarendon Press, 1986), and *Middlemarch*, ed. Bert G. Hornback (New York: W. W. Norton, 1977).

5. I have since then been unable to relocate the offending commentary. Probably we were not the only ones to notice.

Standing against the effects of ineptitude and mischievousness, though basic, is only a first function of textual criticism. There is then the task of restoring integrity to texts that have fallen afoul of the inept and mischievous. For this task, proofreading is not enough; one must have emenders who know better what the text, in its details, should be, or textual scholars who can comb variant texts for more authoritative versions, or philologists who can bring etymology, paleography, linguistics, and other forms of erudition to bear on questionable texts and cruxes to improve the copy, either to restore a more authoritative form or produce a text better by some criterion than that found in the extant copies.

For example, in Thackeray's "three-decker novel" *The History of Henry Esmond* (1852), there is a scene near the end of volume 1 depicting Henry coming home on holiday from university and being greeted with joy by his foster mother, Rachel Esmond, and her two children, all of whom soon troop up to see Henry's room, freshly prepared by Rachel. In every edition from 1852 to 1989, we read that Henry and Rachel go up "hand in hand." The phrase is not unusual, but Rachel is in a difficult marriage, Henry is only a few years younger than she, and in volume 3, they marry. So, a careful reader might be justified in seeing this hand-holding as an early indication of things to come. In the manuscript that served as setting copy, however, the first word in the phrase "hand in hand" is squeezed in, almost illegibly, at the margin and in fact says "hat"—Henry goes up "hat in hand." As a significant phrase about the relationship between Rachel and Henry, "hand in hand" comes far too early and the material evidence of the extant manuscript points strongly to the conclusion that the compositor created an adventitious reading—or let's just say it: an error.[6]

A similar situation, already well known, occurred in the novel *White Jacket* (1850) by Herman Melville. The title refers to a very dirty white coat always worn by a sailor himself known as White Jacket. Just off the coast of Virginia, White Jacket falls overboard. In a state of utter confusion, "of a sudden some fashionless form brushed my side—some inert, coiled fish of the sea; the thrill of being alive again tingled in my nerves, and the strong shunning of death." The encounter with the coiled fish was no inconsiderable event for White Jacket. In perhaps the most famous critical commentary on

---

6. The manuscript of *Esmond* is in the Trinity College Library, Cambridge, UK. The manuscript reading is recorded in Edgar Harden's edition of the novel (New York: Garland Publishing, 1989), on page 91.

this novel, F. O. Matthiessen performs a sort of rhapsody of admiration, for he sees connections between the dirty jacket, the sailor's guilty conscience, and what he calls "the soiled fish."[7] He claims that only Melville could have thought to brush the guilt-ridden man with a soiled fish. Melville, however, wrote "coiled fish"; the word "soiled" appeared in the text for the first time in 1922 in the Constable edition, long after Melville's death.[8] Matthiessen didn't notice. Nor would it be easy for the citizens of many a university town to notice. Although this error was first pointed out in 1949, and although all the copies of *White Jacket* available in the libraries of Leicester, England, where I was when I first wrote this, were printed after that date, all have the erroneous reading: soiled.

It has been argued in print that though it may be true that Melville did not write "soiled fish," he should have. "Now there some something singular" as Mr. Brooke, by a similar strategy, has been made to say. Perhaps Thackeray, too, should have written "hand in hand." Should the world at large be grateful to textual scholarship for correcting these errors? Or should the world regret the intrusion of niggling though verifiable facts that interfere with the free flow of accidental and imaginative criticism?

The issue is complicated somewhat when every copy of a work seems faulty. What can one do, for example, for a text that seems not to make sense as it stands and for which no authoritative alternative exists? What does one do in Thackeray's *Vanity Fair* (1847–48) when, at the bankruptcy auction of the Sedley household goods, Captain Dobbin at first appears to be interested in the sale of Becky Sharp's drawing of Jos Sedley riding on an elephant simply because he remembers the comic scene of its creation? The auctioneer of course believed Dobbin to be an interested bidder, but when Dobbin blushes and turns awkwardly away, we read in the text of the first edition that

7. F. O. Matthiessen, *American Renaissance* (New York: Oxford University Press, 1941), 392.

8. Only the first American and first English editions have any authority, both of which say "coiled fish." The substitution of "soiled" for "coiled" was introduced by the Constable edition of 1922. Matthiessen's error was first pointed out by John W. Nichol, "Melville's 'Soiled' Fish of the Sea," *American Literature* 21 (November 1949): 338–39. A good account of this critical error and its exposure is found in Gordon N. Ray's "The Importance of Original Editions," in *Nineteenth-Century English Books: Some Problems in Bibliography*, ed. Gordon Ray, Carl J. Weber, and John Carter (Urbana: University of Illinois Press, 1952). The issue is resurrected and rehearsed from a different point of view by James Thorpe in "The Aesthetics of Textual Criticism," *PMLA* 80 (1965); repr. in *Principles of Textual Criticism* (San Marino: Huntington Library, 1972), 3–49.

"the auctioneer repeated his discomposure."[9] Some editors have tried to fix this nonsense by simply deleting the phrase altogether; others have followed the lead of George Saintsbury, who in 1908 changed the word "repeated" to "respected" so that in regard to Dobbin the auctioneer now "respected his discomposure." Nothing but common sense supports this speculative emendation, whereby an auctioneer famous for repeating things and getting in the face of reluctant bidders is transformed into a kind gentleman respecting the discomposure of an erstwhile bidder. Can anyone do better with this text that is so obviously wrong?[10]

Or take a case from my graduate school days when, to put bread on the table, I worked as a research assistant on the scholarly edition of the works of William Gilmore Simms, an author so famous and well known I need not further identify him. The editor, my professor, had encountered the word "sprinkt" in a novel that, if memory serves, went something like this: And the recent raindrops, sprinkt on every bush, soon wet her garment. Since the *Oxford English Dictionary* does not give the word sprinkt as a possible rendition of sprinkled, the editor was inclined to assume that a compositor had made an error. He emended to "sprinkled," much to my disgust. A few days later we found the same word, spelt the same way, in a poem by Simms. One can hardly resist the temptation to do good in a world beset by ineptitude, mischief, and corruption, regardless of our belief that literature is written by creative geniuses who, among other things, use words we have not yet learned.

One almost admires David Erdman's decision, when editing William Blake's *The Book of Thel*, to leave the apparent nonsense word "Mne" in the phrase "The daughters of Mne Seraphim." Many editors have changed "Mne" to "the," though Erdman argued that "Mne" was clearly and deliberately put there by Blake when he engraved the plate from which the poem was printed, and that although he, Erdman, did not know what it meant, he knew it was Blake's deliberate work, not an error by a compositor or other person.[11]

Without detracting in any way from the good intentions or even the benefits of speculative emendations, I think of Henry David Thoreau's declaration that "[i]f I knew for a certainty that a man was coming to my house

9. W. M. Thackeray, *Vanity Fair* (London: Bradbury and Evans, 1847–48), 145.

10. In despair, I followed Saintsbury's emendation (London: Oxford University Press, 1908) in my editions (New York: Garland Publishing, 1989; New York: W. W. Norton, 1993).

11. William Blake, *The Complete Poetry and Prose of William Blake*, ed. David V. Erdman (Berkeley: University of California Press, 1982), 3, 790.

with the conscious design of doing me good, I should run for my life, as from that dry and parching wind of the African deserts called the simoom, which fills the mouth and nose and ears and eyes with dust till you are suffocated, for fear that I should get some of his good done to me—some of its virus mingled with my blood."[12] Thackeray describes a similar feeling when he notes that "[t]he wicked are wicked no doubt; and they go astray, and they fall, and they come by their deserts: but who can measure the mischief which the very virtuous do?" (Or so it says in the manuscript; in the first edition, "measure the mischief" becomes "tell the mischief".)[13] In short, copy-editors and scholarly editors, exercising their roles as textual critics monitoring the copying and dissemination of texts, can do as much damage as good. No doubt editors do the best they can. Is it enough to say, in the great tasks of preserving and restoring textual integrity, that I am doing the best I can with the gifts available to me? Who is there on the planet who could not make such a claim and ask in that way to be forgiven for doing work that, although inadequate, could still be described as the best they could do with what they had? Is it okay for a university to set up shop and just do the best it can with what it has? Is there no more sturdy standard below which as professionals we should not fall?

There is more to textual criticism than these two fundamental functions of textual criticism—preserving the integrity of texts and restoring or improving the integrity of texts. Before continuing, I ask, to what does the phrase "integrity of texts" refer? Integrity implies a desirable singularity and stability, as if it could be assumed that a work is best represented in its most accurate text and as if the stability of that text as a text were a most desirable thing. As long as such assumptions go without saying, the tasks of the textual critic are well defined, and the importance of textual criticism in all fields of knowledge is well understood as a validating and maintenance task preliminary to real criticism.

Reflection on the processes of composition and revision, on the conflicts, as well as the cooperation, between authors and publishers, and on the history of the disciplines and practices of the scribal and printing professions soon exposes the plasterwork and wallpaper that covers the cracks in the foundational myth of textual integrity. No text is "the original"; every copy *is* a copy.

---

12. H. D. Thoreau, "Economy," in *Walden Pond* (1854), ed. J. Lyndon Shanley (Princeton: Princeton University Press, 1971), 74.

13. *The Newcomes* (1854–55); the manuscript is at Charterhouse School, Godalming.

Yes, there is such a thing as error, and yes, texts can be misrepresented; yes, there are wrong ways to edit texts. But is there only one right way to edit them? Consider the problems of composition, revision, and production, which entail individuals changing their minds about the text, and conflicts and compromises between individuals about what a text will say. Take note of the ample opportunities for careless or malicious errors. A social awareness of the political power of text manipulation and distribution as well as a sensitivity to the way authors and publishers shape their work for anticipated audiences and reshape them for newly anticipated audiences contribute to our sense that the texts of a work are multiple and fluid. In addition to the multiple opportunities for things to go wrong, works also develop in ways that cannot be rejected as mere error. Texts are fluid and changing in ways that attract our scholarly interest to answer questions about why the text has taken specific forms, who were the agents of change, what effects did different texts of the same work have on different audiences, and what social forces affected the processes of textual change.

All these considerations lead us away from the notion that there is a best text of a work that is best for all times and circumstances. They lead us away from the notion that a work can be taught or understood as a text that is either correct or flawed. A couple of examples out of hundreds that could be brought up might demonstrate this for us. Yeats's poem "September 1913" was first published in the *Irish Times* with the subtitle "On Reading Much of the Correspondence against the Art Gallery" and, fortuitously but not irrelevantly, printed next to the front-page headline "Dublin Labor Troubles."[14] Dated September 7, 1913, it appeared on the eighth, during one of Dublin's worst and most violent labor strikes, which was aimed ultimately at the same man who stood primarily in the way of the Art Gallery. The two disputes are linked in ways that allow the poem to speak with one voice against anticulture and antilabor: "What need you, being come to sense, / But fumble in a greasy till / And add the ha'pence to the pence," and so forth. In that form the poem was part of a dialogue conducted in the *Irish Times*; it is very similar to a letter to the editor. Extracted and published without its subtitle, first in a book titled *Poems Written in Discouragement*, then in another titled *Responsibilities: Poems*

14. For full details, see George Bornstein, "Yeats and Textual Reincarnation: 'When You Are Old' and 'September 1913,'" in *The Iconic Page in Manuscript, Print, and Digital Culture*, ed. George Bornstein and Theresa Tinkle (Ann Arbor: University of Michigan Press, 1998), 223–48.

and a Play, then in *Collected Poems*, and subsequently in practically every anthology of twentieth-century English poetry, it has ceased to be part of a newspaper dialogue, fraught with political engagement, has taken on the mantle of high art—still political, of course, and still local in its references, but now detached and universalized. Not the same poem.

Or take an example where the answers are less clear. When one text of *Hamlet* has the young prince sigh about his "too sullied flesh" (Q1), while in another he sighs about his "too sallied flesh" (Q2) and in yet another about his "too solid flesh,"[15] are we to assume that one is correct and the others are wrong? Can we assume all three are in error? Will it help to have a little context, so we know that (except that Q2 has sallied for sullied) Q1 and Q2 agree that the prince says: "O that this too much grieved and sullied flesh / Would melt to nothing" (Q1), while in the Folio he says: "O that this too, too solid flesh would melt / Thaw and resolve itself into a dewe" (F1)? Would it help even more to know that this speech by Hamlet is twenty-four lines long in the Quarto but thirty-three lines long in the Folio and that the two versions share in common only three of those lines? Can we believe that Shakespeare revised the text so that at different times each was correct? And, if so, what does it do to our concept of the integrity of the work *Hamlet* if we have two correct but very different texts? How can we take advantage of that multiplicity in other acts of criticism?

When John Fowles revised *The Magus*, he wrote, among other things, that the first published version represented a failure of nerve to include explicitly all that he really wanted to put in it.[16] The statement implies that the revised version is the correct one, which the author would like for readers to read. Is it not obvious, however, that, in order to understand precisely what constituted the failure of nerve, one must read both versions, noting the differences? That would be an act of textual criticism by which an appreciation for and understanding of one version of a text is enhanced by knowledge of another.

---

15. Images of Shakespeare's quartos can be seen in the British Library's Treasures, http://www.bl.uk/treasures/shakespeare/homepage.html, accessed March 7, 2007. The First Folio (1623) can be seen at http://www.perseus.tufts.edu/cgi-bin/ptext?doc=Perseus%3Atext%3A1999.

16. First published in Boston by Little, Brown (1965), and then in London by Jonathan Cape (1966); the revised version appeared in London, published by Jonathan Cape (1977), and in Boston by Little, Brown (1978).

Beyond the accuracy and adequacy of a text to represent the work, the functions of textual criticism extend to the accuracy and adequacy of the representation of various significant texts of the work—the work conceived not as a single entity but as an entity that has a developing form through time at the hands of a variety of agents of textual change who might have different levels of interest to us as students of texts and of history. Each text of the work represents in some unique way the historical circumstances of its production as a social, political, economic, and literary event that might be significantly misrepresented by some other form of the text.

The myth of "the integrity of text," whether singular or multiple and fluid, is matched by the myth of "the death of the author." In the mid-twentieth century, textual criticism famously and influentially was devoted to making scholarly critical editions designed to capture, restore, or recreate authors' final intentions. As Hardy might have said, while was fashioning this creature of cleaving wing, the French were preparing a sinister mate for her, a shape of philosophical ice, constituted from bits of structural linguistics, sociology, and cognitive studies. In Arnold's terms literary theory shed a current of fresh ideas on the monolithic notion of the integrity of texts. The death of the author argument freed critics from the responsibility to find historical and/or authorial meaning. It left an open playing field in which to pursue interesting misprision, or, if one felt the old tug of missionary zeal, the pursuit of what Frank Kermode once dubbed "involuntary meaning"— the exposures of ideological jingoism, racism, chauvinism, and carelessness about the environment embedded in the works of our revered authors. In this brave new world, any text would do because we no longer were constrained by what authors meant or meant to mean or by what the text had meant to its original audiences—audiences often inured to the same ideological blind spots that misled the authors. All was not well, however. As David Greetham once pointed out, though it may be the case that any text will do, it remains a question, *what* will it do? Will each text of a work do the same as any other?[17] And, if one is going to castigate the author for not knowing what he or she was saying, does it not follow that one first must know what the author did think was being said? Furthermore, would it be right to criticize an author for a locution that had been introduced or changed by a publisher or by some

---

17. D. C. Greetham, "A Suspicion of Texts," *Thesis: The Magazine of the Graduate School and University Center* 2, no. 1 (1987): 18–25.

previous editor, so that the force of one's indignation against an author or the society he or she represented should more appropriately be directed against the editor, the real author of the offending word? Indeed, any text will do, but not every text will do the same thing.

That being the case, what is the role of textual criticism? Is it to say, the world has gone awry and we must return to our roots, producing texts that will accurately reflect the author's intentions? No discipline can or does stand still. Change and progress and, to quote Arnold again, the free flow of fresh ideas is necessary to the intellectual health of any discipline. The enthusiasm of critics for new ways to read and new conclusions to draw need not be opposed. What needs to be opposed is the facile conclusion, the thoughtless method, the inaccurate identification of the materials on which new knowledge stands. Textual criticism agrees that any text will do but insists that each text will do only that which it can do: it can represent the historical event and the agents of textual change that produced it. *The Norton Anthology of English Poetry*, like all anthologies, reproduces all of its poems in the same type font with approximately the same margins and spaces between the lines. It represents raw English poetry about as accurately as picture books represent paintings or as a CD of best-loved highlights represents musical works. Does that make anthologies repositories of bad texts? I don't think so. But it makes them repositories of anthologized texts, and that is about as different as one can get from reading a manuscript poem by Wordsworth or a poem by Yeats published as a letter to the editor of the *Irish Times*.

A brief rant is in order about modernizations and regularizations and the imposition of consistency for the sake of the reader. In an edition of Walt Whitman's *Leaves of Grass*, the masculine pronouns "he," "him," and "his," in all instances that did not refer specifically to a male, were changed to "hu," "hem," and "hus"; generic references to "man" have "been humanized where appropriate [by substituting "human" or "person"] when the context clearly indicates no sexual reference is intended."[18] The editors seem to think that readers are delicate and literal-minded creatures. Should 1990s political sensitivities trump 1850s poetry? If Whitman's text is thought to be morally or

---

18. Walt Whitman, *The Original 1855 Edition of Leaves of Grass*, ed. A. S. Ash (Santa Barbara, Calif.: Bandanna Books, 1992). One wonders what the word *Original* in the title means.

politically damaging, would a little bit of factual information about the text not serve the same purpose?

The task of the textual critic is to help students and critics of literature to know which text of the work they are using—to reveal what its salient features are vis à vis other forms of the work, to be accurate and relevant, to avoid making mountains out of mole hills, and to show the way by which the knowledge of multiple, unstable, appropriated texts make a difference in the enjoyment of and the critical conclusions reached about any given work. It is not to tell the critic what to do with the text, but to let the critic know the factual status and condition of the material text(s) being used.

To summarize, the textual critic is a proofreader, an emender, an identifier of the unique features of any text, one who points out both the differences between texts and suggests their significance, one who helps all readers know which text is in hand and what its particular characteristics are. These tasks lie very close to those of other scholars whose job may be to write historical or critical introductions or to write explanatory notes. Beyond that, other scholars examine how language works, how punctuation developed, how handwriting affects composition, how book making, typography, book design, papermaking, marketing, and distribution might affect the work. All these textual elements affect readers and index the social interactions at different moments in a work's textual history. These tasks in turn lie next to others that all together form the community of scholarship in the humanities.

To put all that into the words of Samuel Johnson, taken from a manuscript discovered and first published in 1995:

Every man [or should one substitute "person"?] has his task assigned, of which, if he accepts it, he must consider himself as accountable for the performance. The individuals of this illustrious community are set apart, and distinguished from the rest of the people, for the confirmation and promotion of rational knowledge. An academick is a man supported at the public cost, and dignified with public honours, that he may attain and impart wisdom. He is maintained by the public, that he may study at leisure; he is dignified with honours, that he may teach with weight. The great duty therefore of an academick is diligence of inquiry, and liberality of communication. Of him that is appointed to teach, the first business is to learn, an unintermitted attendance to reading must qualify him to be heard with profit. When men whose active employments allow them little time for cultivating the mind, and whose narrow education leaves them unable to judge of abstruse questions, may content themselves with popular tenets, and current opinions, they may repose upon their instructors, and believe many important truths upon the bare authority of those from whom they received them; but the academick is the depositary of the public faith, it is required of him to be always able to prove what he asserts, to give an account of his hope, and to display his opinion with such evidence as every species of argument admits. Our colleges may be considered as the citadel of truth, where he is to stand on his guard as a sentinel, to watch and discover the approach of falsehood, and from which he is to march out into the field of controversy, and bid defiance to the teachers of corruption. For such service he can be fitted only by laborious study, and study therefore is the business of his life; the business which he cannot neglect without breaking a virtual contract with the community. Ignorance in other men may be censured as idleness, in an academick it must be abhorred as treachery.[19]

If you like anachronisms, imagine Matthew Arnold nodding in agreement on the platform behind Samuel Johnson as he intoned this high mission statement. We should not go there. Nor should Johnson's stirring words mislead us about what can or cannot be done—or what should be done. It may be true that the standard for accuracy in academics is higher than for politicians and business persons whose decisions are driven by deadlines. But it is also true that the business of literary criticism and of textual criticism and of critical thinking of any sort, no matter how firmly built on research and knowledge, is, at the end of the day, criticism and not fact—inference and not truth. Not only could there be relevant information as yet unknown to us or lost forever from recovery that would lead to different conclusions, but there is also the problem of difference in purpose and method, which can make critics value and use the same facts differently.

To Samuel Johnson's abhorrence of ignorance in the academic, I would add that ignorance is the academic's most intimate familiar that can never be

---

19. Samuel Johnson, "On the Character and Duty of an Academic," in David Fairer, "J. D. Fleeman: A Memoir," *Studies in Bibliography* 48 (1995): 24, http://etext.virginia.edu/bsuva/sb/.

banished. Though our goal is to know, we live with not knowing. What we think we know, we know tentatively, we question constantly, and we ask only what Matthew Arnold asked, that we seek to keep flowing a current of fresh ideas; for "[t]he little that is done seems nothing when we look forward and see how much we have yet to do."

Responsibility for Textual Changes in Long-Distance Revisions

In an essay developed with Dirk Van Hulle of the University of Antwerp, we defend the legitimacy of a range of different models and goals for scholarly editions. We emphasize the old rule of editing, that each method requires that an editor have rationales, preferably stated ones, about what a text is, to whom it belongs, and what precisely is represented by the edited text of the edition. We argue that all methods of editing, regardless of their benefits, entail losses and "slants" caused by the desires or orientations of the editor. Editors cannot fulfill the goals of all methods in a single edition.[1]

Critical scholarly editing is not an objective process, and the varying results of editing have varying critical consequences. The first variable we considered is to whom the text belongs—by which we mean the person or persons who have, or share in, the authority to change the text. Occasionally, persons of no authority whatsoever make changes in texts, which is why it is important to have a working notion of who, if anyone, has the "real" authority. There are disagreements, however, about who owns a text or for how long and for what purposes their authority holds sway. The text could belong solely to its author, to its first editor or publisher, to its audience, or be shared by all in some form. For most modern books, enough textual variation survives to produce at least three different texts based just on this concept of ownership. In addition, the text could represent an early version, a revised version, a censored version, an edited version, or even an adaptation. That might give us four or five additional versions. As an editor, what does one hope to recover? Authorial genius? The production design and genius of book manufacture? A record of cultural influence on the forms and wordings of a work through

Originally presented at Loyola University Chicago, March 2014, and, in Spanish, at La Universidad de Los Andes, Bogota, May 2014.

1. Dirk Van Hulle and Peter Shillingsburg, "Orientations to Text, Revisited," *Studies in Bibliography* 59 (2015): 27–44.

time? An edited book can purport to represent one version or a progression of texts. It can aim to establish one version or reveal two or more versions. A major question is, then, what does the evidence in hand suggest about the possible ways to edit the work, or what does the evidence suggest about which text would be the one an editor would like to foreground in a clear reading text or in the form that Internet readers are most likely to encounter first? Regardless of how carefully one makes such decisions or how clearly one argues the case for them, there is always the question of how such decisions affect critical engagements with the work.

Many critics treat whatever book they are exploring as an object with a stable text. Some critics believe that the text of their paperback copy, heavily marked for both analysis and teaching, is the most valuable copy (indeed, heavily marked personal copies are not to be sneezed at). Every paperback contains some, we hope legitimate, version of the work, which might do—though we might not be clear about what it will do. Not all copies of a book say the same thing. It is possible that for some of the works we teach, we really don't know which text our teaching text represents—or in what ways it differs from other texts of the same work. What a text says is actually what some actor on the text says it should say: authors write and revise, publishers' editors tinker, and copyright issues, censorship, and the technologies of book production intervene with demands that affect the text in the copy you hold.

Problems arise both when we do not know who is responsible for changes in the text and when, although we *do* know who made the changes, we think that perhaps the reasons for the changes were local and extraneous to what we consider to be legitimate creative concerns. My first example is from William Makepeace Thackeray's *The Newcomes*, the second from Virginia Woolf's *To the Lighthouse*. I see no single right way to edit or single right way to look at these textual problems. It matters, however, because how one edits—or declines to edit—affects how others read the work.

The textual problems here involve the uncertainties entailed in conducting business at a distance. When Thackeray began writing the serially published *The Newcomes*, he had a new experience, that of being well into the writing before publication began. In fact, for the first four months of publication, Thackeray was three months ahead in the writing.[2] Having seen the fourth installment through the press in London, he took his two daughters to Rome for the winter, leaving his friend Richard Doyle in charge of illustrations

2. W. M. Thackeray, *The Newcomes* (London: Bradbury and Evans, 1847–48, published serially; reissued in two-volume form, 1848; revised in one volume, 1853).

and another friend and fellow contributor to *Punch Magazine*, Percival Leigh, as his representative in London should anything go wrong with the text. Because each installment had to be exactly thirty-two pages long (two octavo gatherings), something could easily go wrong. As we will see, something did. Doyle could be counted on to adjust the length of an installment by adding or subtracting illustrations or by making bigger or smaller ones to drop into the text. Publication of installment number five went without a hitch because Thackeray had written two pages more than were actually needed and Leigh had only to decide how to cut two pages out. Unfortunately, for installment six, the postal service intervened and lost a three-page passage that Thackeray had sent in separately. At the time, he did not know that his manuscript for installment five had been too long or that three pages intended for installment six would be lost.

The year was 1854; the month was February. The publishers, Bradbury and Evans, had set in type the manuscript in hand but kept waiting for the added pages until the 11th, when they gave up waiting and sent the twenty-six pages of proofs, which clearly was too short to be adjusted with just Doyle's illustrations. The proofs arrived in Rome the day after Thackeray and his daughters left for Naples. Proofs finally caught up with him on the 21st, which was a Tuesday. February had twenty-eight days, leaving seven days until publication on the morning of March 1st. Five of those days would be required for mailing the proofs back from Italy to London, one day at the print shop for correcting and setting type, one day for printing, and one day for binding—that is eight days out of seven without counting any time for Thackeray to read the proof and write at least three new pages of text. Thackeray could not know why the proofs were only twenty-six pages, since he had sent in enough text, not knowing that the last three pages never arrived in London. On the 25th, he threw up his hands and wrote to Percival Leigh, saying there was no time and adding: "I hope you have eked out the number somehow: and trust in the Lord." Part of my question is, does the phrase "and trust in the Lord" constitute authorial endorsement of whatever happened to the text of installment six of *The Newcomes*?

In London, on the 11th of February, when Bradbury and Evans, the publishers, sent proofs to Thackeray, they must have known it would take five days for proofs to arrive in Rome. They would have surmised that Thackeray would take a day to read proofs and write three more pages, Richard Doyle would prepare a few extra illustrations to drop into the text if needed, and the proofs would return by about the 22nd or 23rd, giving compositors and pressmen plenty of time to correct errors, set three pages of text, and print fourteen thousand copies by the morning of March 1st. They could not know in London that Thackeray would not be in Rome when the proofs arrived there on about the 16th and would have to be forwarded to Naples. And so, February 22–23 came and went, but no proofs returned from Italy. One imagines Percival Leigh sharpening his pencil. Somebody, probably Leigh, rescued the two pages that had been cut from installment five; someone then divided one chapter into two, which added two half-blank pages because each new chapter started part way down a new page; they then set one chapter heading lower down the page in order to make the last page of that chapter wrap over to a new page; the compositors and Leigh then stretched out a few paragraphs by adding spacers between words here and there and/ or adding a phrase so that some paragraphs wrapped over onto a new line; and on several pages, the compositors placed one line fewer than usual. Finally, Richard Doyle included an illustration of three characters standing, elongating them as if in imitation of El Greco saints. All well and good, because the number was printed on time with the requisite thirty-two pages for serial publication.

174   THE NEWCOMES   *March 1854*

tuous conversation. The Colonel likewise danced quadrilles with the ut-most gravity. Waltzing had been invented long since his time: but he had[6] practised quadrilles when they first came in about 1817 in Calcutta. To see him leading up a little old maid, and bowing to her when the dance was ended, and performing Cavalier seul with stately simplicity— was a sight indeed to remember. If Clive Newcome had not such a fine sense of humour: he would have blushed for his father's simplicity—As it was, the elder's guileless goodness and childish[7] trustfulness endeared him immensely to his son. "Look at the old boy, Pendennis," he would say. "Look at him leading up that old Miss Tidswell to the piano. Doesn't he do it like an old duke? I lay a guinea[8] she thinks she is going to be my mother-in-law—all the women are in love with him, young and old. 'Should he upbraid'—There she goes—'I'll own that he[9] prevail. And sing as sweetly as a nigh-tin-gale!' O you old warbler! Look at Father's old head[1] bobbing up and down! Wouldn't he do for Sir Roger de Coverley? How do you do, Uncle Charles—I say, M'Collop, how goes[2] on the Duke of Whatdyecallem starving in the Castle—Gandish says it's very good." The lad retires to a group of artists. Mr. Honeyman comes up, with a

FIG. 5.1 Illustration from Thackeray's *The Newcomes* (London: Bradbury and Evans, 1854). Image reproduced from the 1996 edition (Ann Arbor: University of Michigan Press).

Except that it was not all good, because collation of the manuscript and the printed text shows that someone (it could not have been Thackeray; I believe it was Percival Leigh) introduced almost three hundred verbal changes that do not correct errors and do not help adjust the length of the number. I imagine Leigh getting more and more worried about the number as the days ticked off, and he began fiddling.

When I edited the novel, I was confronted with the question "What parts of the printed version represented Thackeray's work and what did not?" My object in editing was to produce what Thackeray wrote or wanted. Clearly, the publication format required thirty-two pages, so, even though Thackeray was not there to accomplish the changes required to make the serial part fill the required space, his intention is not ambiguous in that regard. But what about the three hundred verbal changes not required by that intention? I imagine what a "social editor" might say: "Texts are socially produced documents, so one prints what was produced."[3] I would disagree with the implications of the premise; works of art may require assistants to help the author, but the work of production personnel is not all of a piece with that of the author. Furthermore, if one prints what was produced, it is called a reprint, not a critical edition. My solution, in the absence of conclusive evidence, was to edit the sixth number two ways—first, for its proper place in the novel, I eliminated the three hundred or so verbal changes probably introduced by Leigh, and, second, I re-edited the number, accepting the verbal changes as if Thackeray had either made them himself or somehow authorized Leigh to make them. I tucked that version at the back of the volume.[4]

Turning to Virginia Woolf's *To the Lighthouse*,[5] I first want to acknowledge the Woolf Online website (www.woolfonline.com), which I and a team of technical and scholarly partners have put together, because everything from here on derives from that surrogate literary archive. For this novel, the author willingly cut out two and a half pages of text that she originally wrote and subsequently corrected at proof stage, fully intending them to be part of the finished work, before the printer pointed out to her that the text was too long to be printed efficiently as set. Woolf did the required cutting, but she

3. Social and sociological impulses in editing are discussed in essays 3 ("The Semiotics of Bibliography") and 10 ("Scholarly Editing as a Cultural Enterprise").

4. W. M. Thackeray, *The Newcomes*, edited by Peter Shillingsburg and R. D. McMaster (New York: Garland Publishing, 1996).

5. Virginia Woolf, *To the Lighthouse* (London: Hogarth Press, 1927; New York: Harcourt Brace, 1927).

never would have done it, had the printer not requested it for format's sake. My question in this instance has to do with what was lost by a cut dictated by factors having nothing to do with artistic or creative considerations, even though the author herself executed the changes. It helps to clarify thinking about the process if one imagines two writing campaigns: the first ends with the correction of the first two copies of proofs (one sent to Harcourt Brace in New York and the other returned to R. and R. Clark in Edinburgh); the second campaign began with the unexpected realization that two and one half pages would need to be cut from the final gatherings of the novel.

Woolf's manuscript, which survives, is actually an early draft. It is a full draft, but it was the basis of a typescript, which for the most part no longer exists.[6] That lost typescript was the basis for at least one new typescript (now also lost) that was sent to R. and R. Clark for typesetting. These two known, but missing, typescript stages of textual revision stood between the extant manuscript and the next extant stage: proofs for the British edition. Two copies, one full set and one partial set, of the first proofs survive; these are the copies Woolf sent to America—the ones she sent back to R. and R. Clark are missing. There might have been more intervening typescripts, but none have been found. The text of the proofs, therefore, contains authorial as well as compositorial interventions. Because two known-to-be-missing typescript stages of authorial revision are now represented only in the proofs, many editors would choose the proofs as a base text, if choosing only between proofs and manuscript.

An analysis of production and revision shows that the choice is actually more complicated. At R. and R. Clark, design and production personnel chose a type font and type size, and then compositors set the book and pulled multiple sets of already-paginated page proofs. If there were galley proofs, Woolf never saw them and they no longer exist. Each successive batch of proof was stamped "first proofs" and dated. Both surviving copies of proofs are identical; that is, all surviving proofs were pulled from type as set, and none are from revised type composition. The proofs end on page 322, which becomes very significant. The Edinburgh printer sent at least two full sets to Woolf in London, where she set to work correcting and occasionally revising on two copies, one to send back to R. and R. Clark to correct type already

6. The part that does exist, corresponding to book 2, "Time Passes," was sent to the translator of the French excerpt.

set for the British edition and one to send on to Harcourt Brace in New York for setting type anew for the American edition.

A quirk of the American copyright law passed in 1891 and not revised until 1954 required that in order for a foreign work to be protected by copyright in America, it not only had to be typeset and printed in America but had to be published in America first. That law, therefore, dictated the schedule for the manufacture and publication of *To the Lighthouse*, which was published on both sides of the Atlantic almost simultaneously on May 5, 1927—at least technically first in America.

The batches of proofs sent from R. and R. Clark to Woolf are date-stamped January 31 through February 12. They appear to have been sent to Woolf as each became ready. We do not know if Woolf corrected and returned the proofs in batches or if she waited to send proofs of the whole book back at once. We know, however, that the last pages of her corrected proof arrived in America on March 10, nearly a month after Woolf received them from Clark. The proofs sent to America are the only ones now extant.

Note especially the fact that Woolf had worked her way through the whole set of proofs, in two copies, correcting and approving what she found. She sent one copy to New York. The other copy, no longer extant, she sent back to R. and R. Clark. Woolf marked both copies similarly but not identically—the resulting editions therefore differ. There was a problem, however, caused by the book production staff at Clark, whose choice of type font and type size resulted in a book 322 pages long. This was a problem because the book was to be printed in octavo format, eight leaves or sixteen pages to a gathering. Twenty gatherings comes to exactly 320 pages, which means that pages 321 and 322 were the front and back of a single leaf—the first leaf of a new gathering, the rest of which would be blank. That single leaf of text, from the printer's point of view, required as much printing effort as a whole gathering. To avoid that additional expense, Clark asked Woolf to cut two pages, and they sent her two more copies of the last three gatherings of the original proofs, on which she could indicate where the cuts were to be made.

My main concern here is with the motive for the cuts. The decision to make the cuts did *not* originate with Virginia Woolf. Her changes did not, at least initially, represent a response to considerations for style, narrative, or artistic aims. The changes are not even responses to suggested improvements by an editor or objections from a censor. The initial motive, pure and simple, was to recover from a mechanical miscalculation that pushed two pages of text onto an otherwise empty gathering. The revisions were dictated by book production format and were caused by decisions Woolf had nothing to do with—to wit, the type font and type size used for the first British edition.

It can be argued that Woolf, regardless of the motive for the changes, must have believed the changes were for the good because she made the cuts on the second set of proofs, which she sent to America, as well as on the proofs sent back to Edinburgh. The American designer had chosen a smaller type font, resulting in about 318 pages, so there was plenty of space to accommodate the original text in the American edition. That is, however, a spurious argument, for Woolf never saw proofs for the American edition and did not know that the American edition did not require any cuts. It remains an open question if she thought her new changes were good and should be in both editions, or if she assumed that the problem with the British proofs would be replicated in the American proofs and so she had better shorten that text also.

A first question, in editing this book now, is "Should one restore the originally intended text in the first set of proofs and ignore the cuts made for format's sake on the second set of proofs?" A second question is "Does reading the book as Virginia Woolf first reviewed and approved the proofs create a different effect from reading the book as revised by Woolf in response to the printer's request that she dock two pages?"

Studying the history of revision is one thing; deciding how to edit the novel is another. Should one restore the pre-format-problem version of the work or go with the published version? That depends. It depends on whether one believes the work as published fulfilled a social contract among author, publisher, production crew, and audience such that restoring the earlier version would be a breach of that contract, throwing a spanner in the works of history, so to speak. Or whether one believes that extraneous contingencies influencing the work, whether they be mechanical, such as in this case, or a combination of mechanical and editorial, as in the case of *The Newcomes*, should be redressed to restore the considered and deliberate and determinable wishes of the author at a specific point in time. Suppose the changes were the result of censorship or a clash of wills between author and publisher, as can often happen. As I mentioned at the beginning, it depends on your notion of who does or should "own the text." In this case, the answer is complicated by the fact that the changes were made willingly by the author. That might be enough to make one accept all the changes—unless one thinks about it.

Consider that these final changes were spurred by nonartistic, noncreative conditions, forced on the author, who had not anticipated the requirement while crafting the perfect final product that turned out to be not so final. One can argue that, given the chance thrust on her by production necessities, Woolf embraced the opportunity to improve the work. That leads to our second question.

Suppose one decides one version is better than the other—more consistent with Woolf's artistic development or more to one's taste, fulfilling one's own preconceived notion of Woolf as an artist. Suppose that, as editor, one is inclined to adopt one version over another on critical grounds or is inclined to accept some changes but not others. Most editors will admit that no edition is objective, but, inconsistent thinkers as they almost all are, they are nearly unanimous in finding fault with editors who admit they are exercising their critical judgment in producing an edited text. That is one reason behind my observation that there is not just one right way to edit, and that every way to edit involves distortions of one sort or another. I could argue that the manuscript, the proofs, and the early published editions all already have distorted the work in one way or another.

Pursuing the second question a bit further: Do the two-page-plus cuts near the end of *To the Lighthouse* create two versions with different effects? Effects of reading are determined significantly by a reader's individual reactions and are, therefore, not themselves objective or essential elements of or in the texts. That is, the text alone does not determine effects on readers. However, whatever effects the two versions have on readers are stimulated by one text or another—different texts, each of which is objective and verifiable.

So, let us examine the cuts from the end of *To the Lighthouse* to see what we think about them critically. A brief review will set the context of the cuts.

Book 1 of *To the Lighthouse*, "The Window," can hardly be said to focus on anything, but remarkable in that section are the endless deferral of the trip to the lighthouse, the difficulties Lily has with getting her painting (or anything else for that matter) right, and the relation between Mr. and Mrs. Ramsay, with which the section ends, where Mr. Ramsay's insatiable need for affirmation is pitted against Mrs. Ramsay's reluctance to put what she feels and what he needs in so many words—as dull sublunary lovers might. Most readers of the novel probably are not aware that the American and English editions of "The Window" have sharply different endings, leaving

English readers with a sense of Mrs. Ramsay's triumph and American readers with the fact that Mr. Ramsay knew.[7]

A common view of book 2, "Time Passes," is that it is an impressionistic, philosophical playing with the idea of what happens when nothing happens—the ten-year interval of neglect in which, seemingly without intention or human intervention, everything stops and everything changes, perhaps through something like the quiet ministry of frost or wind and tide.

In the third book, "The Lighthouse," Mrs. Ramsay is dead, as is Andrew, who was killed in the war, the long-deferred trip to the lighthouse takes place, and Lily finally finishes her painting. One other reminder: in book 3, there are only two sentences written in an objective third-person omniscient point of view. The two sentences constitute the whole of section 6 (mislabeled 7 in the British edition[8] and blocked off by square brackets in the American edition and parentheses in the British). The rest of the book is presented in the third person but is limited to the mind and perspective of one character and then another. Thus, a cut is not just a piece of information withheld from the reader; every cut is a cut in the mind of the character. Even if a similar thought is given to the reader in some other place in some other character's mind, it remains lost from the thinking of the character affected by the deleted text.

There are new revisions throughout the last three gatherings, but two full pages are cut from section 8 (labeled 9 in the British edition). The section begins in Cam's mind but settles mostly into the mind of James, who is trying his best to fend off the image of his oppressive father by plunging symbolic daggers into his symbolic heart so that James can retrieve the image of his mother, who, he remembered, said whatever came into her head and thus, perhaps, was the only one who spoke only the truth. This section is a bit like "Time Passes" in that it takes place during a lull in the wind, while the boat sits motionless in the water, the fish lie dead in the bottom of the boat, Cam and James are lost in thought, and Mr. Ramsay reads silently from his book with a mottled cover like a plover's egg.

7. The differences are noted in a number of scholarly publications but can be conveniently reviewed in "The Composition, Revision, Printing and Publications of *To the Lighthouse*" by Mark Hussey and Peter Shillingsburg, Woolf Online (http://www.woolfonline.com, under "Contexts" in the right-hand menu).

8. The English edition skipped numbering from section 1 to section 3, thus misnumbering all remaining sections.

In this section alone, Woolf achieved the entire reduction in text requested by R. and R. Clark for the British edition. However, she took the opportunity to make other changes, too. I will look first at the major cuts.

Readers familiar with *To the Lighthouse* might be reading the following passages for the first time, since they appear in very few places—and not in any trade edition of the novel. The question before us is "Do the cut passages add to or change one's notion of James and his relation to his father?" All the cut passages are in the mind of James, who does not elsewhere in the novel think or express these thoughts. In the text as it was published on both sides of the Atlantic, James thinks about his father's nearing presence (see fig. 5.2).

Originally, the proof version that Woolf thought was the final form was rather different (see figs. 5.3a and 5.3b):

The picture of the first copy of the proof, pages 286–87, has to be imagined without the black pen alterations, which were copied by an editor at Harcourt Brace in New York onto this original set of proofs only after Woolf had altered and sent in the second copy (see figs. 5.4a and 5.4b):

The Harcourt Brace editor accurately recopied onto the first copy of proofs the alterations Woolf had made on the second set of proofs. No problem there, but the major deletion seems to me to be very significant, removing from James's imagination the horror of thinking of his mother with his father near. Readers can make of that what they will; it is not explicit elsewhere in the novel—and, therefore, nowhere in the published book. A

But he pulled himself up. Whenever he said "they" or "a person", and then began hearing the rustle of some one coming, the tinkle of some one going, he became extremely sensitive to the presence of whoever might be in the room. It was his father now. The strain became acute. For in one moment if there was no breeze, his father would slap the covers of his book together, and say: "What's happening now? What

286

FIG. 5.2   First British edition of Woolf's *To the Lighthouse* (London: Hogarth Press, 1927), page 286.

cut of fifty-six lines—all in James's mind—begins on page 288 of the proof. Notice that Woolf initially crossed out most of the first page, and then reinstated the top third. The final cancellation undertaken to save space begins with a horizontal strikethrough. The final paragraph of the cut is uniquely revealing about James's love–hate relation with his father (see figs. 5.5a, 5.5b, and 5.5c).

It is possible that one could infer from other passages in the novel that James resented or even hated his father, even as he acted subserviently to him, but nowhere else do we get a sense of James's suppressed desire to admire his

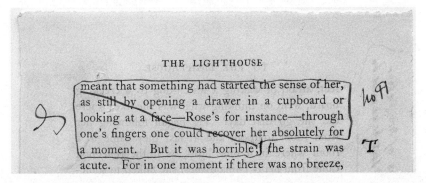

FIG 5.3a   First copy of the proofs of *To the Lighthouse*, page 286, with the Harcourt Brace editor's black-pencil alterations copied from Woolf's violet-ink alterations in the second copy of the proofs (see fig. 5.4a).

THE LIGHTHOUSE

meant that something had started the sense of her, as still by opening a drawer in a cupboard or looking at a face—Rose's for instance—through one's fingers one could recover her absolutely for a moment. But it was horrible; the strain was acute. For in one moment if there was no breeze,

FIG. 5.3b   First copy of the proofs of *To the Lighthouse*, page 287, with the Harcourt Brace editor's alterations copied from Woolf's alterations (see fig. 5.4b).

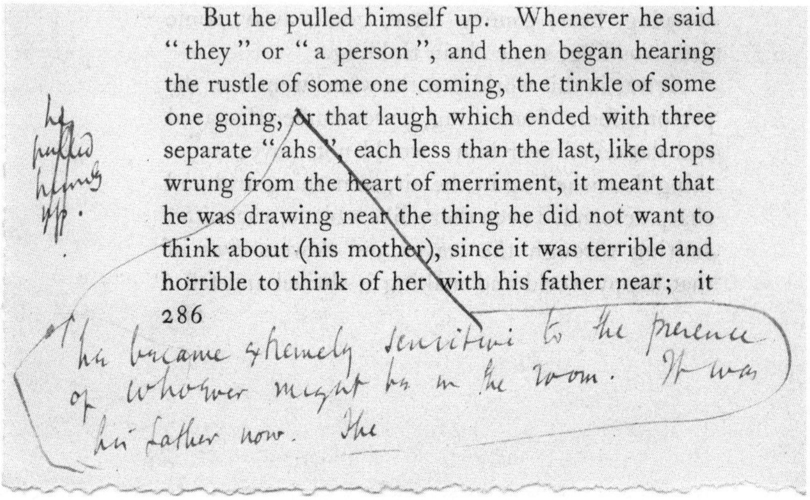

But he pulled himself up. Whenever he said "they" or "a person", and then began hearing the rustle of some one coming, the tinkle of some one going, or that laugh which ended with three separate "ahs", each less than the last, like drops wrung from the heart of merriment, it meant that he was drawing near the thing he did not want to think about (his mother), since it was terrible and horrible to think of her with his father near; it

286

he pulled himself up.

he became extremely sensitive to the presence of whoever might be in the room. It was his father now. The

FIG 5.4a Second copy of the proofs of *To the Lighthouse*, page 286, with Woolf's inked alterations.

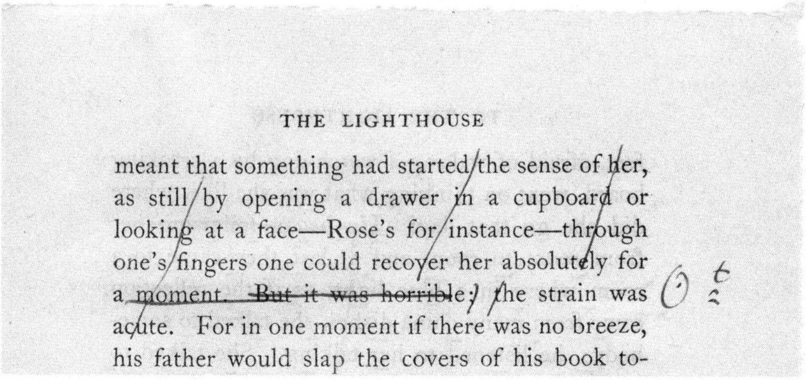

THE LIGHTHOUSE

meant that something had started the sense of her, as still by opening a drawer in a cupboard or looking at a face—Rose's for instance—through one's fingers one could recover her absolutely for a moment. ~~But it was horrible~~; the strain was acute. For in one moment if there was no breeze, his father would slap the covers of his book to-

FIG. 5.4b Second copy of the proofs of *To the Lighthouse*, page 287, with Woolf's inked alterations.

father. Furthermore, the bridge passage that replaces these two and a half pages glosses over the reasons for James's sense of oppression. The shortened result in print is merely this: (see fig. 5.6).

The removed passages strike me as dramatic; they had given to James's stream of thought an ambiguity, uncertainty, and vacillation. In the truncated published version, James's behavior had struck me as merely childish. In the first proof-stage version, he is Oedipal and profound and sad rather than just petulant and immature. I speak as it strikes me—or perhaps only

feet, afraid of waking a watch-dog by a creaking
board, went on thinking what was she like, where
did she go that day? ~~He began following her~~
from room to room and at last they came to a
room where in a blue light, as if the reflection
came from many china dishes, she talked to somebody; he listened to her talking. She talked to
a servant, saying simply whatever came into her
head. She alone spoke the truth; to her alone
could he speak it. That was the source of her
everlasting attraction for him, perhaps; she was
a person to whom one could say what came into
one's head. ~~Now in London, now wherever they~~
lived, they were surrounded by distortions;
lamentations; and long speeches and violence;
and old ladies like Mrs. Beckwith being kind,
and bald men sipping tea and being clever while
bread and butter turned brown in the saucer, and
there one twiddled one's thumbs in the heart of
unreality, sitting in the background on a stool,
and if in the middle of all this sighing and being
clever some one sneezed or a dog was sick, nobody
dared laugh. And the house grew darker, he
thought, and turned the colour of dusty plush,
and there were shrines in corners and nothing
could be moved, and nothing could be broken.
In the depths of the winter, or in those long
twilight months which seemed interminable, his
288

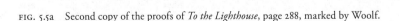

father, standing up very stiff and straight on a
platform in the city (to get there they must dine
early and drive eternally), proved conclusively
(but they could none of them listen) how there is
no God; one must be brave; for there is no God,
he said, while rows and rows of the ugliest people
in the world gaped up at him, in that greenish
hall, hung with brown pictures of great men. If
she had been there now, what would she have
done? he wondered. Laughed? Even she might
have found it difficult to tell the truth. He could
only see her twitching her cloak round her, feeling
the cold. But she was dead by that time. The
war was beginning. Andrew was killed. Prue
died. Still his father lectured. Even when his
hall was full of fog, and only sprinkled with
elderly women whose heads rose and fell, like
hens sipping, as they listened and wrote down,
about being brave, and there is no God, still he
lectured.

Often they quarrelled among themselves after-
wards, what could one say to him? How could
one appease him? For he wanted praise. He
wanted sympathy. He wanted them to go with
him and listen to him, and to say how good it
was; how it was the greatest success. Rose said it,
forced herself to say it, but she said it wrongly
and he was angry; he was depressed. And James

T   289

FIG. 5.5b   Second copy of the proofs of *To the Lighthouse*, page 289, marked by Woolf.

himself wanted to say it, for there he stood very
straight and very stiff, facing that dismal group of
people; one could not help admiring him; and
liking him; as he stood there doggedly sticking
it out about God and being brave. So that sometimes James would have liked to say it himself;
how he admired him; what a brain he had; and
would have done so, only his father found him
once with a book of his and sneered at him for
" it wasn't the kind of thing to interest *him*," he
said; whereupon James made a vow; he would
never praise his father as long as he lived.

There he sat with his hand on the tiller in the
sun, staring at the Lighthouse, powerless to move,
powerless to flick off these grains of misery which
settled on his mind one after another. A rope
seemed to bind him there, and his father had
knotted it and he could only escape by taking a
knife and plunging it. . . . But at that moment
the sail swung slowly round, filled slowly out, the
boat seemed to shake herself awake, and then to
move off half conscious in her sleep, and then she
woke and shot through the waves. The relief was
extraordinary. They all seemed to fall away from
each other again and to be at their ease and the
fishing-lines slanted taut across the side of the
boat. But his father did not rouse himself. He
only raised his right hand mysteriously high in

290

But all the time he thought of her, he was
conscious of his father following his thought,
surveying it, making it thinner & falter.
At last he ceared to think.

FIG. 5.5C Second copy of the proofs of *To the Lighthouse*, page 290, marked by Woolf.

> could say what came into one's head. But all the
> time he thought of her, he was conscious of
> his father following his thought, shadowing it,
> making it shiver and falter.
> At last he ceased to think; there he sat with

FIG. 5.6   First British edition of Woolf's *To the Lighthouse*, page 288.

for the sake of argument to say that an edition that restores the first proofs and rejects the second, shortened proofs might be justified on critical grounds, as well as on grounds of completion of a prior campaign of writing represented by the first set of thought-to-be-final proofs.

However, that would be too simple a choice to make between two documents not otherwise analyzed. For, what would we then do with the notion that, although Woolf may have been required to cut these passages for formatting purposes, she might nevertheless have taken the opportunity to improve the text in other ways.

Take two sentences on page 315 of the first set of proofs in figure 5.7.

Beginning with the sixth line of the photoquote ("It looked like the top of a rock . . ."), Woolf did nothing to the first sentence in the first set of proofs (the penciled-in alteration was made by the editor at Harcourt Brace at a later date when he was copying the changes Woolf made in the second copy of proofs). In the second sentence, Woolf did alter "fruit trees" to "bedrooms" and made other changes down the page. When asked to cut two pages from the text, however, Woolf, who no longer had a copy of what she had done the first time, took the opportunity to change "big wave" to "wave bigger than the rest" in the first sentence and decided that "fruit trees" should be "attics" rather than "bedrooms" (see fig. 5.8).

The copy-editor in America penciled "bigger than the rest" into the first copy, because this was a new change Woolf had not made originally. Probably the same copy-editor penciled a question mark onto the second proofs (barely visible in the upper-right corner) next to "attics" as if he could not decipher the word or could not bring himself to prefer "attics" to "bedrooms." He failed to copy "attics" onto the first proofs, which were used to set type for the American edition. As a result, the American edition says: (see fig. 5.9).

The English edition did not incorporate the phrase about the wave being bigger than all the rest (perhaps because Woolf failed to write that on the copy

> a bird, he spread his wings, he floated off to settle
> out of your reach somewhere far away on some
> desolate stump. She gazed at the immense
> expanse of the sea. The island had grown so
> small that it scarcely looked like a leaf any longer.
> It looked like the top of a rock which some big
> wave would cover. Yet in its frailty were all those
> paths, those terraces, those fruit trees—all those
> innumerable things. But as, just before sleep,
> things simplify themselves so that only one thing
> of all the myriad details that were crowding in
> one's mind just now has power to assert itself, so,
> she felt, looking drowsily at the island, all that
> was fading and disappearing, and nothing was
> left but a pale blue censer swinging rhythmically
> this way and that across her mind. It was a
>
> 315

FIG. 5.7   First copy of the proofs of *To the Lighthouse*, page 315, marked by Woolf and by an editor at Harcourt Brace.

> It looked like the top of a rock which some big
> wave would cover. Yet in its frailty were all those
> paths, those terraces, those fruit trees—all those
> innumerable things. But as, just before sleep,
> things simplify themselves so that only one thing
> of all the myriad details that were crowding in
> one's mind just now has power to assert itself, so,
> she felt, looking drowsily at the island, all that
> was fading and disappearing, and nothing was
> left but a pale blue censer swinging rhythmically
> this way and that across her mind. It was a
>
> 315

FIG. 5.8   Second copy of the proofs of *To the Lighthouse*, page 315, marked by Woolf.

sent back to Clark), but it did achieve the change from "fruit trees" to "bed-rooms." Neither edition achieved the change from "bedrooms" to "attics."

The importance of this sequence is that it supports the idea that Woolf did *not* have a copy of her work on the first set of proofs before her when she worked on the second set, primarily to cut the length of the novel. It also proves that she embraced the opportunity offered by that necessity to make

It looked like the top of a rock which some wave
bigger than the rest would cover. Yet in its frailty
were all those paths, those terraces, those bedrooms
—all those innumerable things. But as, just before
sleep, things simplify themselves so that only one
of all the myriad details has power to assert itself,
so, she felt, looking drowsily at the island, all those
paths and terraces and bedrooms were fading and
disappearing, and nothing was left but a pale blue
censer swinging rhythmically this way and that
across her mind. It was a hanging garden; it was a

FIG. 5.9   First American edition of *To the Lighthouse* (New York: Harcourt Brace, 1927), page 303.

changes not previously made and not required by the press. That is to say, there is not a clear and simple solution to the editorial question "What should we do with the changes introduced when the need to cut two pages offered a chance for other changes?" If we accept "some wave bigger than the rest" rather than "some big wave," why not also accept "attics" instead of "bedrooms" as the change from "fruit trees"?

These are the kinds of problems that some readers and critics seem to want textual editors to resolve so that the text is a simple, linear, final, clear text. It is an oddly uninformed request. It might be more valuable to know which text of the work is represented by one's heavily marked-up paperback edition and to know how that text differs from alternative forms. Students can handle such ambiguities; teachers and critics should, too.

Text as Communication

Communication may not take place at all. A speaker expresses in language a series of words and sentences that more or less satisfy the impulse to express an idea, a command, a request, or some other matter; at least in part, the speaker judges the success of the expression by assessing whether it has or has not adequately satisfied the impulse to speak and may further judge the success by noting the reader/listener's reaction. The speaker may feel happy about having "made meaning." The actual result of expression is either that molecules of air are set to vibrating or that molecules of ink or graphite are distributed on paper or electronic impulses on a computer screen in patterns that other humans have learned to pick up and recognize as speech or writing. The listener or reader then formulates from the disturbed air or distributed sign-patterns a set of understandings about them—meanings, feelings, implications—and recognizes in these formulations a sense of idea, command, request, or other comprehensible concept. The listener then may smile or frown or display responsive behavior to register that the text has been understood—that is, the recipient reacts to his or her own successful (or failed) effort to create a satisfactory arrangement of the audio/visual stimulus. Thus, satisfaction has occurred about "meaning-making" at both ends of a transaction for which there is no guarantee that meaning has been made identically. If mutual satisfaction after speech is communication, then communication has occurred. Both parties may be happy about the transaction, and we call it communication.

In most such transactions, with no guarantee that the meaning generated by the speaker/writer is identical to the meaning generated by the recipient, nevertheless, communication appears to be healthy and successful, appearing

Originally presented at the Society for Textual Scholarship conference 2005.

to produce identical meaning-making on both sides of the molecular divide. Waiters bring what was ordered (most of the time), ticket agents hand you tickets to the destinations you had specified, lovers respond in predictable ways to our love letters (many, if not all, times). Though it is true that different readers do come up with different and perhaps even contradictory interpretations of the same poem or play or other text, it is remarkable how often different readers come up with the same interpretation. It would also be astonishing if they did not. Indeed, one suspects that if interpretation of texts—if understandings of what a speaker or writer produced—did not lead most often to a predictable response, we might despair of ever communicating, throwing up our hands in frustration and saying, "There is no use talking to you; it's like talking to a wall."

In literary criticism, since the 1960s and the "death of the author" discussions usually associated with the names of Michel Foucault, Roland Barthes, and Jacques Derrida, it has seemed naive to think of literary texts as communications from the author to the reader. The important thing became not that authors write but that readers read and respond. It is not important that the author wrote stimulatingly; it is important that the reader responds creatively. The chief, though not only, justification for this presentism is that no reader can know for certain what the author's intention was for the meaning of the text. Ignorance is freedom.

However, it would be churlish to assume that texts are not communicative just because we cannot know for certain what the author meant. Likewise, critical efforts to read texts, even literary texts, as communications from authors to readers are not naive. So, if only as an experiment in thinking, what follows is an attempt to see what the consequences might be of seriously considering text as communication.

Text as communication raises at least two different notions. The first is that texts serve as a medium of communication, as a social but inert intermediary between two or more people—to wit, between the author and the reader or readers. The second is that, because writing takes place in the absence of readers and reading takes place in the absence writers, there is no immediate social interaction between or among persons who share written texts. Therefore, communication or interaction is between the author and the text in the first instance and the text and the reader in the second. Written "communication" is not immediately social. Wolfgang Iser focuses on this notion effectively when he describes the reader's actions as dynamic involvement in recognizing and filling what he calls the blanks and vacancies of texts with what the reader believes is implied or suggested but left unsaid by the explicit text.[1] For Iser, then, the interaction between the text (as the locus of artistic function) and the reader (as the agent of the aesthetic function) defines the work of art in a way that neither text nor reader alone can provide. Although there is a good deal to say about the interaction between the text and the reader, and even more about the dimension of "the unsaid" in written texts, I focus here on the less popular, more controversial idea of the written text as a medium of (a somewhat distant) social interaction between author and reader—the first of the two notions implied by my title "Text as Communication."

For many textual critics in the past, the idea of text as communication provided an important basis for textual criticism. From the day the serpent explained God's meaning to Eve, through to the Greg-Bowers era, text has been linked to authorial intention. It seemed important to understand clearly and without error what was really meant by the author. Textual critics have focused on getting the text right, rather than on getting the meaning right. Yet, both text and meaning are central to the formulation "authorial intention" because the importance of getting the text right was derived from the idea of understanding the author rightly.

Textual critics of the Greg-Bowers era did not think of authorial intention only or even primarily in terms of what authors "meant to mean." Instead, they thought of intention in terms of what the author "meant to write" or "meant to do." Textual criticism does not investigate an author's intentions to write a great novel, to influence an election, to indicate a love or hatred of the world, or to express feelings about a rose. If such intentions have a visible product, we do not have a way to trace with certainty that product back to such an intention. Even if we could know what the author intended to mean or what the work was intended to accomplish, readers are not bound to judge the result by such intentions. One does not find in editorial introductions or notes the idea that the editor believes that an emendation will get the author's meaning across more clearly. That would be "revision," which scholarly editors do not do. Those meaning-based authorial intentions are different in kind from intentions to use a pencil rather than a pen, to write on lined not blank paper, to inscribe the word *black*, not the word *white*,

---

1. Wolfgang Iser, *The Implied Reader: Patterns of Communication in Prose Fiction from Bunyan to Beckett* (Baltimore: Johns Hopkins University Press, 1974).

because intentions to act can usually be verified empirically, while intentions to mean can only be inferred interpretively.

Even when focusing on the verifiable mechanics of an author's intention "to do," however, the textual critic cannot avoid also asking why the author did it or what the author meant by doing it. For one thing, an initially plausible bit of writing might become problematic only when these two questions are asked. Did the author who first wrote "hat in hand" (manuscript) mean to change it to "hand in hand" (print)? Likewise, an initially implausible-seeming inscription may, on examination of these questions about potential meaning, reveal its sense—maybe. Did Blake actually mean "Mne Seraphim?" Did Thackeray really mean "repeated his discomposure?"[2]

The idea of authorial intention implies an intent to communicate something. Given the unfortunate history of the word *intention* in literary studies, however, it might be safer to consider "literary texts as expression"—rather than as communication, which perhaps implies too optimistic a notion of success. Expression suggests that the text belongs to the author. A textual scholar strives to verify the author's expression, rather than trying to ensure that communication actually occurs. And, yet, this avoidance of the word *communication* does not help determine whether Thackeray changed his mind about "hat" (in *Esmond*) or really meant to write "repeated his discomposure" (in *Vanity Fair*). It can also be argued that expression can only be judged by the tools of communication. In trying to determine the presence of textual errors, both approaches involve an attempt to understand "what was written" (the marks on the page), "how it was written" (the tools and processes of inscription), and "why it was written" (purpose and, possibly, audience for the writing).

The primary difference is that "communication" implies a desire on the part of both writer and reader to connect with a "mutual understanding and/or appreciation" of the writing, while "expression" implies only a desire on the part of the writer to satisfy a personal goal without any necessary regard for a reader's reaction. Writers sometimes declare that they do not care if readers understand them; they write because they cannot help themselves or because writing is satisfactory in and of itself. Readers might, therefore, be justified in not caring what the author was bent on communicating.

The concept of intention, and hence of communication, has taken a beating from many quarters since the publication of Wimsatt and Beardsley's

---

2. These examples are discussed in essay 4, "Some Functions of Textual Criticism."

"The Intentional Fallacy" (1946).[3] The result has been the development of a critical idiolect that avoids the word *intention*. To some extent, the avoidance of the word *intention* has coincided with an avoidance of the word *communication* as an element of literature. The question "What is the author saying to the reader?" becomes the questions "What does the text say" or "What is the reader getting out of the text?" All of these questions are about meaning, but the latter two formulations skirt the issues of authorial intention and of communication between author and reader.

Beardsley and Wimsatt's argument about the "intentional fallacy" is *not* based primarily on the notion that intention is private to the author and therefore inaccessible to others. They did not contend that an author might not know or remember his or her own intentions. Proscribing the intentional fallacy was, in their case, based primarily on two propositions: first, that a text cannot be taken to mean what the author wanted it to mean just because it was the author's intention to mean it and, second, that a work could not be valued as a success just because the author wished it to succeed. In other words, an author's intention, even if it were clear and present and palpable, could not be used as a tool by which to judge the effect or success of the work. Given the distinction between intention to mean and intention to do, it turns out that Beardsley and Wimsatt, who analyze only the former, have no bearing on the pursuit of an author's intention to write a certain text.

Incidentally, no one denies that authorial intentions are involved in the production of literary works. The questions are: What legitimate use can be made of the fact of authorial intentions in editing or interpreting literary works? Has not the editor who abandons the pursuit of the author's text appropriated the work for some other purpose than to understand the work as the author wrote it?

Among textual critics, the concept of "text as communication" took a second hit from developments in literary criticism in the last quarter of the twentieth century. With the death of the author and the advent of post-structuralist concerns, the focus of both literary and textual criticism began to shift from questions such as "What did the author mean?" and "What did the author write?" to "What does this text hide?" "What are its unintended meanings?" "What cultural influences are evidenced—possibly inadver-

3. W. K. Wimsatt and Monroe Beardsley, "The Intentional Fallacy," *Sewanee Review* 54 (1946): 468–88, repr. in Wimsatt, *The Verbal Icon: Studies in the Meaning of Poetry* (Lexington: University of Kentucky Press, 1954).

tently—by this text?" and "What is the most interesting use to which this text can be put?" Thus, for many readers and some editors, the text has become a provocateur or, more passively, a signifying material or cultural artifact rather than a communication from author to reader. This shift of emphasis from text as communication to text as a locus for imaginative uptake and readerly play or as a locus of multiple social and cultural interactions has had a striking effect: neither approach requires any truck with intentions or determinate meanings.[4]

Against the idea of text as communication is the propensity of persons to think of communication only in the terms suggested earlier and to see resurgent interest in it as an old-fashioned rejection of critical theory of the last thirty years—a nostalgic return to good old simple days when texts meant what authors meant. The idea of text as communication is, however, much more nuanced and complex than that; for, in addition to including the work of authors who deliberately set out to write clearly what they hoped readers would understand in the ways intended, it includes authors "intending" to write indeterminately or openly or provocatively in ways that encourage readers to appropriate the texts for their own purposes. Authors sometimes appear to have intended their texts in these open ways and usually communicate that intention in some way. It is too simple to say that all literature should be taken as something other than communication, either because it can be or because some literature offers itself obviously (intentionally?) to be taken as something other than communication. It may be difficult to distinguish between an intention to shut the reader out by deliberate obscurity (e.g., early Auden poetry) and an intention to open the work for reader appropriation, but then what is the good of a theory of literature that cannot deal with difficult texts?

Furthermore, the idea of text as communication includes two other rather subtle possibilities: (1) that authors sometimes, perhaps frequently, communicate inadvertently that which they had intended to suppress and are often "understood" in ways they had tried to avoid, and (2) that readers might choose willfully to refuse the intended communication and willfully misunderstand by a rejection of the meanings overtly offered. In neither case has text ceased to be a means of communication, though hostility rather than sympathy might characterize the ambiance of such texts and text uses. Further-

---

4. Another view sees the shift from an emphasis on text to one on document. That discussion is elaborated in a clutch of essays edited by Barbara Bordalejo, "Work and Document," *Ecdotica* 10 (2013).

more, neither is a rejection of the importance of intended texts, for in neither case can the reader operate without some notion of the author's intentions. One cannot claim something to be unintentional without also claiming to know what was intended, nor can one refuse what was intended without knowing it was intended in order to refuse it. Perhaps it should also be pointed out that a reader who "sees" that an author has tried to "hide" something is very different from a reader who "sees" the hidden meaning but does not realize that it was a hidden rather than an overt meaning. The former claims to perceive the author's intentions for the text, and the latter does not, though both may otherwise understand the text in the same way.

I venture to say, whatever else it might also be, every text that was ever written is communicative and open to be read as a communication from an originating agent or agents to an audience or audiences. Writing is not a found object like a piece of driftwood on the beach, open only to fanciful interpretation, but writing can be like a message in a bottle also found on the beach, open both to fanciful interpretation and the subject of investigation into its origins and intended purposes. It may be that the understanding of a text's communicative effect involves a realization that it was meant to communicate nothing. In that case, one proper and even historical response to the text would be to recognize its intended purpose, which was to be without purpose. Even though some texts are *not* expository and seem *not* to have been intended to communicate clearly and precisely some determinate proposition or opinion or feeling about a proposition, it is irrational to conclude, first, that these texts were not meant to communicate, and, second, that therefore any response to them is as good as any other response to them, or, third, that therefore the accuracy of the text of such works is unimportant or that any text of the work will do as well as any other text of it.

Whatever else readings of texts are, they are also apprehensions of some communication. That communication might be that the text is a gift without strings attached, to be done with as one wishes without further regard to the originating agent's wish to be ignored. It is difficult to see, however, how a reader of such a text, doing with it as he wished without regard to the author's wishes, could avoid fulfilling those authorial wishes. It is also the case that authors who wish for their texts to be understood in a certain way will occasionally have their texts read in contrary ways. If a reader exercises that freedom in direct opposition to the author's wish, it is difficult to see how that rebellion is not an acknowledgment that a communication has been received and is being rebelled against. If readers are genuinely insensitive to the wishes of the originating agent and proceed to do as they wish with the text, there is nothing and no one to stop them. Communication, understood as an exchange between sentient beings, will have failed in that case, but we can only know that it has failed if we believe that the text was intended to mean something. Likewise, if a reader genuinely seeks to fulfill the originating agent's wish to be understood but misunderstands the text, communication has also failed. Neither of these failures indicates that the text did not have communicative functions; both stand as testimony to the mundane truth that texts often fail to communicate the ideas, feelings, or wishes of their originators.

Post–Beardsley and Wimsatt criticism and post–Barthes, Foucault, and Derrida critical theory have not claimed that authorial intention did not exist or that authorial intention did not influence the composition of texts. What has been claimed, instead, and with general acceptance, is that the functions of literary texts are not limited by authorial intentions. That is not a claim that intentions did not exist; it is not a claim that intentions were not important in the composition, revision, and production of texts. It is not even a claim that the purposes, intentions, or wishes of originating agents of texts cannot be important in the uptake of those texts. It is only a claim that other responses to texts are also possible. The philosophical, biological, and/or sociological difficulties in ascertaining for certain what intentions, purposes, or wishes were encoded in texts cannot logically be turned into a conclusion that intentions do not or cannot matter to readers. These difficulties are not sufficient reason to proscribe attempts to determine what an author had tried to express.

Let us suppose for a moment that a critic, despairing of ever determining the author's meaning for a text, decides to focus on the most interesting interpretation that could be derived from the text. Lack of certainty drives the critic to this other task. Having failed to determine the author's intention, will the critic be able to determine beyond doubt which interpretation is the most interesting one? Which of these provides the more firm foundation? Isn't the pursuit of certainty in interpretation simply a pointless, unachievable goal?

I do not wish to weigh the merits of one critical methodology against another, but rather to follow out the logical consequences of the proposition that texts are, among other things, also communicative, which makes *mis*-understanding possible and important. In order to engage with authorial meanings, or at least with plausibly historical meanings, what sort of information would a scholar or reader need about a written text?

There is no limit to what we might want to know about variant versions and the contexts in which they were generated to help with such an enterprise. Two points bear further clarification. The first is that some forms of writing, particularly, for example, much lyrical poetry, seem to succeed in being understood in common and consistent ways both by persons with great access to additional information and by those with little extratextual information. It is not often the case that extratextual information misleads readers about how to read such texts, though I would not put that beyond the pale of possibility, some readers being capable of misunderstanding any and all texts with equal dexterity. Nevertheless, persons without special knowledge often hit on the received or standard historical and critical responses.

The second point, however, is that communications of the everyday sort usually take place between persons who know each other or who know the position, rank, or function of each other. Such exchanges take place in environments that are understood by persons on both sides of the communicative nexus in which a number of things go without saying. An illustration of this point is given in Steven Pinker's *The Language Instinct*, where, to illustrate how disjointed, complex, and wondrous human language communications can be, Pinker offers a full-page quotation of a conversation between P and D.[5] Sentences are begun, interrupted, and littered with pronouns for which there is no antecedent and other references that seem obscure. After the quotation, Pinker reveals that this is a transcript of the Watergate tapes. The speakers are President Nixon and John Dean, and the references are to x, y, and z. With all this extra information, one can go back to the conversation, and that which was opaque, fragmentary, disjointed, and incoherent falls into place.

Insofar as texts are communication, they are usually enabled as communication by things that go without saying because the originators of the text addressed a designated audience whose shared general knowledge and perhaps whose shared specific knowledge could be assumed. As time passes and new unforeseen audiences take up the text, some of that which went without saying ceases to go without saying. New audiences then begin making up, from their own knowledge and experience or from their imagination, plausible substitutes for the bits that went without saying. They invent plausible contexts to give coherence to the texts. From these new, adventitious but

5. Steven Pinker, *The Language Instinct* (New York: William Morrow & Co., 1994), 222–23.

effective bits of invention, the meanings of the text are determined anew and differently. Reader meaning replaces author meaning.

The "unsaid" here is different from the blanks and vacancies that Wolfgang Iser writes about as gaps in the text where the explicit text implies or suggests things that readers are to fill in as they "commune" with the text. What goes without saying is that which is assumed to be shared knowledge between writer and assumed reader. They need not be hinted at by the text nor implied by the text; the author assumes them as the natural context, supporting what is written in the text. The immediate, intended audience, for the most part, gets it because they belong to the same interpretive community.

This principle for understanding authorial or historical meanings, significances, and purposes is of equal importance in exploring the way an author's language betrays his overt or intended meaning. No one, except by guessing, can know what the author was betraying unless it is first determined what the author thought he was saying. So, intention and authorial meaning are central issues, regardless of whether one is a historical critic in search of the wisdom of the past or a deconstructive critic ferreting out involuntary meanings.

It is the function of scholarly editions not only to provide accurate texts and information about significant alternative texts so that readers can know which text they are reading, but it is also incumbent on scholarly editors to provide historical backgrounds in essays or annotations that will help shore up the text with that which at one time went without saying but has been forgotten. The purpose for this is *not* to force any critic to read the text as communication but to make it possible for those who wish to read it in that way to do so.

Considering text as communication involves direct confrontation with authorial intentions, production personnel's intentions, and reader's intentions. It does not require that we be literal-minded or that we take leave of our sense of linguistic nuance, indirection, irony, or deceit. "Text as communication" may involve conveyance of meaning, feeling, or purpose from writer to reader, or it could also involve recognition of deliberate authorial provocation to open-ended reader responses. Reading as a discipline (i.e., criticism) is impoverished, not enriched, by the abandonment of authorial or historical readings. We need tools, perhaps even crutches, to support the construction of interpretations that engage with the implications of the intentional acts of all agents of text, whether they inscribe, transcribe, or unscribe the text.

To consider text as communication, and thereby incur an obligation to consider intention and "author meaning," is to reject the easy road of editors who say, in effect, "Don't look at me; I'm just telling you what the text says." Instead, considering text as communication forces editors to act critically, to take risks, to have the courage of their convictions, to be straightforward and explicit about the editorial procedures and decisions taken. Above all, it requires them to adopt a tentative tone that invites readers to consider the evidence, to understand the options and decisions, and to disagree at will.

This is dicey business, I admit, because it can be said to give license to eccentric editors to impose their views of what should have been historical (but somehow cannot be proven to be so) or to impose, through editing, a personal and singular view of what is or was best. Unfortunately, the alternative is open to the same criticism. Sticking to what the documents say literally or compiling archives of texts in images and diplomatic transcriptions requires that one *choose* to proceed in that way. Choosing to make no change in the text is no less an intervention than choosing to emend. Choosing *not* to emend may be the refuge of the timid who prefer recording and rerecording while pretending that scholarship and integrity are fulfilled by self-effacement and a refusal to emend. In effect, it is impossible to avoid what Bowers called the "duty of editors to edit." It can, of course, be argued that a documentary fact of history is, at least, "factual" and not made up. That would seem, however, to imply that scholars must never infer that which cannot be seen, or that raw evidence must always trump interpretation. Surely there is middle ground.

Revisiting Authorial Intentions

To produce a scholarly edition rightly is to do so self-consciously and explicitly. There being no single correct way to edit, one ought to edit in the light of alternative legitimate methods and goals, declaring one's own procedures in relation to them. There are, nevertheless, wrong ways to edit—un-self-consciously and surreptitiously, for example. It is wrong to edit without knowledge of alternative viable methods or without declaring one's methods and goals. It is wrong to edit without knowledge of all the materials witnessing composition, revision, or transmission of texts. It is wrong to edit without sufficient regard for the need to proofread. It is insufficient to argue: I am a scholar; therefore, my edition is scholarly. "Trust me" is an inadequate explanation of editorial methods. I take *scholarly editing* to mean "prepare a historical text for publication and use by others"—a task that entails proper product labeling. If *edit* means write an introduction for a reprinted text or one prepared by a commercial publisher for the general public, then nothing in this essay is relevant. My primary audience, then, is scholarly editors, but readers might take note, since they are always at the mercy of editors for what they read.

Scholars unaware of the complexities of textuality nevertheless are sometimes drawn to editing. One reason to edit is that a scholarly edition signals the canonical status already achieved by, or asserted or desired for, an author or a work. Even though editing is often judged by academic departments to be a lesser, mechanical sort of scholarship, a well-received scholarly edition of a canonical writer can benefit its editor's career. Scholarly editions are not normally undertaken for ephemeral literature or for so-called minor works.

Originally presented at the European Society for Textual Studies in Vilnius, Lithuania, on November 22, 2007.

Editors of texts designed for use in teaching also explain their desire to edit in terms of their love for the work being edited. They say, "This literary work was not available at all, or not available in a decent edition, when I undertook the project." I have elsewhere explored and assessed additional reasons that draw noneditors to editing.[1]

Developments in scholarly editorial methods in the last twenty-five years have complicated the situation by establishing new goals for editions. Looking at the range of legitimate options might keep us from thinking we must throw out previous goals and methods just because we are now attracted to others. Evidence of a scorched-earth approach to new editorial methods can be found even in what sound like offhand remarks. W. Speed Hill once approvingly quoted Jerome McGann to the effect that the copy-text school of editing is "dead as a dodo."[2] Increasingly, the arguments against the editorial practices established by Greg, Bowers, and Tanselle are conducted on a level of invective, without regard for logic or understanding. The terms *authorial intentions*, *eclectic editing*, and *copy-text editing* have become little clubs with which to denigrate editions that do not accept the newer dogmas of multiple texts, social contracts, or bibliographical codes. I am on the board of a projected scholarly edition originally proposed as an eclectic edition, which an internationally known publisher initially rejected unless the editorial policy was changed to adopt either the first or last lifetime edition as copy-texts for each volume and limited emendations to corrections of the text reflecting the time of the copy-text's original publication. The ascendency of "social editorial methodology" was cited as the reason. It is not a bad policy, but the original proposal, I would argue, was just as good if not better—or just as bad, depending on one's point of view.

Richard Bucci has begun reexamining the Greg-Bowers school of editing by making more explicit and more accessible arguments first mounted by G. Thomas Tanselle, demonstrating that "copy-text editing" is a misnomer invented by those who appear to have misunderstood those editing principles.

1. Peter Shillingsburg, "Hagiolatry, Cultural Engineering, Monument Building, and Other Functions of Scholarly Editing," in *Voice, Text, Hypertext: Emerging Practices in Textual Studies*, ed. Raimonda Modiano, Leroy F. Searle, and Peter Shillingsburg (Seattle: University of Washington Press, 2004), 412–23; repr. in Peter Shillingsburg, *From Gutenberg to Google: Electronic Representations of Literary Texts* (Cambridge: Cambridge University Press, 2006), 161–72.

2. My argument is in *From Gutenberg to Google*, 152–53; Hill's quotation is from a review in *Text* 6 (1994): 370–81, where he approves of McGann's remarks in *New Directions in Textual Studies*.

Critical editorial methods often involve, but do not require, selecting a copy-text. Despite their mechanical implementation by some editors, the editorial principles developed by Greg, Bowers, and Tanselle never required the reduction of textual criticism to the practical aims of producing final authorial, intention-clear texts.[3] Nevertheless, many scholars since the 1990s have quoted or repeated McGann's dismissal of "intentionist editing" without examining the evidence for themselves.[4]

One argument for preferring documentary reproductions rather than emended texts is that historical texts accurately reflect the social complex that produced the original edition(s) and are, therefore, the proper objects of research into textual history. Editions designed to make such study possible cannot introduce emendations or mix readings from one material form with that of another. Another, less ideological argument supports a similar approach. It values the historical record over reconstructions of intended texts because a record of textual variants collects historical facts. It objects that emended texts reflect editorial opinions, which can be, maybe always are, eccentric. Edward Vanhoutte, quoting Dirk Van Hulle approvingly, used the word *copy-text* in a way that reflects German historical critical practice: "'Traditional scholarly editing focused on a text's afterlife, choosing a copy-text in order to edit and use it as the "invariant" against which all other versions could be compared; the variants were presented in an apparatus variorum.'"[5] It is not clear what Vanhoutte means by "to edit," since the idea that the

3. See Tanselle's comprehensive analysis in "The Editorial Problem of Final Authorial Intention," *Studies in Bibliography* 29 (1976): 167–211, repr. in Tanselle, *Selected Studies in Bibliography* (Charlottesville: University Press of Virginia, 1979), 309–53, and in "Greg's Theory of Copy-Text and the Editing of American Literature," *Studies in Bibliography* 28 (1975): 167–229, also repr. in *Selected Studies in Bibliography*, 245–307. Richard Bucci elucidates the concept in "Tanselle's 'Editing Without a Copy-Text': Genesis, Issues, Prospects," *Studies in Bibliography* 56 (2003): 1–44. See also Tanselle's "Editing Without a Copy-Text," *Studies in Bibliography* 47 (1994): 1–22; repr. in Tanselle, *Literature and Artifacts* (Charlottesville: Bibliographical Society of the University of Virginia, 1998), 236–57.

4. Two additional steps in reassessing the shift from eclectic to more documentary forms of editing are found in the third essay in this collection, "The Semiotics of Bibliography," and in Sarah Neville's "*Nihil biblicum a me alienum puto*: W. W. Greg, Bibliography, and the Sociology of Texts," *Variants* 11 (2014): 91–112.

5. Edward Vanhoutte, "Traditional Editorial Standards and the Digital Edition," in *Learned Love: Proceedings of the Emblem Project Utrecht Conference on Dutch Love Emblems and the Internet, November 2006*, DANS Symposium Publications 1 (The Hague: DANS, 2007), 166, is quoting Dirk Van Hulle, "Compositional Variants in Modern Manuscripts," in *Digital Technology and Philological Disciplines*, ed. A. Bozzi, L. Cignoni, and J.-L. Lebrave (Pisa and Rome: Istituti editoriali e poligrafici internazionali, 2004), 513–27.

copy-text is an "invariant" or standard, against which to record other textual forms, seems to avoid emendation as an editorial method. The Anglo-American use of "copy-text," as established by W. W. Greg, indicated that the text chosen, not as an invariant standard but as a port of last resort, relied upon only when convincing evidence about what an author wanted, is lacking. Neither Vanhoutte nor Van Hulle can be fully represented by such a brief quotation, but the implication that "copy-text" editing was a mechanical process with a narrow goal lurks here, seeming to echo McGann's and Hill's dismissive tone.

One reason it may have seemed useful to employ a reductio ad absurdum attack against so-called copy-text editing was to make room for McGann's initially much-resisted arguments in favor of a broader and more socially, politically, and economically based historical approach. His arguments were and remain convincing about textual scholarship in general, especially about production and reception histories. They were and remain less convincing about editing in particular. Disparaging the principles of textual investigation and scholarly editing developed by Bowers at least called attention to an alternative in a scholarly atmosphere dominated by the pursuit of the author's final intentions and implemented in some cases by a mechanical application of rules for editing. Greg's and Bowers's "rules" were not rules but principles, which were not fully understood by all the editors who employed them. It has not been difficult, furthermore, to point out the logical inconsistencies and oddities of decisions made by even the most knowledgeable editors for some of the volumes approved by the Center for Editions of American Authors (CEAA) and by the MLA's Committee on Scholarly Editions (CSE) in the heyday of Bowers's advocacy of scholarly editing.[6]

Now, decades after the publication of the opening salvo of McGann's attack on "copy-text editing" in *A Critique of Modern Textual Criticism* (1983), we can reexamine the widely accepted denigration of the role of intention in scholarly editing to see what its real sins were, other than that it dominated the field and was often treated as the one right way to edit in America in the

---

6. The CEAA was replaced by the MLA's CSE in 1976. See, for example, my review of the Northwestern Newberry edition of Melville's *Moby-Dick*, "The Three *Moby-Dicks*," *American Literary History* 2 (Spring 1990): 119–30. See also the reviews listed in G. Thomas Tanselle's "Part 5: Some Noteworthy Reviews of Scholarly Editions," in his Introduction to Scholarly Editing: Seminar Syllabus (Columbia University, 2002; online from The Rare Book School, University of Virginia, http://www.rarebookschool.org/tanselle/syl-E-complete.090302 .pdf2002), 53–59.

1960s and 1970s. A conventional history of textual studies of modern literature might reach back to the end of the eighteenth and early nineteenth centuries, in order to begin with Lachmann's theory and practice, although his ideas were developed for work on classical texts—for which a lost archetype, not unfulfilled authorial intentions, was the goal of editorial reconstruction. A. E. Housman's early twentieth-century advice, which has been much quoted since then, also aimed at classical rather than modern texts. In that short history, textual studies reflects a steady progression from one dominant methodology to another, from one most-favored form to another, arriving in the late twentieth century at ports in various countries: historical critical editing in Germany under the leadership of Siegfried Scheibe, Gunter Martens, and Hans Zeller,[7] and variations of that approach in Italy, Spain, and the Netherlands. In Anglo-American countries, scholarly critical editing (once proudly touted as eclectic editing) followed the lead of R. B. McKerrow, W. W. Greg, Fredson Bowers, and G. Thomas Tanselle.[8]

Anglo-American editing began fragmenting in the mid-1980s. Some editors sought to establish a single dominant text (e.g., representing an early version, as was favored for a variety of works by Hershel Parker in his book *Flawed Texts and Verbal Icons*,[9] or representing a late authorial text, as generally preferred by editors working with the CEAA). Other editors insisted on the importance of a multitext approach—a group represented variously by Donald Reiman in "Versioning," Paul Eggert in "Document or Process as the Site of Authority," and Robin Schulze in her edition of the early poems

---

7. A good English-language introduction to historical critical editing is *Contemporary German Editorial Theory*, ed. Hans Walter Gabler, George Bornstein, and Gillian Borland Pierce, 125–52 (Ann Arbor: University of Michigan Press, 1995), especially essays by Scheibe, Zeller, and Martens. A summary of varying contemporary views of editing is Dirk Van Hulle and Peter Shillingsburg, "Orientations to Text, Revisited," *Studies in Bibliography* 59 (2015): 27–44.

8. A convenient retrospective collection of essays representing this approach is *Anglo-American Scholarly Editing, 1980–2005*, ed. Paul Eggert and Peter Shillingsburg with Kevin Caliendo, published as a special issue of *Ecdotica*, an Italian journal of textual studies (2010; dated 2009). See also the earlier collection edited by Ronald Gottesman and Scott Bennett, *Art and Error: Modern Textual Editing* (Bloomington: Indiana University Press, 1970); repr. by Oak Knoll Press, http://www.oakknoll.com/pages/books/61707/ronald-gottesman-scott -bennett/art-and-error-modern-textual-editing.

9. Hershel Parker, *Flawed Texts and Verbal Icons* (Evanston: Northwestern University Press, 1984).

of Marianne Moore.[10] In Australia, the Anglo-American editorial scene was further nuanced. Adapting flexibly to the individual authors in the Academy Editions of Australian Literature, the editorial methods and goals reflect the unusual editorial experience of its general editor, Paul Eggert, who edited not only traditionally canonical works by D. H. Lawrence and Joseph Conrad but edited fifteen or sixteen lesser-known Australian writers, represented in the Colonial Texts Series and Academy Editions.[11] By contrast, many scholarly editors have developed their notions of the "right" way to edit by working on only one, two, or three writers.

Prominent in our own day are other editorial programs opposed to any emendation policy that is designed to improve or enhance a literary work, even when such efforts are seen as restorations of lost historical forms and not as the fulfillment of unrealized intentions. Instead, these new most-favored methodologies variously prioritize documentary historical snapshots of texts in progress, texts in documents with particularly important historical impact, so-called bibliographic codes[12] or so-called social contracts as the goals of

10. Donald Reiman, "'Versioning': The Presentation of Multiple Texts," in *Romantic Texts and Contexts* (Columbia: University of Missouri Press, 1987), 167–80; Paul Eggert, "Document and Text: The 'Life' of the Literary Work and the Capacities of Editing," *Text* 7 (1994): 1–24; Eggert, "Document or Process as the Site of Authority: Establishing Chronology of Revisions in Competing Typescripts of Lawrence's *The Boy in the Bush*," *Studies in Bibliography* 44 (1991): 364–76; Eggert, "Textual Product or Textual Process: Procedures and Assumptions of Critical Editing" in *Editing in Australia*, ed. Eggert (Sydney: University of New South Wales Press, 1990), 19–40; repr. in *Devils and Angels: Textual Editing and Literary Theory*, ed. Philip Cohen (Charlottesville: University Press of Virginia, 1991), 124–33; and Robin Schulze, ed., *Becoming Marianne Moore: The Early Poems, 1907–1924* (Berkeley: University of California Press, 2002).

11. See Paul Eggert's "Canonical Works, Complicity and Bibliography: A Case-Study," *Variants* 1 (2002): 159–73. For a sense of changing methods and goals, see the Academy Editions themselves or see my reviews in *Text* 12 (1999): 264–73 and in *Script and Print* 31, no. 2 (2007): 118–22.

12. Bibliographic codes, minted by Jerome J. McGann (in "Theory of Texts," if not before), came under fire from Paul Eggert, who questioned the codification of such "codes," and from David Hoover, who questioned whether such "codes" could ever be sufficiently standardized to be recognized by computational means. To refer to them as bibliographical indicators of social, generic, or economic conditions, themselves always in a state of flux, seems less conducive to misunderstanding. See Eggert, "Text as Algorithm and Process," in *Text and Genre in Reconstruction: Effects of Digitalization on Ideas, Behaviours, Products and Institutions*, ed. Willard McCarty (Cambridge: OpenBook, 2010), 183–202; and David Hoover, "The End of the Irrelevant Text: Electronic Texts, Linguistics, and Literary Theory," *Digital Humanities Quarterly* 1, no. 2 (2007): n.p.

textual criticism for scholarly editions. To my knowledge, no one quarrels with the goals of these new projects because faithfulness to historical documents has a long tradition of value in textual studies. It follows that to study texts representing the work of each and every participant in the production of historical documents is a legitimate pursuit in the sociology of texts. I do not know of anyone now who still argues against D. F. McKenzie's broadening of the bibliographical horizon to include an interest in the workings of textual players other than the author, though I do know several who still argue against some of McGann's applications to the editing of McKenzie's bibliographical observations.[13]

It is of first importance in textual scholarship to understand, describe, and record accurately the range of historical documents that represent a work's transmission and dissemination. Therefore, the replicating work of microfilming, scanning, photocopying, and other forms of accurate imitation of documentary originals is important and, as I take up in other essays, finds its best expression in digital archives.

It is also important to keep one's definitions of editing clearly in mind. Transcription, which in normal parlance is not "editing," is nevertheless an interpretive task; markup for electronic representation is also interpretive.[14] Producers of accurate reproductions of historical documents frequently also construct apparatuses to represent alternative historical documents—that can be both critical and creative. These tasks are interpretive and entail the art, not just the mechanics, of editorial attention. Replication and reproduction do not, however, involve the criticism of textual criticism or the editing of scholarly editing. There is a significant difference between painstakingly accurate recording of textual information and the well-reasoned production of desirably edited texts whose characteristics are not to be found in any single historical document or, when found there, are found in mixed or etiolated forms.

Much ink was employed in the last quarter of the twentieth century to demonstrate—successfully, I believe—the value of historical, documentary,

13. McKenzie himself did not explicitly refute McGann's usage, but his edition of *The Works of William Congreve* in three volumes (Oxford: Oxford University Press, 2011) is edited to fulfill Congreve's intentions for the works in ways not achieved by any historical edition—a policy compatible with Bowers's principles and ignoring McGann's. See also T. H. Howard-Hill, "Theory and Praxis in the Social Approach to Editing," *Text* 5 (1991): 31–48.

14. See Dino Buzzetti's attempts to analyze the nature of such actions in "Digital Representation and the Text Model," *New Literary History* 33 (2002): 61–88.

sociological approaches to textual scholarship, but in establishing the value of such studies it was unnecessary and even foolhardy to characterize authorial concerns as no longer legitimate. It was especially unworthy to do so with ad hominem tactics rather than meticulously considered argument. To be fair, McGann, who is often credited with initiating this sweeping action, was careful, in *A Critique of Modern Textual Criticism*, to indicate that the author should not be the only agent of textual change to whom we look for textual authority—thus preserving an interest in authors while extending it to production processes. Much of what was subsequently written in the field about authorial intention simply bows to McGann on one hand and to Beardsley and Wimsatt[15] on the other, before dismissing authorial intention as irrelevant to the concerns of scholarly editors.[16] When the argument does involve details, it most often alleges that because authorial intentions are inaccessible, lodged irretrievably in the past, all efforts to recover intentions are limited to the editor's personal critical preferences. Although we might feel the need to sweep away the current fashion to make room for something that was being neglected, we might not have been justified in doing so. It is not just totalitarian governments that progress as if the new cannot live in the same air with the old.[17] Politics as well as scholarship shape the actions of editors, publishers, production personnel, and even publics for reading. In order to make room for the historical/critical/social text, it seemed to some that the author's sole control over his or her work of art had to be brought down.

The first argument in that process was to insist on the importance of social and economic forces in the production, not of art (aesthetic objects) but of books (material commodities). For the democratizing spirit that sees value in the will of the people involved in the production of books, it was not enough to recognize and champion the importance of all the players in the production and transmission of texts. It seemed necessary in addition to

15. W. K. Wimsatt and Monroe Beardsley, "The Intentional Fallacy," *Sewanee Review* 54 (1946): 468–88, repr. in Wimsatt, *The Verbal Icon: Studies in the Meaning of Poetry* (Lexington: University of Kentucky Press, 1954). See essay 6 ("Text as Communication") for an analysis of the intentional fallacy.

16. Among the favorite so-called arguments against eclectic editing are: "mongrel edition" (used in an internal review against my edition of *Vanity Fair*), "never seen on land or sea" (indicating an edition is bad because it is not the replication of an existing text), "neither fish nor fowl" (ditto), and "dead as a dodo" (already mentioned).

17. See Paulius Subačius on the history of textual scholarship in Lithuania during Soviet occupation from the 1940s to the 1980s: "Canonisation as Impediment to Textual Scholarship: Lithuanian Postcolonial Experiences," *Variants* 7 (2008): 23–35.

overwhelm and dispel the elitist spirit of the solitary genius author and the priesthood of artistic taste and value represented by those in the academic world who stood at the gates to keep out the hoi polloi. That is one way to explain why the author is no longer seen as the authority over his or her own texts. The author is dead not only as the arbiter of what the text means; the author is no longer even allowed to determine what the text says.[18]

Important though it might have been in the 1960s to kill the author and recognize his death, interest in the author is not dead. Tides that sweep out have a habit of sweeping back in, usually bringing other matter with them. Of at least as much interest as documentary historical editing, in the last quarter of the twentieth century, *critique génétique* became widely known as a methodology deeply involved in textual criticism, focused on the genesis of the texts, but with no interest in editing them, because the two main goals of their investigations were the writing process itself and the potential interpretive consequences of observing and analyzing the genesis and revision of literary works. Genetic studies drew a sharp distinction between textual criticism and scholarly editing, insisting that textual criticism neither stops with establishing historical records nor necessarily ends in the production of a scholarly edition. Rather, a textual history can reveal the writing process, thus serving the purposes of criticism, interpretation, and understanding of the literary work both as art and as individual and social behavior. While persons interested in genetic criticism might find their work enhanced by editions designed to reveal genesis, not all editions whose primary purpose is to "establish or set the record straight" are designed to reveal the progress of genesis. Although the information is in the scholarly edition, it is often difficult to extract the narrative of genesis because the apparatus was designed not as a record of dynamic textual change but, rather, as a record of static documentary difference.[19]

18. The debates among textual scholars resulting from attempts to understand the implications of French literary theory to editing processes are best surveyed in David Greetham's *Theories of the Text* (London: Oxford University Press, 1999). See also my "Textual Angst: Literary Theory and Editorial Practice," chapter 2 of *Resisting Texts: Authority and Submission in Constructions of Meaning* (Ann Arbor: University of Michigan Press, 1997); and Paul Eggert, "Introduction," in *Biography of a Book: Henry Lawson's "While the Billy Boils"* (University Park: Penn State University Press, 2013).

19. An introduction to *critique génétique* in the context of alternative editing methodologies is in Dirk Van Hulle and Peter Shillingsburg, "Orientations to Text, Revisited," *Studies in Bibliography* 59 (2015): 27–44.

Genetic studies focus on genesis—the creation and development over time—of works of art, whether literary, theatrical, in film, or other work involving revision and production. Best known for their work on manuscripts—the exogenesis and endogenesis of works before publication—geneticists also trace postpublication development or epigenesis. Whereas avant-texts are usually largely authorial, production naturally involves the work of others. The description of the scope and aim of genetic criticism emphasizes the narrative of textual change rather than emphasizing the agencies of change. The emphasis on autographs leads one to believe that interest in authors and authorship is the primary motivating force. Literary critics, too, seem to avoid expressing their interest in authors by stating that they are interested in the meanings of the text, as if the text were not tethered to its author. Critics who investigate texts for the ways in which authors inadvertently expose themselves, however, are also investigating authorial intentions. Acknowledged or not, the identities of the agents responsible for texts still influence what critics and readers take the text to signify.

The point is not that authors are necessarily and always more interesting or more worthy of attention than other textual workers, but rather that sweeping away "agency for texts" as a means of making room for an interest in the "materiality of texts" and the "sociology of book publication" was a mistake. Those interests supplement rather than replace interest in agency. When, in *A Critique of Modern Textual Criticism*, McGann asked that the author be pushed from the center of attention in order to make room for other agents of change as indicators of textual conditions, he might have done a better job than he intended (if I'm allowed to guess at what he intended). While no one denies that authors are important agents of text production, fewer editors now seem to care what the author might have wished for the text. The material results of production are empirical; the intentions or desires of authors not so much.

In the mid-1960s, a great deal of attention was focused on analytical bibliography and textual criticism. That was the heyday of Fredson Bowers's career at the University of Virginia, when his editions of Thomas Dekker and of Beaumont and Fletcher provided the first practical demonstration of the theories of textuality that he and others were elaborating in the pages of *Studies in Bibliography*. The newly established CEAA had its headquarters at the University of South Carolina under the direction of Matthew J. Bruccoli. The situation as then seen was both simple and significant. Modern literature, just as much as classical literature, was in need of a rigorous textual methodology that would produce texts worthy of the kind of critical attention that was dominant in the United States at midcentury: the New Criticism with its close attention to text. New Critical practice rested on the premise that the author/genius/creator of the great and perfectly crafted poem is worthy of very close attention and also on the second premise that everything one needs to know about a poem is packed into the text of that poem. One would consequently think that it was important that every word and every point of punctuation in this work of art (a well-wrought urn) be authentic, as it was intended to be by the genius who created it. Given these views, the duty of the textual critic was simple: the right way to edit was to produce, in a clear text, the poem as it was finally, in minute detail, intended to be. Thus, collecting and examining all historical forms of the text, compiling the details of the author's biography, and determining printing-house practices gave the textual critic the evidence needed in order to proceed eclectically. An informed editor's power of *divinatio* could lead to the (more or less) perfect fulfillment of authorial intention through emendation. The result should fit the needs of the New Critic, who assumed the poem to be perfectly realized and to contain all that was needed for a fully aesthetic engagement with the work of art.

In such a paradigm, the function of the textual apparatus was to show, in a "Historical Collation," what the material evidence for the text was. Furthermore, honesty required the editor to reveal in a "List of Emendations" everything that had been done to the historical texts in order to produce the newly perfected critical text.

As one "right way to edit," eclectic critical editing was very complex. It was also perfectly coherent and utterly responsible. In the hands of a knowledgeable and competent scholar-editor, the results were impressive. In the hands of editors struggling to fulfill what they conceived to be the mechanical rules of editing, the results could be bizarre. Either the inappropriate application of the principles of critical eclectic editing, creating disappointing editions, or the natural development of interest in new points of view propelled, in the 1980s, objections to this methodology. One review of a critical edition began: "This edition is the result of riches running wild—first the riches and then the running wild."[20] The objection began with the notion

20. Hershel Parker, review of the Kent State University Press edition of Charles Brockden Brown's *Wieland*, in *The Eighteenth Century: A Critical Bibliography*, n.s., 3 (1981): 177–79.

that the grant money lavished upon the Charles Brockden Brown project was excessive and misdirected. The reviewer concluded that the editorial goal and methods had utterly failed to produce an edition worthy to be used. Very likely every country and every literature has produced such an edition and such a review. Sound objections to editorial practice abounded in part because of real errors and omissions of evidence, but more often because of the myth of one right way to edit.

My own rebellion against the editorial policies promoted by the CEAA and its successor, the CSE (of which I was successively coordinator, board member, and chairman), may seem minor, but to me it was momentous. Focusing on the writings of William Makepeace Thackeray, my biblio-graphical and textual analyses of surviving documentary evidence for *The History of Pendennis*, *Vanity Fair*, and *The History of Henry Esmond* demon-strated to me that no existing Thackeray manuscript could be considered a fair copy. No other historical form of these works represented Thackeray's own work—the printed texts were overproduced by editor/compositors who supplied far more alteration than was required by the underpunctuated manuscripts.

The methodology then prevailing called for choosing a copy-text as a standard for accidentals, and then emending substantives by reference to other historical texts. The result was unsatisfactory to me on two counts. First, following the manuscript's accidentals would produce a text seriously under-punctuated and therefore nearly unreadable, but choosing a printed edition as copy-text would produce a text seriously overpunctuated by agents who repeatedly exercised an iron fist and a roughshod insensitivity to the beauties of Thackeray's rhetorical dexterity. Second, the textual apparatus for either method would foreground the textual work of compositors and the scholarly editor while burying the evidence of Thackeray's own revisions in haystacks of changes introduced by other hands.

When I began work on Thackeray, the only other Victorian scholarly editions under way were John Butt and Kathleen Tillotson's edition of Charles Dickens and Gordon Haight's edition of George Eliot. In most available classroom editions, I found that editors made decisions based on their under-standing of the prevailing rules for "editing the right way," but too often they illustrated A. E. Housman's remark that textual criticism "is not susceptible of hard-and-fast rules . . . you can have hard-and-fast rules if you like, but then you will have false rules, and they will lead you wrong; because their simplicity will render them inapplicable to problems which are not simple but complicated by the play of personality."²¹ What struck me was the number of editors who reluctantly made decisions according to the rules that they thought were the correct, hard-and-fast rules, and then they apologized to the reader for the result.²² Mechanical application of rules will always result in bizarre and embarrassing editions that then become the examples used to justify the abandonment of the methods, as if the methods, not the execution, were at fault. What eclectic editing does not promise to produce is editions that are "correct"; critical scholarly editions do not render all other editions obsolete. Nor do they replace authoritative original editions. It did not help that eclectic editors occasionally made such claims.

For Thackeray's works I wanted a reading text that was different from the manuscript by supplying missing punctuation, but that rejected the excessive punctuation of the printed texts. Although Thackeray worked rapidly and relied on compositors, he was not sloppy or careless. The punctuation that he did supply reveals delicate rhetorical nuance and an ear for conversational English. My eclectically edited texts of *Pendennis*, *Vanity Fair*, and *The Newcomes* find middle ground between the manuscript and the first printed texts. Eclectic editing requires editorial powers of divinatio and *emendatio*; it is for others to say if my editions demonstrate such powers. Whatever might be said in principled objection to this method, the resulting edited text involved both textual criticism and scholarly editing. I am neither a microfilm machine nor a copy-editor; I am, instead, a textual critic and scholarly editor. Each edition creates a text that had not existed before because such a text was lacking.

Or so I thought—but not all the world agrees. It is the case that textual critics who exercise divinatio and emendatio produce texts that no other

---

21. A. E. Housman, "The Application of Thought to Textual Criticism," *Proceedings of the Classical Association* 18 (1922): 67–84; repr. in Housman, *Selected Prose*, ed. John Carter (Cambridge: Cambridge University Press, 1961), 131–50; see 132.

22. I have cited examples from Hans Zeller on Goethe ("A Resistance to Contemporary German Editorial Theory and Practice," *editio* 12 [1998]: 138–50); from Gordon Haight on George Eliot (in a review of *The Mill on the Floss*, ed. Gordon S. Haight, *Journal of English and Germanic Philology* 80 [1981]: 590–92); and from Sylvère Monod on Dickens (in *Scholarly Editing in the Computer Age: Theory and Practice*, 3rd ed. [Ann Arbor: University of Michigan Press, 1996], 5). But see also Monod's explanation for not restoring a manuscript reading, even though the printed change was caused by a compositor's error and Dickens's correction was, in Monod's opinion, inferior to the original, in Monod, "Between Two Worlds: Editing Dickens," in *Editing Nineteenth-Century Texts*, ed. Jane Millgate (New York: Garland Publishing, 1978), 26.

textual critic, even those bent on similar aims, would achieve precisely. It follows that the result of such work is always one person's opinion of what the text should be. If all editors followed these principles, we would, so the argument goes, live in the chaotic conditions described in the Bible in the book of Judges, when "every man did that which was right in his own eyes." We are no longer prepared to acknowledge with A. E. Housman that

> [t]extual criticism, like most other sciences, is an aristocratic affair, not communicable to all men, nor to most men. Not to be a textual critic is no reproach to anyone, unless he pretends to be what he is not. To be a textual critic requires aptitude for thinking and willingness to think; and though it also requires other things, those things are supplements and cannot be substitutes. Knowledge is good, method is good, but one thing beyond all others is necessary; and that is to have a head, not a pumpkin, on your shoulders, and brains, not pudding, in your head.[23]

In orderly, disciplined societies, this sort of freedom is not tolerated. Editors must not produce editions according to principles that are right in their own eyes only. I am not sure the alternative is preferable either. By multiplying the rules of editing, can we make textual editing safe, even for blockheads?

This hyperbolic case in defense of eclectic critical editing was prompted by attacks on it. What room, it has been asked, has romanticism, aesthetics, or intention in the workshops of rigorous, disciplined, historical, documentary modern editors? Have not computers enabled us to increase the repetitive checks and the amount of information that can be brought to an edition, revealing precisely and accurately the history of composition, revision, and production of the texts? Are these not the actual texts that people have read—indeed, the texts that, upon being published, supplied the livelihood of writers working in an economic community of workers to produce the reading materials of a culture? Editing a work to reflect a single author's desires ensures that the text neither represents precisely its source documents nor the culture of which it was a part. Eclectic critical editing, it was said, just muddies the stream of textual history by offering one editor's opinion about a romantically conceived ideal text.

---

23. Housman, "Application," 150.

The first and easiest answer is that the electronic archive has changed the goals of editing profoundly.[24] Yes, the electronic archive is the perfect venue for increasing access to the documents of textual history. Digital archives can provide images of historical texts, searchable transcriptions, and the added value of commentary and markup systems. That seems perfect for the student of textual composition, revision, production, and dissemination of texts in an environment lending itself generously to an understanding of the socio-economic and political life of literary texts. I do not, however, see why that should cause the demise of critical editions, reflecting lost or unachieved textual forms. The electronic archive has room for edited texts as well as historical ones. The question now is, was it right to try to rule the eclectic edition out of court? Apparently not. Despite three decades of objections to eclectic editing, and although German historical critical editorial principles object to emendation because it mixes text from more than one source, most Anglo-American print editions published in the last ten to twenty years still strive to create texts reflecting authorial preferences. It has been insufficient to object that intentions are inaccessible, that eclectic or emended editions irresponsibly mix the documentary evidence, that the result represents the critical opinions of an individual editor, or that "copy-text" editing is "dead as a dodo."

I offer three arguments against these charges. The first returns to an earlier point about facsimile reproductions that replicate extant historical documents. They fill gaps in libraries that do not own material originals. While such products involve textual criticism only minimally, the importance of archives of replicated original documents for textual criticism cannot be overemphasized. Scholars are deeply grateful for microfilm series and digital reproductions such as Early English Books Online (EEBO), Eighteenth Century Collections Online (ECCO), and Google Books, even though such resources give no access to the paper, the texture, the smell, the heft, or the bibliographical structure of the originals, and they seldom, if ever, provide commentary or indicate textual variations. These are not criticisms but acknowledgments of the limitations of digital replications of original documents. Accurate reproductions for wider dissemination, important though such projects are, do not constitute textual criticism. Though far more reliable

---

24. A very good account is Kenneth Price's "Edition, Project, Database, Archive, Thematic Research Collection: What's in a Name?" *Digital Humanities Quarterly* 3, no. 3 (2009).

than transcriptions, their photographic characteristics still pose serious limitations on investigations into the books and texts they represent. Texts, whether original or in facsimile, require the discipline of textual scholarship to identify which text each documentary form contains, to indicate textual development and variation, and to give context and basic information about the texts.

One gains a sense of empowerment when one turns from simple straightforward, though massive, reproduction projects to the scholarly and delightful full-color reproductions of rare materials in electronic repositories such as the Blake Archive, the Rossetti Archive, the Whitman Archive, Woolf Online, and other repositories. That sense derives from the wealth of bibliographical and textual analyses as well as from the images and transcriptions. And yet, without original material documents, it is impossible to establish the textual records of composition, revision, and production. Textual criticism cannot be conducted, and scholarly editions cannot be constructed without first attending to the basic work of bibliography—collecting, analyzing, and storing.

Original documents enable us to ask "Where did this come from?" and "Is the source of this text authentic and reliable, one with some authority?" The denigration of the aforementioned digitization is not against the necessity or usefulness of digital reproductions and records of textual histories. Rather, it is about thinking that the work of textual criticism and scholarly editing is completed when the record of textual histories has been established. It is not.

The second answer to the arguments against editorial interest in the author focuses on the function of inference in rational argument. Science deals with the fact that much that needs to be analyzed and "observed" cannot be seen or measured or pinned down directly. Paleontologists infer the size, shape, and living habits of extinct animals from fossils; oceanographers infer the depth of oceans from sound waves; and atomic scientists infer matter from traces left in cloud chambers. It does not seem a stretch to apply similarly indirect methods to literary works for which the only material trace is paper with inked symbols. It is a triumph of rational thought that observable evidence can be analyzed in order to point to facts that are not themselves observable. That is one important meaning of the word *conclusion*—that it is a fact or a proposition that could only be reached by argument and inference from known, observable evidence. It is generally agreed that authorial intentions (indeed, intentions of any kind) are inaccessible for direct observation or analysis. It does not necessarily follow that intended texts cannot be the goal of editing. It is not denied that texts result from deliberate acts *intended* by writers (and indeed by others). This fact does not get us very far, but we know that texts, especially manuscript texts, for which the bibliographical, textual, and biographical records of genesis and transmission have been established, provide evidence upon which rational analysis can be exercised to infer intentions. The simplest of cases makes the point. I do not believe there is anyone who, given the sentence,

> All meg are created equal.

would be so lacking in confidence as to be unable to infer that an error had been made and that the intended reading was

> All men are created equal.

There are ambiguous cases, but even here, inference is possible:

> There are gardens to bed ug.

could be

> There are gardens to bed up.

or

> There are gardens to be dug.

These acts of inference are not simple. They involve a highly sophisticated grasp of the conventions of language and the history of its use, and in the case of "bed ug" some acquaintance with dropped type and movement in the form. In some imaginable context, "meg" might be right—suppose "meg" was short for megabytes of storage, and the speaker-writer meant to suggest that storage is storage. There is often more evidence brought to bear than is found in the text itself. In the example for *Henry Esmond*, given in essay 4, "Some Functions of Textual Criticism," I examined the line that in the manuscript says,

Rachel took Henry hat in hand to his room.

where all the printed editions have

Rachel took Henry hand in hand to his room.

I noted that the word *hat* in the manuscript is squeezed in almost illegibly at the end of a line. The question "How did *hat* become *hand*?" cannot be answered from direct evidence. We did not see it happen, or note who did it, or know where the author was when it happened, nor can we know if the author was aware of it or approved it afterward. Both phrases are common in the language; there is no demonstrable error. Did the author intend *hand* to replace *hat*? The ambiguity persists because revisions often take place between manuscript and print stages, and because authors often overlook small matters in proofreading. We look, therefore, to a range of contingent evidence and draw an inference, perhaps a series of them. We know that the compositors were paid by the amount of type set but that errors were charged against them. They had cause to be careful, yet time was sufficiently important to cause speed. In his hurry, a compositor could easily have "seen" the common phrase "hand in hand," whereas deciphering the minutely handwritten *hat* would have taken precious time. We can then ask if *hand* makes sense and fits the rest of the text. At the end of volume 1 of *The History of Henry Esmond*, where this scene is found, Esmond is about eighteen or nineteen; his stepmother, in a loveless marriage, is about twenty-six; and in volume 3, after the death of her husband and long years of acrimony and guilt, she marries Esmond. It seems unlikely that these two characters would have gone anywhere "hand in hand" at this early stage of the story. A hint of suppressed love rather different from mother-son love does, however, occur at the end of volume 1, when Rachel visits Esmond in jail to rail against him for his part in the duel in which her husband is killed. She takes a button from his coat, a fact not revealed until volume 3.[25] The weight of evidence favors "hat"; it is an inference, not an observable fact, but one I feel confident about. Incidentally,

25. See the Garland edition (New York, 1989) edited by Edgar F. Harden, page 91, and the rejected substantives recorded on page 656. Actually, the edition fails to record the fact that "hat" is nearly illegible in the manuscript, which is in Trinity College Library, Cambridge. In an electronic edition with images of the manuscript, the fact would become obvious.

any other answer to the question "Did the author intend *hand* instead of *hat?*" would also be an inference. The observable facts—that the manuscript says *hat* and the print edition says *hand*—do not require textual *criticism*. What are we to do with these facts? Even if one believed that *hand* was the act of a compositor, could one say the compositor deliberately made the change, or was it just a misreading? If it were a misreading, would respect for the workman require us to accept it—or reverse it?

Although an author's intention can sometimes be inferred with a high degree of confidence, editors cannot go through a text changing this or that willy-nilly because they do not like one thing or prefer another or because they pretend to know the mind of the author. They can, however, exercise their rational analytical skills on a range of material evidence that points to that which cannot be observed directly. Two weak reasons lead editors to refrain from exercising such analytical skills. The first is that the editor is only pretending to be a textual critic but does not actually have the skills. The other is that the editor with such skills lacks the courage to use them. A legitimate reason to refrain from emendation applies when the goal of the "editing" is to replicate the historical record rather than to analyze it in order to recover a lost or damaged form of the work. Replicated texts are properly called reprints, not edited works.

A third answer to those who say that criticism must be curbed in textual criticism and that editing must be restricted in scholarly editing involves the role of aesthetics in literature. It is true that in many research projects, investigation is undertaken in the first place for its own sake. Knowledge for its own sake has a privileged tradition. We do our research by asking questions and seeking evidence without regard to the consequences. We want to know just because we want to know. I doubt, however, that what motivates readers, students, and teachers of literature can be summed up in the statements "in order to know" and "in order to be useful." Why do we read, study, and teach literature? Why do we conduct literary research? Love of knowledge and the desire to be useful can probably be better fulfilled in fields other than literature. Ask students why they have chosen literature for their major, and most will say "Because I love to read." That might also point to certain kinds of utility: I love to read because it broadens my appreciation for what it means to be human, or because I believe it will make me a better person. More often, however, the answer is something like "Because I enjoy engaging with the thoughts and feelings of great writers or of the characters about whom they write." The answer points to aesthetics, to pleasure, to beauty.

If we read for pleasure, for beauty, for engagement with the thoughts and feelings of writers, then we want texts that will maximize these goals. When a work has achieved the status of a scholarly edition, it is almost certain also to be a work that fulfills these desires. For the purpose of such pleasure, we do not *primarily* want a text that is an accurate representation of a historical document. In particular, we do not want such accuracy if the historical document's text is a damaged or distorted or corrupted text, interfered with by a mélange of agents of textual change. Instead, we want an edited text reflecting the considered judgment of a textual critic who has the analytical skills and courage to employ divination in a process of emendation, leading to a text that fills a desideratum—a text more probably intended by its author. Perverse as it might sound, the pleasures of such reliable texts "from the horse's mouth," so to speak, can be enriched by knowledge of the textual genesis and development of the text.

The preceding argument equates the aesthetic and the authorial. Occasionally, however, authors are not the best judges of the aesthetic potential of their works and have benefited from the ministrations of others, including their publishers' editors. It is not difficult to name authors such as Byron, Dreiser, or Fitzgerald, who, in the eyes of scholarly editors such as McGann and James L. W. West, have been helped by their original commercial publishers. Nor is it difficult to name authors such as Dryden, Housman, or Twain, who railed against the ineptitudes of compositors and printers.[26] The electronic archive provides the historical texts in these cases—both pleasant and unpleasant. Historical archives alone do not, however, supply the critical analysis or editing needed to adjudicate between extra-authorial help and interference.

It can be objected that a scholarly editor might, on occasion, consider the opportunity to improve on the author's efforts by offering emendations from his or her own superior sensibilities. It is right to object to such editing.

26. *Lord Byron: The Complete Poetical Works*, ed. Jerome J. McGann, 7 vols. (Oxford: Clarendon Press, 1980–93); Theodore Dreiser, *Sister Carrie*, The Pennsylvania Edition, historical editors John C. Berkey and Alice M. Winters, textual editor James L. W. West III, and general editor Neda M. Westlake (Philadelphia: University of Pennsylvania Press, 1981). See also James Thorpe, *Watching the Ps & Qs: Editorial Treatment of Accidentals*, Library Series 38 (Lawrence: University of Kansas Libraries, 1971).

Editors who actively collaborate with an author to produce an aesthetically superior text should be called adapters, not editors. The fear of such interferers is not so great as to require our profession to shackle the hands of all scholarly editors to prevent them from following in disciplined ways the rules of evidence leading to the creation of a text inferred from the historical evidence but not found whole in any one historical document. The existence of an electronic archive of historical texts would make it easy for dissenters to avoid any and all critically edited texts. Disciplined eclectic editing does not involve tolerance for everyone's favorite emendation. Once created, critically edited texts become historical documents in their own right, occupying space in the historical archive of texts, each desired by some if not by all. A reader's assessment of any one text can only be sharpened and enriched by a knowledgeable comparison of that text with its historical and critically reconstructed alternatives.

To conclude, as long as the comprehensive documentary evidence is made available (digitally or otherwise), as long as the records of variation and contexts are accurately compiled and described, and as long as the editor explains and exposes his or her work, it does not matter which way one edits. Every edition fails in some way. No matter how hard one tries and no matter how many images, records, or arguments one presents in an edition, there will always be something lost or left out and something that cannot be done with the results. There will always be something that was done better by the edition one is trying to replace. If pushed to say what I thought the right way to edit was, I would say it is right to edit accurately and often.

How Literary Works Exist

Literary works are not known without media; they are known only by means of copies. There is no original of which all other exemplars are copies; the original is itself just the first copy. What are they copies of? The work. It is like a mystery: No copy *is* the work; every copy *is* the work. Each copy represents the work; no copy represents the work fully. Documents and texts exist as material objects, copies. Works, on the other hand, come into and go out of existence as mind objects, engagements with copies. Textual scholars care for material objects because they are the necessary media for the mind objects we all care about. Copies are seldom, if ever, identical. Because we care about works, we must care for documents and texts. It is not a mystery; it is a subject for analysis and debate.

This essay reexamines the nature of the "material things" that "convey" texts and the ways in which producers and readers interact with material texts. It focuses on that which textual scholarship identifies, analyzes, and curates. A clear understanding of *material texts* will clarify how best to represent them as *virtual texts* in digital scholarly archives and editions. Virtual archives are copies of copies.

Material Texts and Digital Representations

The crossover period from print to digital publication of texts and documents entails momentous and expensive decisions about libraries, about electronic

Revised from a lecture presented at University College London, February 2007, and subsequently published in *Text and Genre in Reconstruction: Effects of Digitalization on Ideas, Behaviours, Products and Institutions*, ed. Willard McCarty (Cambridge: OpenBook, 2010), 165–82.

access to books, and about the construction of electronic scholarly editions and digital archives. Are we sure we know what we are doing?

If we ever come to believe that digital representations of physical books are adequate or complete representations, then textual studies, bibliography, and history of the book will have lost the battle to persuade us to understand how books exist, how communication happens, and how understandings of texts are achieved. If, on the other hand, textual studies, bibliography, and history of the book fail to embrace the challenge of electronic representations of books, they will have lost a valuable opportunity to broaden and enhance the understandings they have developed of books as physical objects, media of communication, and loci of understanding. Digital textuality must not only deal with all three of these issues but inject them into the public debate about digital objects and their uses.

Public policy, as represented in the expectations of funding agencies for electronic dissemination of scholarly editions and archives, did not begin with extensive or successful efforts to get the relationship between physical texts and electronic representations rightly understood. Our ability to get that relationship wrong is not limited to some simple opposition between physical and electronic books. We can make poor choices in the practical ways we embrace the development of electronic books, even as we continue to collect and protect physical books. Funding agencies often and understandably base their judgments about edition and archives projects on the soundness of the scholarly investigations and on the perceived importance of the works being edited. Completion dates are set and, almost as an afterthought, a request is made for electronic access and dissemination. Scholars comply because they, too, care primarily about the texts and textual scholarship. Electronic dissemination can seem like a relatively simple job of porting to the screen what traditionally was printed. For this transfer, assistance in the form of a "techie" might seem sufficient. Even now, agencies and scholars sometimes assume that thoughtfully constructed long-term electronic vehicles exist for presenting the fruits of editorial scholarship. Despite XML, TEI, and SSLT, there are not. Yet, few editors with a funded completion date ask for very long "What is the best way to construct a digital scholarly edition?"—a question swept away by the more practical question "What is the best way, given our deadlines, to mount a presentable digital version of this research project?" Five hundred years of print experience influenced this tendency with its settled procedures. Print projects had defined limits because publication required separate book design and production for different audiences. Digital interface and dissemination has capacities unknown in print. When textual research questions and electronic dissemination questions are treated together, it becomes clear that, in the electronic world, catering to differing audiences, such as fellow researchers on one side and general readers on the other, no longer has to affect the design and structure of content. Document images, text transcriptions, and analytical data and commentary can have basic forms to be invoked in different ways by different users. Interface design, not content design and structure, tailors access to common resource materials. Further, when digital structures and methods of dissemination are well coordinated from the beginning, the foundations of a project can be launched before completion of the whole. Digital media allows planning for the long-term, open-ended project; print publication is limited to the short-term end product.

Mitigation of the imbalance of priorities between project content and scholarship, on one hand, and digital mechanisms for structure, storage, access, and dissemination, on the other, was marked by the establishment at the National Endowment for the Humanities (NEH) of the Office of Digital Humanities to support infrastructure development. That the fields are related is evidenced further by textual scholars participating in digital humanities conferences and the inclusion of textual studies in publications such as the *Digital Humanities Quarterly*. New funding policies can lead to something better than deadline-driven local solutions to local problems.

Goals of Critical Editing

Digital dexterity is also important because not everyone expects the same thing from scholarly editions and virtual archives. Three major editorial approaches, referred to as "critical editing," "historical critical editing," and "social textuality," are demonstrated.

Critical editing attempts to create texts that restore lost original forms or to emend an existing text so that it resembles what the editor thinks the author aspired to, but was thwarted by various agents or circumstances. Both types entail emendation and eclectic constructs; neither aim can be achieved definitively, and so the results are frankly and explicitly labeled *critical* editions.[1] In both, editors aim to create texts that represent works better than they are represented by any of the extant historical documents. In the last quarter of the twentieth century, the methods for constructing these archetypes and fulfilling authorial intentions were intensely challenged by European, especially German, historical critical editors, who focused on editions that accurately represent extant documents and that trace their relationships. Social textuality also rejects critical and eclectic emendation as an interference with historical forms. Both of these challenges to critical editing curb editors' use of critical judgment. Two aspects of historical documentary approaches nevertheless continued to require editorial judgment and interpretation: the preparation of transcriptions and the preparation of critical apparatuses that trace and explain relationships among historical texts.

By rejecting most if not all emendation, both the historical critical and the social textuality approaches limit themselves to *documentary* issues; neither approach attempts to deal with the *work*, the mind object. Both replace the ideal of authorial authenticity and of aesthetic sensitivity, which were central to critical editing, with documentary facts and social awareness. They both locate value in documentary texts as intrinsically interesting, but for somewhat different reasons: historical critical editing because of the historical status of documents and social textuality because documents index the social conditions of authorship, publishing, and reading through time.

Two related developments simultaneously affected textual criticism. One involved shifting attention from the (dead) author's intention for the work to book production and its personnel, on one hand, and to readers and reception, on the other. The other development shifted attention from questions about how to edit for print publication to those about how to edit for electronic publication.[2]

1. Paul Eggert refers to critical editions as "arguments" in "Writing in a Language Not Your Own: Editions as Arguments About the Work—D. H. Lawrence, Joseph Conrad and Henry Lawson," *Variants* 9 (2012): 163–84; I first heard him use the phrase in 2006, in his Master Classes lecture at De Montfort University. Burghard Dedner, in a conference paper delivered in Japan in 2015, refers to the critically edited text as "an editorial hypothesis."

2. Key texts in the shift of attention from author to reader include Roland Barthes, "The 'Death' of the Author," in *The Rustle of Language* (1968), trans. Richard Howard (New York: Hill and Wang, 1986), 49–55; Michel Foucault, "What Is an Author?" trans. Josué Harari, in *The Critical Tradition*, ed. David H. Richter (New York: St. Martin's Press, 1989), 978–88; Stanley Fish, *Is There a Text in This Class? The Authority of Interpretive Communities* (Cambridge, Mass.: Harvard University Press, 1980); G. Thomas Tanselle, "Textual Criticism and Deconstruction," *Studies in Bibliography* 43 (1990): 1–33; and D. C. Greetham, "[Textual]

Each of these three approaches is valuable in its own right, and alone each is incapable of serving the needs of the others. Social textuality provides critical analyses of sociocultural conditions by examining historical evidence. Conduct of its research requires original documents. High-resolution digital images are an almost-acceptable substitute. Social textuality cannot support an editorial strategy, however, because new editions are witnesses to the new social conditions of their own production. No new edition can be a witness for the production of any previous edition it might be trying to (re)present because the new edition can represent only itself. The term *social edition* is, therefore, an oxymoron; either every edition is a social edition or none is.[3]

Historical critical editorial policy is basically archival. Its goal is to bring comprehensive order and understanding to the surviving documents that represent a work. Hence, its primary goals are analysis, preservation, and representation, not editing in the sense of correcting or improving texts. Its principles translate very well to the production of digital archives, which serves the same purposes. The sociology of text and social modes of production and reception are basically bibliographical and historical. Their interests are best pursued as bibliography and book history. Critical editing aims to create texts that support reading experiences that correspond to a view of the work—the mind object—that either was supported in a now-lost document or that would have existed but for the interference of accident or incompetence or malice.

Both historical critical editing and social textuality reject critical emendation. That is tantamount to rejecting interest in forms of the text in documents that no longer exist or in forms the text might have taken, had the vicissitudes of history not interfered. Those lost or unachieved texts do not exist. Any attempt to "see" them has to be mediated by critical emendation and new representations. Readers, however, continue to be interested in authors far more than in production personnel or in other readers. As a result, critically emended editions continue to be produced. It seems more productive,

<hr />

Criticism and Deconstruction," *Studies in Bibliography* 44 (1991): 1–30. My discussion of the shift from print to digital forms, in *From Gutenberg to Google: Electronic Representations of Literary Texts* (Cambridge: Cambridge University Press, 2006), is part of a continuing discussion. The arguments in the present essay did not occur to me until after I had published that book.

3. My main argument that social and sociological interests in books are the concerns of bibliography and book history, not the editorial concerns of textual studies, is elaborated in essay 3, "The Semiotics of Bibliography."

therefore, to see the aims of historical critical editing and the interests of social textuality as complementary interests rather than as methodologies that supplant eclectic goals and methods of critical editing.

Shifts in academic interest from art to culture, from creators to consumers, from aesthetics to economy have affected many aspects of the profession of letters. Enthusiasms often come at a price and can blind one to the losses involved. We do not need to adjudicate among the goals of textual criticism as if one were right and the others wrong or inferior. Just as every thoughtful curation of textuality reveals something about documents, texts, and works that was not apparent before, so every editorial decision, including the decision not to emend, or even a decision to do nothing, entails loss. By asking how literary works exist, I hope to see how images and text transcriptions representing works should be or could be prepared for electronic representation—either with minimal loss or at least with self-consciousness about losses.[4]

How Do Literary Works Exist?

Applying to textual works the words *implied*, *represented*, and *interpreted* will lead to clearer notions of how literary works might be edited and represented digitally. It also demonstrates that time, money, and expertise to pursue digital tools and project designs are needed *before* undertaking a literary digital project with a deadline. Projects for which the outcomes are analyses of current best electronic practice have begun to attract attention and some funding. Digital textualists are not yet united in their recommendations for

---

4. Arguments about the nature of "work" in relation to "texts" and "documents," and whether the literary work is essentially a concept or a physical object form the chief dividing lines separating editorial methods. Key texts are W. W. Greg, *A Calculus of Variants: An Essay on Textual Criticism* (Oxford: Clarendon Press, 1927) and "The Rationale of Copy-Text," *Studies in Bibliography* 3 (1950–51): 19–36; G. Thomas Tanselle, "Reproductions and Scholarship," *Studies in Bibliography* 42 (1989): 25–54; Jerome J. McGann, *The Textual Condition* (Princeton: Princeton University Press, 1991); Gunter Martens, "What Is a Text? Attempts at Defining a Central Concept in Editorial Theory," in *Contemporary German Editorial Theory*, ed. Hans Walter Gabler, George Bornstein, and Gillian Borland Pierce (Ann Arbor: University of Michigan Press, 1995), 209–31; Bodo Plachta, "In Between the 'Royal Way' of Philology and 'Occult Science': Some Remarks About German Discussion on Text Constitution in the Last Ten Years," *Text* 12 (1999): 31–47; and D. C. Greetham, *Theories of the Text* (London: Oxford University Press, 1999). A summary analysis of competing theories is in Peter Shillingsburg, *Scholarly Editing in the Computer Age: Theory and Practice*, 3rd edition (Ann Arbor: University of Michigan Press, 1996).

new electronic environments (addressing fundamental questions about interface design, coding practices, file structures, analytical and presentation tools, and potentials for extending and repurposing content) and the economics of development, dissemination, access, and maintenance.[5]

Although I am a textual critic and editor, I speak here primarily as a student of literature, interested in the materials that contain or convey literary works. We are interested in authors, publishers, and production personnel who composed those materials; we are interested in the discourse communities in which the words were written; we are interested in the people who bought and read the works, not only at the time of first publication but through the years and into our own time; we are interested in literary works as material objects currently reimagined and marketed; and we are concerned about how our modern identities and "presentness" affect our reception of literary texts. In short, one way to put the problem of electronic editing is that we wish to serve the needs of people who want to understand the work of art in a variety of artistic, critical, historical, material, social, and intellectual ways.

Literary projects that reexamine and revamp the computer infrastructure within which to mount archives and editions need clear understandings of the relations among material data, binary data, and the diverse categories of information about them. I want to consider the question of electronic editions in that light. The aim is definitely *not* to discover how our understandings of literary works can be contained in humanities computing. The question is, rather, how can humanities computing support and enable our understandings of literary works?—though it would be even better to think of it as a two-way street.

Literary works are variously *implied* by their material representations; they are *represented* materially and virtually, and they are *interpreted* variously by authors, publishers, editors, and other readers. These three characteristics, though analyzed here separately, invade each other at every point. Digital editions and archives need to address all three.

---

5. Tools projects with interesting potentials for scholarly editions and archives include Peter Robinson's "Textual Communities" (http://www.textualcommunities.usask.ca/); John Bryant's "TextLab" (http://mel.hofstra.edu/textlab.html); "Easy Tools for Difficult Texts" (http://easytools.huygens.knaw.nl/); "Australian Electronic Scholarly Editing" (http://austese .net/); and "Humanities Research Infrastructure and Tools" (HRIT, https://sites.google .com/a/ctsdh.luc.edu/hrit-intranet/home).

The Work Implied

My colleague, Price Caldwell,[6] attempting to understand my views about notes, drafts, manuscripts, magazine publications, and book publications, asked if I meant that the work consisted of the sum of all these things. I imagined an edition that added all the versions to produce a work that was a sum of its variant parts. I rejected the notion out of hand. "Oh," he said, "perhaps you mean that the work is implied by these material documents but is not equivalent to any one of them?" Exactly. No one copy represents the full work; each copy represents the work in some way. The work is not equivalent to any material representation of it but is (partially and particularly) represented by each material instantiation of it.[7]

If the work is *implied* by the documentary text, it cannot itself *be* the documentary text. Each document represents some version of the work, but is a *version* equivalent with the text found in a document? Can the document *be* the version itself, or does the document only represent a version of the work? Take, for example, the case of a second edition heavily revised by the author but in which both first and second editions are riddled with typos and each suffered from censorship: two versions, neither well represented by extant documents. Some documents are incomplete and do not represent a whole version. Manuscripts can represent more than one version: original, intermediate, and last, intermingled on the page. Sometimes a version becomes recognizable by being extracted and constructed eclectically from texts found in more than one document. If the work and its versions were identical to the material texts representing them, it would follow that the work and its versions are just as flawed as their material forms. Or, contrarily, it would mean that the material form of the text, being identical with the work, cannot be flawed. The work would be a different work, but each perfect, in each different document. (I do not accept that argument.) If, on the other hand, the work is implied by the texts found in documents, then material

6. Caldwell's interest in ordinary language led him to develop a system he called "molecular sememics" as a way of understanding the functional dynamics of natural languages (five essays between 1989 and 2006). I applied this theory to script act theory in chapter 3 of *From Gutenberg to Google*.

7. See recent discussions in "Work and Document," edited by Barbara Bordalejo in *Ecdotica* 10 (2013), especially essays by Hans Walter Gabler, "Editing Text—Editing Work" (42–50) and Bordalejo, "The Texts We See and the Works We Imagine: The Shift of Focus of Textual Scholarship in the Digital Age" (64–75).

texts can be flawed and are subject to emendation in new texts. The result is a curated text, a critical text, an editorial hypothesis, a critical argument about the work. These are not pejorative labels.

New questions arise. Does the work consist of a series of snapshots found in material *things*, each document a static entity in a series of material objects? Or do the documents represent a developing series of attempts to construct a final static object? Is each document an iteration of the work as a temporarily final form to be studied as a historical event? Are each of these views viable? Perhaps it depends on the circumstances of the work's various productions. Or it might depend on who is asking the questions. In common speech, we refer to a work of art, whether as short as a sonnet or as long as *War and Peace*, as if the work were a thing as a whole, for which some document can stand as a snapshot. This view of the work as a static material object or series of objects is rather simplistic. A complex view holds that the work is like a machine: a tool for making our way bit by bit sequentially (mostly) through the work that is only implied by any one form of the variant machines that represent it.[8] From an experiential point of view, a literary work is seldom, if ever, looked at as "a whole." Readers travel through literary works more or less linearly, focusing on smaller units in a sequence that achieves a sense of wholeness only in our memory of the experience of reading. The writing and manufacturing of literary works are accomplished in similar focused sequences. The idea of a snapshot version of the work as a whole is at best a metaphor on the verge of collapse, held in place by paper and ink, not by one's apprehension of that which paper and ink signifies. I hold that a document is a document, not a work. A book is a book, a historical artifact, not the work of art that it only implies—sometimes imperfectly. The work, on the other hand, is performed into existence sequentially and ephemerally in the reading process. Flaws and differences in various texts affect that process. Thus, textual editing, while producing a copy, is not just copying.

When one reads one version alongside another, rather than reading a single text in isolation, one frequently gets a bigger bang for one's buck. The late Professor Julia Briggs brought two good examples to my attention. Chapter 18 of *To the Lighthouse* (the last in the first section titled "The Window") in the American edition ends with Mr. Ramsey's aloof detachment registered as his ability to know; the same chapter in the British edition ends instead

---

8. The tool comparison permeates Willard McCarty's *Humanities Computing* (London: Palgrave Macmillan, 2005).

with Mrs. Ramsey's triumph. Both versions contain approximately the same statements but in different climactic orders. Alone, each of these versions has whatever effect the reader derives from that particular arrangement of the details. In opposition to each other, a reader encounters tensions of dissent and difference that raise a range of questions: Who did this? Why was it done? What difference is being made? Was it an accident? Do the versions target different audiences as conceived by the author? Do they only represent different potentials? Is one version actually the "right one"? A "right one" renders the other one wrong. In that case, it would be an act of editorial kindness to readers to suppress the erroneous reading. The surviving evidence does not indicate that either one is wrong in this case. We know that Americans read one version and the British read another. For persons reading only one version, this range of questions will not be raised or addressed. Further, if such a single rightness were desirable in a scholarly edition, it would have to be created in its single rightness by an editor who, first as a reader, enjoyed the richness of the tension offered by the two versions in opposition, spoiling the experience for other readers by making a decision on their behalf. Each version implies the work in a different way; in juxtaposition, the versions imply the work in a more complex way.[9]

The other example Briggs brought to my attention was from Thomas Middleton's *The Second Maiden's Tragedy*. The husband spends his life in passionate suspicion of his wife, who, in fact, is unfaithful to him. Just as he dies at the end of the play, in the first version, he is convinced by his wife and her lover that they are innocent, and the husband dies in the blissful belief that his wife is truly his. He simultaneously feels the sad truth that his whole married life has been wasted and embittered by groundless suspicion—never mind the fact that the audience knows that is false. In the alternative ending, the wife and lover come clean at the deathbed, admitting all, and so the husband dies in the full satisfaction that he was right in his suspicions all along and in the sad certain knowledge of having been cuckolded. Now, we might think that one or the other ending is better, more authentic, or more final, but the ironic twists revealed by contemplating both endings in tension against each other might be better than either of them alone.

9. See Mark Hussey and Peter Shillingsburg, "The Composition, Revision, Printing and Publications of *To the Lighthouse*," Woolf Online, (http://www.woolfonline.com/?node =content/contextual/transcriptions&project=1&parent=45&taxa=47&content=6955& pos=3; particularly section III).

The argument contends, so far, that the work is not a document. It is not a single text. It is not the sum of all of its texts. It is implied in part by the text in each document, as well as by the texts of versions that can be extracted and constructed editorially from documents. In some instances, it can be implied differently by the tensions between two or more versions at once than by each single version in isolation. Works as wholes exist in inert potentials in documents (material objects), or they exist as wholes ephemerally in the memory of those who have read the whole work (mind objects). Works exist most immediately as performances in progress.

The reader's performance is dependent on the documents and information in hand. The reader's success depends on the satisfaction derived from the performance. From an editorial point of view, however, the questions are: What forms of the text will be represented? How will they be represented? What effect is being sought by that type of representation? The editor is in charge of the decisions that have to be made in constructing the edition. Readers have no choice but to accept the editor's decisions. Readers variously wish to understand the work of art in historical, documentary, social, intellectual, and aesthetic ways. Editors determine the reader's access. That is a grave responsibility. If we wish to create digital representations that enable this variety of sensibility, we must develop some sophisticated sensitivity to the multiple condition of literary works (their implied forms *and* their chronologies of dynamic existence). An electronic archive with digital images of documents and searchable transcriptions is a good start. Is it good enough?

The Work Represented

Imagine you have gone to one of the world's great libraries to see the manuscript, or the first edition, or the even rarer third revised cheap edition of a work. You fill out a call slip, pass it to the librarian's assistant, and in due time you are handed a typed transcript. After a moment of speechless surprise, you say, "No, no. Please, may I see the original?" "But," says the librarian, "look: this is not just any transcription. See. There is a full header recording who prepared the transcript and how it was proofread. Not only that," says the librarian, "but it is from a TEI conformant XML encoded original file." "No, no," you say. "I don't care who transcribed it or how many times it was proofread. I don't care if it is TEI conformant. I want to see the real original." Thank goodness librarians do not act that way. So, when we come to the digital archive/edition/work site as a place to study a work of literary art online and we click on the icon or hotlink to "The Blessed Damozel," or *The Songs of Innocence*, or *The Origin of Species*, or *Vanity Fair*, why do we get a transcript? We do not want a transcript; we want an image—and not just any image. We want a choice of the manuscript, the 1821 newspaper, the 1848 first edition, or the 2002 critical edition. What we get when we make the choice should be an image of what we asked for, not a transcript and not the image of some other document with the same title, which well-meaning but misguided persons think is the same thing. Furthermore, we want to know where the material source text is housed.

This idea does not go without saying. Many electronic sites offering literary works offer only transcripts. Many websites offering literary texts do not identify the source text for the transcript or say who transcribed it, how it was transcribed, how it was proofread, or when it was transcribed. Most electronic literary works were mounted by people who think that a text is a text is a text; any text will do. Some sites identify a particular source text but offer only a transcription, as if the transcript and the source were interchangeable equivalents. They are not. They do not imply the work in the same way, as has been argued many times by the followers of D. F. McKenzie and Jerome J. McGann.

Digital *transcriptions* are valuable things. They enable searching and computerized analysis. Unfortunately, each transcript is a new edition that reprints the text from a material document. A collection of digital transcriptions does not constitute an archive of anything other than an archive of digital transcriptions. There is also the disadvantage of OCR (optical character recognition) not getting everything right. When one performs a machine search of a raw scanned text, one will miss all the instances of the search words that have been mistranscribed. Textual scholars do not, however, expect machines to do what they are supposed to do before releasing a digital project to the public—in other words, proofreading, double-checking, vetting, verifying, and approving the transcripts first.

Digital *image* archives are a slightly different matter. Digital images are what we have done best in digital editing. We may not have done it perfectly; we have occasionally done it imperfectly. Yet, there is a sense of satisfaction about the potential for electronic archives that makes us think that if we are not there yet, we are almost there. A digital image collection, too, is only an archive of digital images—copies of copies. At its best, a virtual archive contains the images not just of the text but of the medium on which the text was written or printed, so that we can know something about the paper, the margins, the condition of the material, the quality of the printing, the sense of design, and the sense of the document's age. The virtual archive, in two respects, can surpass a real one: first, by collecting images from multiple physical repositories and, second, by producing images of high enough resolution that the virtual reproduction can reveal more than the original reveals to the naked eye. Certainly, virtual archives can be better than microfilm, which has served our profession so well, but which has also taught us lessons about the inadequacies of photo reproductions.

Virtual archives can surpass material archives in other ways. Internet storage devices are capacious and open ended. Projects no longer need to be completed before being launched because the ability to add to them is never cut off. Even better, we have licked the distribution problems, too: unlike material archives, the digital library can be made available everywhere via the Internet. Scholars have less reason go physically to academic institutions with great archives—or if they still have to, we feel that in time they will not have to.

The electronic age has reached one milestone: *texts* and *documents* can now be represented digitally in scholarly, reliable, and useful ways. What can we say about the representation of *works*?

One answer is that works *are* represented in texts and documents; without documents, there are no works. Since various documents and texts imply a work differently, such that the work is not equivalent to any one document, documents need curation in more ways than one. The complexity of works exceeds the sum of historical texts and documents. Archival representation requires more than digital imitation of handwritten and machine-printed texts. Archives also need emended texts representing lost and unachieved forms, and they require the information about the material evidence and the critical arguments that help to establish what the *work* is or can be.

Textual debates have not questioned the need for images, transcriptions, and information about historical texts. The denigration of critically edited eclectic texts, however, needs further examination.

Critically edited texts are drawn from two or more extant historical documents and are informed by other contextual data. They aim to provide a version of the text approximating what was in some now-lost form or to fulfill what would have existed but for interventions by persons of dubious authority to make changes. There might be more than one such critical edition, none of which is truly "final" or "definitive" in any sense yet may be useful for displaying otherwise unavailable conceptual versions of the work as an editorial hypothesis.

Despite being widely criticized, critical editing is still, for English-language texts, a frequently practiced form of scholarly editing. Editors who want to produce the most artistic, or most politically correct, or most aesthetically pleasing form of the work are guided by aesthetic or commercial interests. Their methods may be eclectic but are usually also "enhanced" by speculative emendation. Before leaving them aside as not relevant to historical critical editing, I note that *all* variants, except those produced by the author, were originally speculative emendations by persons acting as editors. In its most defensible form, eclectic editing seeks to incorporate in one text the guiding influence of the person or persons to whom the greatest authority for the text is now attributed. It is an approach used in attempts to reconstruct archetypes when all the historically extant documents are chronologically and transmissionally distant from their originals, or where many documents claim some authority. It is also used when manuscripts, proofs, and authoritative printed documents bear the evidence not only of revision but also of carelessness, censorship, or inept or well-meaning but heavy-handed interventionist editing.

The fact that responsible scholars continue to practice this editorial approach suggests its methods are not dead as dodos. One can find examples of poorly edited texts, but, regardless of what that says about an editor, such editions do not demonstrate that the methods themselves are at fault.

Diversity of opinions about the nature of works and about uses for documentary materials require that we develop capable tools for electronic editions and archives. The tools and the display capabilities need to be adequate for the needs of scholars who use any or all of these approaches. Works are implied and represented, but who determines what was implied by each representation?

The Work Interpreted

If the work is implied by, rather than fully inherent in, the documents that represent it, then the only way to know what is implied by each form is to interpret that form and to say what one thinks is implied by it. When one does that, one is confined to saying what is implied by the particular copy of the work one is reading. One's interpretation of the copy in hand does not necessarily apply to other copies nor is it necessarily generic to the work as a whole. This range of variation is caused only in part by the unpredictable differences among readers who bring to bear different experiences and expectations to a work. Texts of a work stimulate different responses through textual differences, through the implications of their bibliographical design and materials, and through the different contexts that attended composition, production, and reception.

Examples of how differences between copies of a work can lead directly to conflicting interpretations are discussed in several essays in this book. For bibliographical particularities, one need only mention the differences between authorized and pirated editions of works by Byron or Goethe. For lexical particularities, one needs only to say "coiled fish" versus "soiled fish," or "too sullied flesh" versus "too sallied" or "too solid flesh," or "early editions of Henry James" versus "the New York edition of Henry James," or to refer to the examples from Middleton's *Second Maiden's Tragedy* or Virginia Woolf's *To the Lighthouse*, already described.

Interpretive differences also arise from knowledge or ignorance of the contexts of origination surrounding the significant events in the production of copies of the work. That which is implied by a Yeats poem published in the *Irish Times* at a time of incidental public turmoil of 1913 is not what is implied by that same poem safely ensconced in the Norton Anthology of English Literature, volume 2, in 1997 or 2007. It might be enough to mention Keats's "Oh, Attic shape," taken as a reference to a vase in grandma's attic. If we are inclined to use locutions such as "What Shakespeare did so well here" or "Only Melville could have thought to use such a word," we should be sure not only that the author is responsible for the locution being quoted but also that we know enough about the circumstances of its utterance to know that our insight is supported by evidence about what "went without saying" for the author, production crew, and first readers of that copy of the work.

The complex task of interpretation is rendered both more complex and more precise by attention to the particularities of the copy being read and to its lexical, bibliographical, and contextual differences from other copies.

Author Meaning Versus Reader Meaning

If we avoid sounding as if we knew what the author had meant by claiming instead that "the text says so and so" or "the text means so and so," we not only speak the nonsense that paper and ink molecules have independent volition but also assume that the text we are quoting is identical to that in all other copies. Texts do not mean things; people mean things by texts. Readers create or assign meaning to texts by invoking contexts in which the texts make sense. In the absence of knowledge of the contexts that supported meaning at the time of composition, readers invent plausible contexts. In order to produce *informed* reader response, readers need texts that are particular, that look like what they are, and that are surrounded or supported by the materials that at one time went without saying but now do not.

Readers are, of course, not required to be informed. Asking readers to express their opinions about texts concerning which they have no information about the contexts of origination is like asking anyone you might meet on the street to express an opinion about when the United States will pull out of some conflict, or whether it will rain tomorrow, or who will be the next president. People usually have no difficulty in expressing opinions about things they do not know, but one had just as well ask a crystal ball or a cat. Such opinions are acts of the imagination, unimpeded by knowledge, rather than the result of analysis of the full panoply of relevant evidence. It is not good enough to offer readers a historical text without also offering the fruits of scholarly research into the contexts of origination.

Digital Options

If, as I have argued, the work is implied, represented, and interpreted in relation to the particular copy (or copies) in hand, it follows that the work itself exists only in deferred forms—not in immediate, transparent, unambiguous forms. A text is never a *mere* text, or a *simple* text, or a *correct* text, not even if it is well edited. Locutions such as "the work itself" are empty rhetorical nonentities, for the work exists only in our constructs of it. While *documents* are clearly material and the *texts* on them, though variable, are fixed, the *work* is a mental construct and ephemeral. The German historical critical editors make this same point by distinguishing, in the words of Gunter Martens, between textual evidence called findings (the textual document) and the aesthetic object called interpretation (the work extracted from the material evidence).[10] Historical critical editors err, I believe, in assuming

10. Gunter Martens, "(De)Constructing Texts by Editing: Reflections on the Receptional Significance of Textual Apparatuses" (1975, in German); trans. in *Contemporary German Editorial Theory*, ed. Hans Walter Gabler, George Bornstein, and Gillian Borland Pierce (Ann Arbor: University of Michigan Press, 1995), 125–52; Martens, "What Is a Text?" 209–31.

that editors can focus their attention on the textual evidence and leave the aesthetic object for critics to worry about. For, when editors detect an error in a document, they must appeal to the aesthetic object and the intentions behind it to divine a correction. Editors, like other readers, are prevented from immediate, transparent, and uncritical interaction with the work because textual evidence is evidence for the work—not the "work itself." The "work itself" is ephemeral, various, and conceptual, as it is raised variously from the texts of documents by interpretive performance. I hold that informed performance is better than uninformed.

Though texts and documents can be digitized, the *work* will never be nailed down and made fixed forever—not in print and not digitally. Because textual conditions lead inevitably to disputes about how to interpret and how to re-present works, digital archives and editions must be constructed to meet many different expectations.

While our job as editors is most immediately with the material evidence (documents and texts), we must acknowledge the elusiveness of works when we make decisions about how to represent the evidence electronically. An archive of representations of a work is a beginning, providing the foundation for full engagement with the work. Adequate electronic designs for archives and editions will enable (but not guarantee) literary criticism that is broadly based in relevant texts and contexts.

In the print world, editors were prevented by economics and the limitations of paper from making text and context *invitingly* available to critics. Important textual differences and revealing contextual facts were buried in apparatuses and introductions. Digital productions promise better presentation and better interface designs to help readers achieve greater understanding of texts. However, we still have formidable infrastructure and design problems to solve.

Digital infrastructure and design problems arise naturally in a new medium without traditions. Project directors seeking quick and cheap ways to mount projects are frustrated or settle for compromises. Unsurprisingly, we find electronic projects following the print model—finished projects presented to users not as dynamic growing sites for scholarship but as products to be seen and not touched. In the book world, every project was cut down to size by compromise. Digital projects still compromise in similar ways because of the size of hard discs, the speed of downloads, the size of budgets, the availability of funding, and the flagging energies of scholars. The incunabular period of digital archives and editions suffered from a failure of imagination, failing to see the problem as a whole or to recognize the short-falls of local solutions for local problems. We thought too small. The goals of digital archives and of digital editions are too great for any one editor or one small team of editors to fulfill. We need to see electronic editorial projects as partial contributions to work sites where our best collaborators may have only just now been born. We need to see that our colleagues in computer science are our partners, not our assistants. Long-term design can allow textual crit-ics to begin with foundations to be built on by other scholars who can attach their own scholarly work to the existing site as developing contributions to knowledge.

Conclusion

Editing is an attempt to deal with a complex set of materials for which there are a variety of viable and necessary approaches.

Editing in the electronic world is a task that should not end with one project's vision of the product but instead should serve as a foundation for new scholarship. Project directors should foresee a future community of scholars who can contribute to basic editorial work, to the construction of contextual matter, and to the structure of critical understanding of the works represented in our electronic archive of editions. That requires agile structures and enduring maintenance, repair, and replacement management far beyond the capacity of any one person.

These conclusions have much to say about how we do our work. In order for scholarly editors in the electronic medium to make a difference in the way students and critics read and interpret texts, they must do the following four things:

1. Make access to texts in scholarly editions as convenient and inexpen-sive as paperbacks, as stand-alone components, tethered (linked) to their archival sources.
2. Construct editions that enable readers to both see and touch, and manipulate, alter, and personalize their copies in whatever way they wish.
3. Construct editions so that other scholars can participate in the further construction of the work site by adding new materials, new links, new

comments, new information, new texts, new tagging, new views. If necessary, establish ongoing editorial boards to adjudicate growth.

4. Protect the integrity of the original textual foundation and the discreteness of each contributor's offering while accomplishing points two and three. This will require an environment as well as a storage and retrieval system for electronic projects that separates text images from text transcriptions; that separates text data from markup and commentary by means such as standoff markup; that protects file integrity by means such as checksums; that tracks individual engagement histories for users; that ensures site longevity by multiple distributed online storage; and that provides for spontaneous aggregation and integration, and display of texts, contexts, and scholarly commentary, both original to the project and newly contributed.

Finally, funding agencies need to support development of a collaborative literary research electronic environment. We have had enough of electronic editions and of archives created as look-but-don't-touch products, closed, finished, and ultimately abandoned.

Convenient Scholarly Editions

Convenience can hardly be overemphasized. Literary critics and students most often use their own cheap paperback copy with the turned-down page corners, underlining, and marginal notes, or they use e-books and Project Gutenberg—texts, usually, of sources unknown or misidentified, proofed cursorily, if at all, printed in random fonts and formats. Why do they do that? Because it is convenient. In some cases, they do not have access to a good library. If the Internet provides inferior goods, is not something better than nothing? Convenience is, in practice, one of the most important qualities of a text. All else being equal, students and critics probably care about the quality of texts. Given an equal choice, none would say "I prefer an inaccurate text of unknown origin." Given easy access to contextual information about the texts being studied, few would say "I really do not want to know." In practice, however, many proceed without knowing because it is convenient. They also might not know the consequences of not knowing. How can complex, sophisticated textual awareness be made convenient?

Having sketched in the previous essay relationships between *documentary* materials of literary *texts* and immaterial constructs of a *work*, and having acknowledged multiple uses and points of view that scholar-critics bring to documents, I turn to the nature of the virtual things being created as digital

Initial ideas for this essay appeared in *From Gutenberg to Google: Electronic Representations of Literary Texts* (Cambridge: Cambridge University Press, 2006). I am indebted to discussions with Professor Hussein Zedan (computer engineering), Mr. Stephan Brown (knowledge media design), Dr. Nicholas Hayward, and Dr. Takako Kato at De Montfort University, and with Paul Eggert. Earlier versions were trialed at King's College London (June 2006) and at the Digital Textual Studies: Past, Present and Future conference at Texas A&M University, September 2006. That version appeared in *Digital Humanities Quarterly* 3, no. 3 (2009), in the special issue "Digital Textual Studies: Past, Present and Future," ed. Amy Earhart and Maura Ives, http://digitalhumanities.org/dhq/vol/3/3/000054.html#.

correlatives to material forms. Porting text from book to screen is not at all simple nor, despite some impressive efforts, has anyone adequately achieved it. Project builders have done the best they can with finite resources and time. The results can be beautiful and sometimes innovative. The best methods are still developer-unfriendly, user-unfriendly, and maintenance-unfriendly. When we have achieved convenience in development, use, and maintenance, we will have fully functional tools and a generalizable environment for constructing digital scholarly editions.

To develop this model, we first need to describe objectives in ways that are not driven primarily by deadlines or the desire to get a specific project finished and posted to the Web. Digital archives must begin with images of all the documents (visual surrogates for the originals), because even accurate transcripts are not surrogates but new editions or reprints. Transcriptions need to be linked to corresponding images. Relational links (collations and textual histories) are basic information about variant texts. Textual content (the archive) should be structured so that relevant scholarship can be published as part of the site. Convenience requires that the tools that make virtual archives possible be useable by laymen—just as are typewriters, word processors, and analytic tools. Everything in the surrogate must be designed to make long-range extendibility possible for future textual and literary scholars. Design and documentation should make site maintenance a pleasure for future technical partners. For safety's sake, knowledge sites should be distributed (mirrored) widely. Safety would be enhanced if an authenticator warned users when the content of a file has been altered. Implementing these desirables will make possible continuous scholarly and technical development beyond the tenure of the initial developers of these projects. Users can exercise their own judgment.

It is no disparagement of the fine and complex electronic editions under way or recently accomplished to say that they are not convenient, fully functional, generalizable environments for scholarly editing and archiving. Projects such as those on Nietzsche, Wittgenstein, Rossetti, *Piers Plowman*, Blake, Dickinson, Beowulf, Boethius, the Dead Sea Scrolls, the Codex Sinaiticus, Archimedes Palimpsest, Woolf Online, and the *Canterbury Tales* each represent in one or more ways the leading edges in digital editing. These pioneering, innovative projects in digital humanities and computer science pave the path to further digital capabilities. They do not yet fulfill the potentials of the medium, nor do they share enough in common to be called a united front.

One reason digital editions and archives tend to be finished megawholes to be looked at but not touched is that the design and structure of content and links among the parts focused, naturally enough, on what textual scholars wanted to see and on how humanists would use the site. A newer alternative structuring method focuses on how computers store and give access to minute bits of data understood at the binary and pixel level. The humanist's concern with how it looks and how it is used is an interface issue, not a content structure issue. Content viewable exactly as the originators desired is less tied to their vision and lies in wait for display and use in new ways yet to be discovered. New materials and new visualizations can be added collaboratively.

Collaboration is one of the most difficult aspects of the digital world for scholars to grasp and exploit. There is little tradition for it in the humanities. Sharing the results of labor, while good, is not the same as developing projects collaboratively.[1] Modularity is key to collaboration. To be collaborative, a project's content (documents, texts, textual relations) must remain free of scholarly markup and commentary. That kind of critical analysis and commentary about the archive needs its own repository as content of a different kind. Interface will enable retrieval and combination of text data and markup. Combining different contents in single repositories has limited interoperability and repurposing. In the long run, interpretive content structures kill projects. The modules (small units of content) require an environment rendering them connectable and extendible, such that the parts can be enhanced, repaired, or replaced without damaging the network that comprises the whole—whatever it is that the whole turns out to be. Designed to grow, a project can be added to by many different scholars over long periods of time. Users should be able to see, touch, and appropriate their own displays from the archive of modular data, unrestricted by the uses that initiators foresaw. The intellectual work of the future can be built on the textual foundations laid down digitally if they are clean and neutral, leaving display options to interface.

---

1. Organizations such as the Advanced Research Consortium (ARC) focus on aggregating existing projects and groups of projects (NINES, MESA, REKn, 18thConnect, and ModNets) initially developed in isolation. ARC principles can be viewed at http://wiki.collex.org/index.php?title=Principles_for_Metadata_Reform&action=edit. TEI was thought to be a scholarly standard for digital representations of original documents, but it is increasingly clumsy in its third decade of implementation.

Nothing dates so rapidly as advice about how to achieve goals such as those laid out here. Assuming that TEI or some other markup system survives, we need tagging tools that will allow textual scholars (not just trained technical assistants) to associate their analytical tagging (not only corrections but commentary) as standoff markup. Standoff markup (isolating text data from interpretive commentary) will help maintain the goal of modular structure that is currently often ignored by projects that embed markup in text files. Premixing text and markup in multipurpose files means that every attempt to add tagging or correct errors renders the whole vulnerable to accidental changes. It also inhibits repurposing of textual content. A standoff markup tool will allow multiple scholars to add tagging without affecting base texts or previous interpretive work. As a knowledge site grows—offering complex, complementary, and even conflicting annotation—the interface and navigation tools should enable choices among the annotation categories users wish to have affect their views of the text. Texts, commentary, and record of variation, kept separately and managed by interface, can be corrected, augmented, deleted, and repurposed without affecting the integrity of any other part of a project. The systems that we need for this kind of editing have not been well developed yet. The big first task is to get scholarly editors to give up being control freaks and begin working in collaborative communities. The next is to fund them in partnerships with computer scientists.

Convenience and Thoroughness

The history of scholarly editing is not famous for its attempts to make the fruits of textual research easily accessible to readers. Textual scholars are perhaps the only creatures on earth capable of being enthusiastic about textual apparatuses. Jo Ann Boydston, addressing the Society of Textual Scholarship in the early 1990s, spoke "In Praise of Apparatus."[2] She had just finished the monumental task of editing the works of the American philosopher John Dewey and was impressed by the importance and usefulness of the apparatus. Her paean to apparatuses struck responsive chords in the hearts of historical critical editors, for many of whom the editor's primary task is to bring order and explanation to textual histories. The text itself, according to Gunter Martens, writing in 1975, could be dispensed with or published separately,

2. JoAnn Boydston, "In Praise of Apparatus," *Text* 5 (1991): 1–13.

since the real business of textual criticism was contained in the apparatus.[3] Textual apparatuses support additional textual tasks, as Keith Elliott pointed out relative to eclectic editing for the New Testament. A carefully constructed textual apparatus is essential for the eclectic editorial goals he calls "thorough-going editing."[4] The point has been made countless times by editors from A. E. Housman to Richard Bucci.[5]

We also need flexible ways to deploy basic textual data because textual scholars explain textual criticism and textual histories in a variety of ways. Some scholars see in textual histories the dynamics of composition, revision, and publication; others care more for the complex of social interactions that affect the textual results; others believe such histories help in distinguishing right from wrong readings; others wish to see texts obscured by accidental or ill-informed textual changes; and still others care because they see interpretive consequences unavailable to us when we read a single text in isolation. Textual data is basic to all, regardless of the approach, and needs to be stored neutrally, accessible for display in ways that support a variety of views.

While considerable effort goes into the construction of textual appara-tuses, often little effort is put into using them during the writing of interpre-tive essays. In print editions, where costs and space tended to reduce apparatus to code, this neglect of textual difference was understandable, if not justified. Electronic representation introduces radical changes we need to take advantage of. The labor and cost of creation is not less (probably more). But space is more ample, and replication and dissemination less costly, and navigation of the archive infinitely easier. What in print was compressed and difficult can, with proper design, be as expansive or as precise as needed. Despite the limitations of electronic surrogates, understanding the dynamic textual interactions of literary works may best be accomplished electronically because access to information is greater, faster, and easier than in material

---

3. Gunter Martens, "(De)Constructing Texts by Editing: Reflections on the Receptional Significance of Textual Apparatuses" (1975, in German); trans. in *Contemporary German Editorial Theory*, ed. Hans Walter Gabler, George Bornstein, and Gillian Borland Pierce (Ann Arbor: University of Michigan Press, 1995).

4. J. Keith Elliott, "Reflections on the Method: What Constitutes the Use of the Writings that Later Formed the New Testament in the Apostolic Fathers?" in *The Reception of the New Testament in the Apostolic Fathers*, ed. Andrew Gregory and Christopher M. Tuckett (Oxford: Oxford University Press, 2005), 47–58.

5. It is a central argument of the present book, too, but see *Anglo-American Scholarly Editing, 1980–2005*, ed. Paul Eggert and Peter Shillingsburg with Kevin Caliendo, special issue, *Ecdotica* 6 (2009).

documents. Constructing the environment is not faster or easier—nor as yet available.

There are good reasons to go to the trouble of constructing virtual archives and scholarly editions. As scholar-critics, we want to know the evidence for what we call knowledge. We need to know the answers to the questions "Where did that come from?" and "How do you know?" All literary critics acknowledge that for the study of literature, we need texts. Some also acknowledge that for the study of texts, we need not just any text but specific texts. There are interpretive consequences to knowing or not knowing the specifics of the texts of a work in the form of drafts, manuscripts, typescripts, proofs, magazine publications, books, and revised editions. It seems naive if not irresponsible to think that to understand and interact with a poem, play, or novel, all one needs is a clean, approved text, as if one text should serve all purposes. If we are studying the history of Shakespeare in the eighteenth century, is it not obvious that we would need eighteenth-century editions to work from? If we wish to study the social, political, economic, and daily life surrounding the production and reproduction of a work, we need more than an approved text—more even than a text and guide to variants. For such studies, we could use libraries and travel funds. We do not *need* computers, as Tony Edwards suggested at a conference I hosted at De Montfort University. He said, "Computers are just a convenience." Willard McCarty said to me afterward, "Yes, of course, one can walk from Leicester to London, and in that sense automobiles and trains are just conveniences." We do not go from Leicester to London without convenient vehicles; we do not investigate the textuality of works we study without convenient archives and editions.

Convenience is good, but digital scholars usually want to provide something that could not otherwise be done—something that shows that the electronic world supersedes the print world. Of course, being able to get from Leicester to London in one hour and fifteen minutes is something that cannot be done on foot. If, however, trains at the end of your journey dumped you out onto green park grass with straw in your hair, you might object that the convenience had its downsides. Not so; you get to St. Pancras station and walk out as if nothing unusual has taken place.

So, too, if the scholarly electronic edition, as a convenience, dumped a text smudged and damaged because its source was not acknowledged, its fonts and formats had all been changed, its covers and dust jackets had been torn off and discarded, its contexts of origin had been completely disregarded, and its words and punctuation had been altered in both palpable and impalpable ways, we would say the convenience had its downsides. These are, in fact, the conditions of most electronic texts now available.

Convenience in texts has another very important role. In print, scholarly editions are not only inconvenient; they are so expensive that most people do not own them or consult them. There are rules and perhaps laws against taking a book from the library and dog-earing the pages, or writing in the margins, or, having done that, failing to return the book to the library. Hence, most literary criticism is conducted in the presence of convenient, cheap editions, often paperbacks, with texts that can be dog-eared, underlined, written in, or even torn apart. Unfortunately, such texts often lack accurate acknowledgment of sources and have no trace of original fonts, formats, or forms, or even descriptions of those forms. Hence, much literary criticism is based on texts with dubious claims to textual accuracy, without textual histories, and often without historical contexts. Why are these the tools of choice for literary criticism? They are convenient.

Electronic formats have a chance of providing literary critics with convenience, though we have not yet figured out how to be as convenient as a paperback—as cheap, as portable, or as dynamically interactive, albeit by pencil, as a personally owned printed book. One problem may be that scholarly electronic editions result from attempts to be as good as the scholarly print editions that so few people use. It is said that the likelihood a scholar or student will check the accuracy of a supposed fact is in inverse proportion to the distance that has to be traveled to do the checking. If it can be checked without getting up—high likelihood—across the room—probably but maybe not—out the door across the campus to the library—only if highly motivated, and so forth.

Some people are motivated and do use scholarly editions. However, thirteen years after the publication of Grindle and Gatrell's magnificent edition of Thomas Hardy's *Tess of the d'Urbervilles*, 90 percent of new critical essays on that novel cited other editions.[6] It is not a unique case, nor does the existence and use of a scholarly edition guarantee anything. Scholarly editions are not always better than other editions; if the early volumes of the Ohio Browning edition live up to the denigrations of its scholarship found in the

---

6. Or so Simon Gatrell claimed in a conference presentation, SCMLA, Savannah, 1996; Thomas Hardy, *Tess of the d'Urbervilles*, ed. Judith Grindle and Simon Gatrell (Oxford: Oxford University Press, 1983).

reviews[7] and in the explanation that one of its own board members gave for his resignation, there must occasionally be good reasons not to use that scholarly edition.[8] Furthermore, there is not always a choice; in the case of works for which no scholarly edition has been created, something else must do. It simply is not always the case that doing the convenient thing is bad, but it is natural, and scholarly editions have not had the effect they should have had on criticism, primarily because they are not convenient either in price or structure. Can digital archives and editions be made convenient?

Scholarly editions have not been convenient because textual criticism is complex; because the print medium required that textual scholarship's complexity be compressed and made economical; because the textual condition of a four-hundred-page novel entails some 150,000 to 300,000 words and 1.5 to 3 million characters, punctuation, and spaces, each subject to misplacement or replacement. Levels of complexity are added by variants in the manuscript, the proofs, the magazine version, the first book appearance, and the revised edition or editions and perhaps more besides. In addition, textual and literary criticism both require knowledge of the contexts of textual origination—frames of reference. It is not easy to deal with complex textual histories and contexts period, let alone economically and compactly. That is why scholarly editions are not convenient. The convenience of cheap paperbacks is "purchased" at a great loss. Perhaps students and critics willing to forego knowledge have no idea how much they are paying for their convenience. Reforming them is not our job; making knowledge accessible and convenient may be.

Convenience for *readers*—for students and critics—is not the only goal. Convenience is a necessary goal for *editors* as well. Editing entails a variety of tasks, not all of which have to be intellectually challenging every time. Editorial scholarship is not easy, but the construction of scholarly editions should not have to entail reinvention of editorial architecture every time. Editors have traditionally thought themselves to be in charge of the quality

---

7. Reviews of the Browning edition: Thomas J. Collins in *Victorian Studies* 13 (June 1970): 441–44; Michael Hancher in *Yearbook of English Studies* 2 (1972): 312–14. See also a response by John Pettigrew in *Essays in Criticism* 22 (1972): 436–41.

8. Morse Peckham, "Thoughts on Editing *Sordello*," *Studies in Browning and His Circle* 5 (1977): 11–18; and Peckham, with David R. King, "The Editing of 19th-Century Texts," in *Language and Texts: The Nature of Linguistic Evidence*, ed. Herbert H. Paper, Gerald E. Else, Judith Goldin, and Albert H. Marchwardt (Ann Arbor: Center for Coordination of Ancient and Modern Texts, University of Michigan, 1975), 123–46.

of every detail of their editions. Consequently, they have been very protective of the fruits of their labor. With print editions, battles are frequent between the editor and the publisher. In electronic editions, this protectiveness of editorial work reveals itself in the pains taken to make sure that users of the edition cannot appropriate (i.e., contaminate) the text. Collaborators are not invited in. If you find an error in a print edition, you can cross it out and write in the correction. If you want to add a note, you can do so in the margin. Digital editions are not easily appropriated, personalized, or augmented by "mere users." The convenient scholarly edition needs a new structure and added tools to facilitate not only their original development but the open-ended collaborative action that might lead to editions growing and changing.

Furthermore, convenience for *readers and editors*, good as it is, is not good enough. Scholarly electronic editions need to be convenient for the *technical experts* who not only have to build them but who will have to maintain them, repair them, and transport them to future platforms and software. With more and more libraries creating digital repositories, we need editions that can easily be stored and maintained by digital librarians who simply cannot devote their lives to mastering the intricacies of each individual project. If we do not, the shelf life of electronic editions is too short to justify the investment of time, money, and intellectual labor necessary to produce them. On the other hand, if we limit the complexity of textual criticism to currently easy stuff so that digital librarians can handle the materials, we will have to compromise the projects. Better to admit that we are not there yet. Print books on acid-free paper last centuries; when we have figured out how to do that electronically, we will have something to crow about.[9]

English Poetry Research Carrel

I end with a post-present vision of an English Poetry Research Carrel, which is one idea of how a collaborative literary research electronic environment

---

9. It is worth mentioning here that "the idea of an electronic scholarly archive / edition / work site" is the goal of a number of separate efforts that have not yet been well integrated or even well cross-pollinated. See, for example, Ray Siemens, "Text Analysis and the Dynamic Edition? A Working Paper, Briefly Articulating Some Concerns with an Algorithmic Approach to the Electronic Scholarly Edition," *Text Technology* 14 (2005): 91–98, also available at http://texttechnology.mcmaster.ca/pdf/vol14_1_09.pdf. See also the NINES project, http://www.nines.org; Discovery, http://www.discovery-project.eu/; and the ARC project mentioned previously. These efforts seem more in tune with a future of the methodology than with the deadline-driven development of a single project.

would make a literary work of art look to a user. I am presupposing that content structures conform to best post-present practice in computer science and that the tools for constructing, collaborating, and maintaining the carrel are in place.

In Podunk, J. Q. Scholar sits, keen to learn what can be known of John Keats's "Ode on a Grecian Urn." There is no research library nearby. Curiosity is stimulated but not satiated by the books on Keats that are at hand.

Scholar opens a Web browser search tool, types "John Keats's 'Ode on a Grecian Urn,'" and clicks on the first item: English Poetry Research Carrel, which contains a list of poets. Scholar clicks on John Keats. A Web page appears, looking like a desk surrounded by books with a number of options for finding Keats's poem and materials about it. Available items include facsimiles of four manuscripts, none in Keats's own hand (none exist); a magazine appearance; two book appearances in Keats's lifetime; and a scholarly edition, introduced, edited, and annotated by Jack Stillinger. In addition, there are biographies, bibliographies, and commentaries in "full text." J. Q. Scholar can, with one click, find, open, and begin reading the poem. Any curiosity about the particular edition is satisfied by full bibliographical citation in a pop-up window. A desire to know if any editions differ from the one open is satisfied with a click, producing either textual variants or a variant text—either as image or transcript. Stillinger's account of the textual history is a click away. A bibliography of commentary on the poem, another click away, links to full texts more often than not. Reader curiosity drives access. A search engine across all parts of the carrel is also capable of linking to the Internet at large. On the virtual desktop are the tools for extracting, quoting, highlighting, and selecting texts; for personalizing the Keats Knowledge Site; for adding things from outside the carrel; for storing Scholar's own contributions to his personalized Keats site; and for building Scholar's own critical response to or explanation of Keats's poem.

Having produced his own critical interaction with the poem or discovered new information about the author or context or language of the poem, J. Q. can save a personalized knowledge site and can also submit a scholarly contribution to the Keats Knowledge Site, where the site's review board can vet or have vetted the contribution and add it, if approved, for the benefit of other scholars. In any case, J. Q. can generate study aids for his next class on Keats.

J. Q. Scholar, who is of no certain age, located anywhere—Podunk or OtherSimilarPlace—could be fifteen or fifty-five, a seasoned or beginning researcher. The ways into the carrel are familiar and intuitive; the depth and sophistication of entry should be the user's choice.

This is fiction because, to my knowledge, no such carrel and no such site exists. The goal is to construct the electronic infrastructure that will support the literary and scholarly content as well as the navigational and analytical tools that will provide a place for investigation and dynamic interaction with the carrel's English literary materials.

Scholarly Editing as a Cultural Enterprise

> May he never find happiness who alters the orthography,
> let alone a single word, of the text.
> —Antanas Baranauskas, in a letter to Justinas
> Dovydaitis from January 8, 1900

"German and the Anglo-American textual scholars are speaking different languages," Dirk Van Hulle observed to me one day; "translation between the different schools is urgently necessary." This subject had appealed to me for many years, but particularly since 1999, when I began participating in textual studies meetings in Austria, Switzerland, the Netherlands, Belgium, Germany, Denmark, Italy, Spain, and the United Kingdom. I noticed that home-country solutions to textual problems needed to be defended at international conferences against criticisms leveled by foreigners who, kindly though they might be, did not fully understand the arguments or their applications to national literatures. The defensiveness, I believed, worked on all sides, mine included. My textual studies work in Europe, Australia, South Africa, India, Japan, and Colombia, where I have discussed in depth the editorial problems associated with different national literatures, led me to ask "Can there be such a thing as a 'home-country solution' to textual problems?" Are there cultural aspects to editorial problems? If so, how can they best be addressed? Do editorial goals or methods, specially designed for culturally

Earlier versions presented at ESTS, Brussels, 2009, and published in *Variants* 8 (2011): 247–68. The epigraph, from Antanas Baranauskas, *Raðtai* 2, ed. Regina Mikðytë (Vilnius: Vaga, 1970), 173, is drawn from Paulius Subačius, "The Problem of Polytext," *Literatûra* 49, no. 5 (2007): 134.

specific situations, need to be defended against criticisms from outside the cultural domains that shaped them?[1]

Language differences contribute to the isolation of editorial traditions. Perhaps all editors *should* speak or read all relevant languages equally well, but we do not. The need to translate is not, however, felt urgently by very many German, Anglo-American, or French editors, who often feel a contentment that the important things are all being done in their own native language. The urgency to communicate across borders is felt most strongly by those who speak two or more languages, or who have experienced editorial discussions in multiple cultures and have tasted both the outrage and the exhilaration of a serious conversation across cultural barriers. The desire for intercultural exchanges of ideas has been noted and acted on sporadically. In 1976, a special meeting was convened at Indiana University consisting of a small number of Soviet Russian "textuists" and an equally small number of American scholarly editors. Though much was anticipated, little came of that meeting in subsequent editorial practice in either Russia or America. The differences in perspective must have been too great.[2]

My experience of European editing began when I was a graduate student in the 1960s. Hans Walter Gabler came to the University of South Carolina to talk about an electronically generated and typeset edition of James Joyce's *Ulysses*. He brought with him a prototype of fifty-one pages with seven pages of preliminaries. The University of South Carolina had recently launched a scholarly edition of the works of William Gilmore Simms, a prolific mid-nineteenth-century favorite son author in South Carolina. Our training to conduct such a project came directly from reading everything Ronald B. McKerrow, W. W. Greg, and Fredson Bowers had written about scholarly editing—about choosing copy-texts and emending them. The Modern Language Association of America had just launched its Center for Editions of American Authors (CEAA), which was based at the University of South

---

1. See the fascinating, and at times horrific, relationship between Russian and Lithuanian textual studies recounted in Subačius, "Problem of Polytext."

2. In an email to me of May 4, 2010, Thomas Tanselle noted that meeting with the Russians was considered at the time to be a historic occasion, but nothing tangible was produced as a result of the meeting, and it had no effect on Anglo-American thinking. Also in an email to me, on the same date, Paulius Subačius noted that a current standard work on Russian textual scholarship, A. L. Grishunin's *Investigative Aspects of Textual Scholarship* (Moscow, 1998), has no references to studies in any other languages. A similar Polish work, R. Loth's *Main Terms and Problems of Textual Scholarship and Scholarly Editing* (Warsaw, 2006), lists four Western works in the bibliography but does not refer to them in the text.

Carolina. We believed at the time, therefore, that when Hans Walter Gabler came to visit, he was coming to the newly emerging center of American scholarly editing—an idea that tended to ignore the University of Virginia, Bowers's home institution, or Ohio State University, home of the pacesetting Nathaniel Hawthorne edition.

Gabler's initial impact on editorial thinking and practice in America was very much like the Russians' impact on the American space program when they shot a dog into orbit. As good as we thought we were, we knew that, in a way, we were behind. We had Hinman collators, but we did not have TUSTEP computer collation. We had a computer text comparison project called OCCULT, but no one who knew how to use it had a real project, and no one with a real project knew how to use it.[3]

Perhaps more important, Gabler's demonstration that a complex textual situation could be rendered between the covers of a book without losing any (or much) of its complexity seemed to set a standard for comprehensive scholarly obscurity. The race was on to design an apparatus that was capable of recording every nuance of composition and revision in the most compact possible way. The fact that critics at large resisted comprehensiveness by insisting on simple comprehensibility did not stop Fredson Bowers from writing headache-inducing textual introductions or from inventing a system for reporting alterations in manuscripts in which the explanation was much longer than a photo-facsimile of the manuscript would have been.[4] American scholarly editors were willing to give up clarity and ease of use in favor of exhaustive completeness, compacted for economical publication. Or so we thought.

In the scholarly editorial drive for completeness, American scholars were willing to compromise in ways that German historical critical editors were not. One need only mention the distinction W. W. Greg (an Englishman) had drawn between substantives and accidentals. Greg used the distinction to create a rule of thumb to guide editors in distinguishing, when one could

---

3. See George R. Petty Jr. and William M. Gibson, *Project OCCULT: The Ordered Computer Collation of Unprepared Literary Text* (New York: New York University Press, 1970); and http://www.tustep.uni-tuebingen.de/tustep_eng.html.

4. Fredson Bowers's "Transcription of Manuscripts: The Record of Variants," *Studies in Bibliography* 29 (1976): 212–64 is a nearly, if not totally, comprehensive guide to the kinds of variants and alterations found in modern manuscripts. The TEI has undertaken to elaborate as comprehensive a system for coding manuscript transcriptions, alterations, and variants.

not be sure, variants that were likely to have originated with an author from those likely to have originated with a compositor. His aim was to have a plan for what to do when the evidence was either insufficient or "indifferent." Fredson Bowers went a step further, putting the distinction to use in order to identify variants that were *not* worth reporting as part of the textual history. When Bowers advocated "laying all the editorial cards on the table face up," it turns out he did not mean *all* of the cards; accidentals in post-copy-text forms of the work were excluded as uninteresting, first, because they originated (most likely) with compositors and, second, because they did not affect meaning. Editors everywhere were relieved. That Bowers's use of the distinction between accidentals and substantives, though economically practical, was illegitimate in concept became evident when he invented the term *semisubstantive* for accidentals that *were* worth reporting.

Under the general leadership of Fredson Bowers, American editing was moving steadily in a direction that most European editors opposed: Bowers advocated eclectic principles in pursuit of authorial intentions employing the best intelligence that an editor could exercise in order to make bold editorial decisions. In a drive toward the most fully accomplished representation of the author's work, principles for choosing copy-texts were followed by principles of emending the copy-text. Editorial emendations were made legitimate by reporting them in full and by providing explanations of why the editors had acted. The goal of American editing, to produce new, improved, never-before properly extant texts that would be reliable as the basis for sound literary criticism, was to be achieved by a highly disciplined and fully explicit methodology.

Thus, when Hans Walter Gabler's edition of *Ulysses*[5] produced on the left-hand page a "continuous manuscript genetic text" and on the facing right-hand page the most advanced version of the manuscripts in one continuous and readable text, editors in America did not actually listen to what he said he was doing. Instead, we assimilated his work into our own understanding of copy-texts and eclectic editing so that, for most of us, the left-hand page in Gabler's edition of *Ulysses* (1984) represented a rendition of all the authorial manuscript evidence for the text, and the right-hand page

5. James Joyce, *Ulysses*, ed. Hans Walter Gabler, Wolfhard Steppe, and Claus Melchior; pref. Richard Ellmann (New York: Random House, 1986).

represented the author's final intentions as of 1922. When Gabler told us that was not right, we thought that he did not fully understand his own work.[6]

In general, that is how American editors assimilated European editorial thinking.

European editorial thinking also came to America in the form of a 1975 essay by Hans Zeller.[7] Zeller's work was theoretical rather than practical— that is, his work was presented in English as an argument rather than as a demonstration of his ideas in practice. I do not know of anyone in the United States who, having read Zeller's article, actively disagreed with the argument. Comparing texts to webs, Zeller argued that a change in one spot on the web affected the whole web and rendered all the relationships within the web different. For him, a variant was not an isolated step in a process leading to a finished and polished whole, but rather each variant represented a stage in the process of composition, revision, and publication—each stage constituted a potential wholeness and integrity of text that deserved and required attention. Zeller's work, though widely accepted as theoretically sound, did not immediately affect American editorial practice because it was dismissed as impractical. What in the world, we thought, could come of a work of art edited to show multiple versions of the work—especially when one variant in one point of punctuation could render the whole a new version?

The American tendency to see the purpose of scholarly editing as bringing a text to its greatest fulfillment of authorial intention caused American editors to resist a European tendency to see the purpose of scholarly editing as the work of presenting as clearly and fully as possible the record of the extant authorized historical forms of the work. Americans saw themselves as using the evidence to determine what had gone wrong and to amend the situation by emending the text; the Europeans saw their work as that of accumulating and displaying the panoply of extant evidence and explaining the relationships among documentary texts.

A consequent difference can be seen also in how American and European editors imagined readers using the scholarly editions. Americans imagined

<hr />

6. See Hans Walter Gabler's "Unsought Encounters," in *Devils and Angels: Textual Editing and Literary Theory*, ed. Philip Cohen (Charlottesville: University Press of Virginia, 1991), 153–66; and "Joyce's Text in Progress," *Texte: Revue de Critique et de Théorie Littéraire* 7 (1988): 227–47.

7. Hans Zeller, "A New Approach to the Critical Constitution of Literary Texts," *Studies in Bibliography* 28 (1975): 231–64.

critical readers who were grateful but skeptical and who would first use the newly established text to generate sound criticism and aesthetic judgments, but who would perhaps secondarily examine the textual introductions and tables of variants occasionally in order to validate the purity of the reading text. Europeans, on the other hand, imagined a scholarly reading public who would first examine the textual history and establish a sense of the historical versions of the work, and who secondarily would use that history to influence critical responses to various versions of the work presented. If aesthetic judgment ever entered the picture for the Europeans, it was to be reflected in criticism, not in the edition. Two possible exceptions justify the word *critical* in historical critical editing: the critical analysis required to design and construct a textual apparatus and the limited liberty afforded in correcting demonstrable error (*textfehler*).

These are just generalizations. Exceptions abounded on both sides of the Atlantic, but there is something to be learned from seeing the history of editing on the two continents in this way. For one thing, doing so makes it nearly impossible to point a finger in either direction across the water and say "Over there, they do not know what they are doing" or "Over there, they lack courage or are foolhardy and irresponsible." Instead, this view helped me to see the limitation of any comprehensive solution to textual problems. Each comprehensive solution is comprehensive only within the limits of its enabling theories of text. Historical critical principles of German scholarly editing are remarkable and admirable for the rigor, the organization, the nuance of the arguments, the respect for evidence, and the disregard for the economic consequences of scholarly methods and goals. These inspire awe and perhaps envy—except in a time of declining funding. The German focus on the materiality and historicity of documents, and on the rational analysis and disposition of textual records constitutes an important model for the ethical handling of evidence. The practical criticism of genetic textual studies requires, as a preliminary, the ordering of evidence for which historical critical editing is noteworthy. On that type of foundation, geneticists can focus their attention on the fluidity of texts, on textual relations, on process, and ultimately on critical interpretations of the textual record.

In the late 1980s and 1990s, in the pages of *TEXT*, the annual publication of the Society for Textual Scholarship, articles by German and French textual scholars began to appear, and the barriers to the urgently needed dialogue between Anglo-American editors and Continental editors began to fall. The collection of translated essays published as *Contemporary German Editorial*

Theory in 1996, edited by Hans Walter Gabler, George Bornstein, and Gillian Borland Pierce, also prompted Anglo-American editors to understand the Germanic qualities of Gabler's edition of *Ulysses* and the intellectual and practical appeal of historical critical principles.

In the late 1990s, H. T. M. (Dick) Van Vliet saw the need for transatlantic dialogue on editorial subjects and did something effective about it. He invited me, along with Paul Eggert and David Greetham, to conferences in the Netherlands and Germany. Van Vliet and his colleagues in Den Haag also attended the biannual STS conferences in New York. Dialogue and translation took place at these conferences, and, for me, very memorably with Bodo Plachta, Rüdiger Knutt-Koforth, Burghard Dedner, Dirk Van Hulle, Edward Vanhoutten, Geert Lernout, Christina Urchuegia, Annette Schutterle, Domenico Fiormonte, Luigi Giuliani, Francisco Rico, and others too numerous to mention.[8]

Did Anglo-American editors urgently need to hear from Continental editors, or did Continental editors urgently need to hear what the Anglo-Americans were doing? I think the exchange was fruitful both ways. Attempts to understand the historical development of editorial thinking in the two cultures suggest that their differences arose in part from the schools of thought and practice against which developing editorial practice in each region was rebelling, and in part from the nature of surviving materials that formed the models for editorial practice. One need only contrast the Shakespeare Archive with the Goethe Archive. The former has no manuscripts and a chaotic array of printed exemplars ranging from the spurious to the commercial, none of which were overseen by the author. The Goethe archive, by contrast, has a building in Weimar filled with manuscripts and multiple publications overseen by the author. Furthermore, Goethe's works were published by craftsmen famous for meticulous accuracy. Shakespeare's were produced by members of the Stationers Company, a guild with extensive rules about how to deal with drunken workmen.

---

8. Among the best fruits of the conversations orchestrated by Van Vliet are the dialogue between Peter Shillingsburg ("A Resistance to Contemporary German Editorial Theory and Practice," *editio* 12 [1998]: 138–50) and Bodo Plachta ("In Between the 'Royal Way' of Philology and 'Occult Science': Some Remarks About German Discussion on Text Constitution in the Last Ten Years," *Text* 12 [1999]: 31–47), and individual essays by Burghard Dedner ("Editing Fragments as Fragments," *Text* 16 [2004]: 97–111) and Paul Eggert ("Version—Agency—Intention: The Cross-Fertilising of German and Anglo-American Editorial Tradition," *Variants* 4 [2005]: 5–28).

Another factor that distinguishes the goals of editorial enterprises in different countries has been the funding mechanisms and the arguments that had to be made in order to persuade governments to support scholarly editing. Yet another factor was differences in prevailing notions of critical interpretation of literary texts and different notions of what constitutes the nature of a literary work.

My impulse in the late nineties, when I first read the essays in *Contemporary German Editorial Theory* and first encountered Bodo Plachta, was to resist the influence of an approach to editing that appeared to me to stop when the business of collecting, organizing, and representing the textual evidence had been completed. It seemed to one nurtured in Anglo-American goals for editing that a huge step in editorial practice was systematically avoided by the Germans—actually editing the work. The goal of American editing was to produce a reading text that best served the purposes for which the author had worked. The textual apparatus was supposed to support that reading text by recording the historical evidence and revealing the critical interventions needed to produce the reading text. By contrast, the goal of a German edition was to establish the record of historical variants in a well-ordered apparatus to which a text of one historical document was attached for convenience. To European editors, it seemed that Anglo-American editors, having collected and organized the editorial evidence, went on to do two objectionable things: first, they edited the text by imposing their own critical judgment on the evidence and pretending that their edited text was somehow *the* text, and, second, they created apparatuses of textual history that were nearly impossible to use for the purpose of restoring the historical and documentary order from which they had been constructed.

The center of textual authority on the eastern side of the Atlantic was the documentary evidence of the series of textual events that constituted the work historically; on the west side of the Atlantic, the center of textual authority was the artistic goals of authors in the pursuit of their highly specialized craft. On the east, the documents were history, marred or not, to be recorded; on the west, texts marred by the processes of publication required editing to repair hiccups in authorial aims. Where Germans saw the scholarly editor's goals to be collecting and organizing the evidence in order to enable systematic study of textual histories and investigation of the relationships among the various textual forms of a work, Anglo-Americans saw scholarly editorial goals to be the collection, organization, and presentation of textual evidence in order to identify and restore the artistic purposes that had been thwarted by the imperfections of commercial publishing. The audience for the great German editorial projects consisted of other students of textual history who needed a sound substitute for the primary materials, uncontaminated by new editorial intervention. The primary audience for Anglo-American scholarly editions was taken to be the critics and teachers of literature who wanted corrected texts that fulfilled the purposes of authors and their best supporting production assistants—editions in which the history of inept production and censorship was relegated to the historical textual apparatus. In the end, Americans had a perfected text and might do without the apparatus; Germans had a perfected apparatus and might do without the text.

It is not my place to adjudicate between these views. They are each better for the purposes for which they were created and the goals that appeared most important at the time as well as for the national setting in which they were devised. I suggest, however, that when an editorial goal has been chosen and understood in relation to the culture and history that makes that goal desirable, it is necessary to apply thought, rationality, and wisdom to the methods for achieving that goal. Academic ethics require that editors curb the rhetorical flourishes with which their goal and the methods for achieving it are explained and defended. It is usually not the case that the goal and methods chosen are the only rational or legitimate ones.

Defending ourselves from the incredulous exclamations of editors from a different culture, who are serving different notions of what is needed, has in the past provided us with joyful moments of outrage and righteous indignation. The current of thought and dialogue established by the European Society for Textual Studies (ESTS; http://www.textualscholarship.eu/) has eroded these islands of resistance and isolation. Anglo-American editors and their Continental cousins have learned a great deal from each other. We are more likely to ask of editors that they explain what their goals are, what their methods have been, and what can be done with the products of their labor. We are less likely to ask whether an edition is edited in the right way—which is to say, my way.

Genetic critics often declare that they are not editors, that they do not produce scholarly editions. To conduct their work, however, geneticists require either a scholarly edition or they must collect and record the history of textual variation for themselves. Genetic criticism constitutes a significant aspect of textual studies. Its objectives can be stated in several ways: the study of use of sources, of creative composition or genesis, of revision as an indicator of cognition, and of textual variation for interpretation of texts. Brilliant examples of genetic studies exist relative to works for which copyright restrictions have prevented the production of a scholarly edition. I do not know if genetic study, though most frequently associated with France, actually has a national character. American editors of the mid-twentieth century certainly thought that they were doing genetic study when they transcribed manuscripts, and meticulously recorded alterations in manuscripts, and then tried to sift through the variants produced during printing processes to see who was responsible for the changes and what effect the changes did or could have on the work. Americans did not, however, call it genetic study. It was frequently thought that the purpose of manuscript work was primarily to serve the needs of editors pursuing authorial intentions. This cannot be said of *critique génétique* in France, which serves the desire of critics to trace and understand genetic, creative processes.[9]

Anglo-American textual scholarship produces both edited texts and extensive textual apparatuses. Its only real difference from historical critical editing as practiced in Germany is that the basic archival and bibliographical work of collecting variant texts and displaying variation is not published as such but is followed by a next step, which, like genetic studies, is a highly analytical activity in pursuit of the significance of textual history. It seeks answers to the question "What did the author want the text to be?" It might have served Anglo-Americans better, perhaps, if, like historical critical editors, they had made a pause at the completion of research—when all the relevant texts had been collected and the record of their variation had been completed—in order to freeze the record of historical textual stages. As a separate effort based on analyses of the record, they could then have produced new texts that they could claim were closer to what the author wanted the text to be. These add-on efforts would be judged and criticized as interpretive arguments rather than as corrupted, misguided attempts to be historical records. Americans did not usually undertake these two stages as separate publication goals because funding focused on reading texts, not on records of historical variation or studies of creative processes. The surge in funding in America in the late 1950s and more significantly in the 1960s supported the claim that

---

9. See Jed Deppman, Daniel Ferrer, and Michael Groden, eds. *Genetic Criticism: Texts and Avant-Textes* (Philadelphia: University of Pennsylvania Press, 2004). See also the journal *Genesis: Manuscrits, Recherche, Invention*, devoted to *critique génétique* (Presses de l'université Paris-Sorbonne). An excellent example of the method applied to Argentine writer Jorge Louis Borges is Daniel Balderston's *How Borges Wrote* (Charlottesville: University of Virginia Press, forthcoming).

editors were restoring America's literary heritage to its best and pristine forms. Had American editors claimed to be establishing the historical record without adding new value, they would probably not have been funded. Whether or not resulting from transatlantic influences, the Georg Büchner edition, a major German multivolume project edited by Burghard Dedner, adds an eclectic text to the record of historical texts, constructing text from two sources because neither is without obvious problems.[10]

Because the practice of combining the collection and arrangement of historical textual data with the preparation and presentation of a newly edited text requires the exercise of individual judgment in interpreting the evidence, unevenness in the final results may be inevitable. That is what some German editors told me was objectionable about American editorial practice, regardless of how sensible an editorial approach to the work it might otherwise be. They were right about that. In my own experience, what I produced as a highly principled improvement in editing William Makepeace Thackeray resulted in what my German colleagues considered a contaminated text. In 1996, I published a scholarly edition, *The Newcomes*. That edition was reviewed only once, by a kind friend who nevertheless did not mention that in the explanation of editorial principles and practice I plotted out four legitimate approaches to the editing of the novel. Lamenting that I could edit in only one of these ways, I regretted that those persons who would have liked a different kind of edition would have to work a little harder to change my plan into theirs. Few, if any, other Anglo-American scholarly editions declared themselves as representing just one of several possible editorial solutions, though Paul Eggert's recent edition of Henry Lawson's *While the Billy Boils* does so.[11] Most editors present their results as if the materials, common sense, logic, and perhaps truth itself could be served only by the editorial policy they have chosen. The objection to my practice was that I had mixed the evidence from different documentary witnesses to produce an eclectic text, thus contaminating the orderly presentation of historical textual evidence. That is true. I was not trying to present the historical textual evidence in as

10. Georg Büchner, *Sämtliche Werke und Schriften: Historisch-kritische Ausgabe mit Quellendokumentation und Kommentar* (Marburger Ausgabe), ed. Burghard Dedner and Thomas Michael Mayer, 10 vols. (Darmstadt: Wissenschaftliche Buchgesellschaft, 2000–2013). The volume with the eclectic text is vol. 6, *Leonce und Lena*, ed. Burghard Dedner (Darmstadt: Wissenschaftliche Buchgesellschaft, 2003).

11. Henry Lawson, *"While the Billy Boils": The Original Newspaper Versions*, ed. Paul Eggert, explanatory notes by Elizabeth Webby (Sydney: Sydney University Press, 2013).

orderly a fashion as possible; I was trying to extract an intended text from the flawed materials surviving. It had not occurred to me that anyone would want an edition that was just a historical record. Nor, had I thought about it, would I have believed such a "documentary edition" would, by itself, have been worth creating. In editing *The Newcomes*, I failed, therefore, to add this fifth way to edit to the four methods that I did outline. Had I reprinted a historical text and attached an apparatus that laid out the history of textual development so that my edition could be used as a resource for the study of the history of the text of *The Newcomes*, I dare say I would have escaped criticism. From an Anglo-American point of view, that would have left the major work of analysis and scholarship undone. Lumped together in that orderly arrangement of documentary history was work contributed not only by the author but by workmen in the production process, some of whom were inept and did not serve the author well. Who would sort out the tangle of responsibility for each letter, word, and punctuation point in the text? I think that my edition of *The Newcomes* sorts out who was responsible for the text at every point. In order to do that, I had to subordinate the orderly presentation of documentary differences, which can be done best by treating each document as a whole, in favor of the orderly presentation of the author's own work, which requires an eclectic text. The two goals—documentary representation and agential integrity—are incompatible and, therefore, impossible to accomplish simultaneously in any single printed edition.

The more cross-cultural my experience became, both in geography and in time, the more I saw that different editorial goals are desirable under different cultural, economic, and intellectual conditions. Different goals must be pursued by different methods.

Acceptance of that proposition entails the necessity of applying precise, logical attention to the consequences of adopting one goal over other possible ones, and of suiting a methodology to that goal. Unfortunately, precise logical thought is not something that comes naturally to everyone who wants to produce an edition. Flexibility of purpose is not a license to stop thinking logically or precisely about textual evidence. The discipline of textual studies is universal; the conditions and desires with respect to editions are not universal. Perhaps this will be more clearly expressed through the experiences that have led me to that conclusion.

In 1984, I had the privilege of spending six months at the University of New South Wales branch located at the Royal Military College, Duntroon, the

Australian Army's academy of officer training. Professor Harry Heseltine, a noted authority and pioneer from the late 1950s in the then relatively new field of Australian studies, was beginning to feel the need for a series of editions to bring back into circulation a range of Australian works written and published during the period of colonization that ended in 1900. In the 1980s in Australia, I first heard the phrase "cultural cringe." It refers to the feelings of people who think they are living at the margins of some other more vivid world that is centered elsewhere. The condition of cultural cringe was most easily visible when a person born and raised in a colony would say, upon embarking for England, that he was "going home"—that is, he was going to a place he had never been before in his life, but a place that represented for him the center of his culture. Cultural cringe was also evident in the labeling of goods as "export quality," which implies that for domestic use, items of inferior quality would do. Australia, in the 1980s, was getting very vocal about its escape from cultural cringe, and one evidence of that escape was a flourishing interest in its own native literature, although the word *native* in the 1980s still meant literature written in English. Aboriginal studies flourished later.

The sense of urgency to do something effective meant that the new Colonial Texts Series should be done quickly and cheaply. There is an old saying about being able to have only two out of three desirables: You can have cheap and good, but then it will take a very long time. Or you can have quick and good, but it will cost a great deal. Or you can have cheap and quick, but then it will not be very good. The goal was to get some early Australian texts published at a reasonable price in a reasonable amount of time with a reasonable degree of editorial respectability. How could that be done? Professor Heseltine assigned me the job over five months to deliver five lectures to the English department on scholarly editing and on how to organize and produce this series of colonial texts. Those lectures became *Scholarly Editing in the Computer Age: Theory and Practice* (1984).[12] The section on practice was further defined as "practicalities" because I knew, in all scholarly editions designed for print, that practical decisions had to be made that compromised the ideal solutions dictated by principles.

Not fully reflected in my book are things I found out about the problems faced by editors in a young country that was turning new attention to its own

---

12. First published by the English department of the University of New South Wales, Duntroon, the book has since then been revised twice for publication by the University of Georgia Press (1986) and the University of Michigan Press (1996).

literary past. Since Australia's academic history had previously been focused on the so-called mother country, it meant that library collections had not been sufficiently focused on local book and magazine production. The country's bibliographical tools were not focused on local literatures, and its book production and editorial methodology was not focused on local works. A nation's bibliography has to be done before a selection of works to edit can be intelligently undertaken; bibliography tells us what forms particular works have taken.[13]

The bibliographical record revealed the range of forms colonial Australian writing had taken—often in obscure and deteriorating newspapers and short-lived journals. For Heseltine's project, the next questions were: How much textual work could be undertaken (i.e., afforded)? How much textual information would be included in the new editions (i.e., how much would the publisher tolerate)? Once collations and textual histories had been written, what text would be chosen for reproduction? Once a text was chosen, would it be faithfully reproduced or be emended? Other questions included: Where would the textual information be printed? How much explanatory annotation would be included? What kinds of introductions would be written?

Because in the 1980s typewriters were giving way to computers and photocopy equipment was giving way to digitization, the next questions were about how the research and editorial work would mesh with the preparation of production files for print publication. Once it was established how texts in the series would be edited, the next questions had to do with book design and production: What kind of covers (hard or paper) and paper would be used? What size book? How much would it cost to produce? How much could each copy be sold for? How many copies should the print run be?

My part in all that was relatively easy by comparison with what Professor Heseltine and his editorial team would have to do. All I had to do was think about how to make principled and reasonable compromises such that the end result would be reasonably good (not a full-dress scholarly edition but intellectually thoughtful and respectable), reasonably economical (not free and not out of the purchasing reach of students), and reasonably quick. I gave my lectures early in 1984; the first volume of the Colonial Texts Series appeared in 1989: Ada Cambridge's *A Woman's Friendship*, edited by Elizabeth Mor-

13. In the last thirty years, Australia has filled in many of the gaps in the record of its own print history (see particularly Aust-Lit online, http://www.austlit.edu.au/, which builds on John Alexander Ferguson's multivolume *Bibliography of Australia* [Sydney: Angus and Robertson, 1941–69]).

rison, followed in 1991 by N. Walter Swan's *Luke Mivers' Harvest*, edited by Harry Heseltine. I used Morrison's edition of *A Woman's Friendship* in a course I taught in Australia in 1989. It was the only decently edited Australian novel available at the time. I do not just mean that the text was prepared and presented in a way that inspired confidence. I mean that, as an American in a foreign land, I was grateful to use a book presented and supported in ways that made its text, its meaning, its significance, and its enjoyment more accessible through introductions and notes that placed text in historical context.

Heseltine's job of initiating the scholarly editing of Australian literature soon became easier when he hired Paul Eggert into his department. Eggert not only took over the direction and evolution of the Colonial Texts Series, but he also directed the establishment of the Academy Editions of Australian Literature, which produced a remarkable series of full-scale scholarly editions of major Australian works. There is no tinge of cringe associated with these volumes.

It is remarkable that those who desired to make cheap, quick, good editions took five years to produce the first result. The Colonial Texts Series sprang from the desire of a literary critic to teach literature not currently available in student editions. That is a common occurrence with inadequate results more often than not. We have seen poorly edited, hastily produced editions of works by women and by African Americans and by other colonial writers, all mass produced in response to emerging widespread interest in minority or ethnic literature. Although all works are worthy of careful, if practical, editorial treatment, how often is it that our students have to read from the irresponsible results of cheap paperbacks, or Project Gutenberg texts, or Google Books texts that are poorly transcribed, poorly selected, and unlabeled, poorly labeled, or even mislabeled? As a community of textual scholars, we have high ideals for scholarly editing, but we also have a responsibility in the practical world of student editions. Happily, the Colonial Texts Series came to fruition in a measured way that produced sound editions.

I wrote *Scholarly Editing in the Computer Age* in Australia during a time of personal rebellion against what had increasingly come to look like rigid dogmas for producing eclectic editions reflecting an author's final intentions. I did not object to eclectic editing; I objected to burying the record of authorial revision in tables designed to foreground the editor's work and provide undifferentiated variants in a history of both authorial and compositorial interventions. Five years later, I spent a year in Australia, frequently arguing with Paul Eggert about the nature of texts, of works, of documents, and of signs, and agreeing that eclectic editorial policies had not been perfected. Anglo-American editors everywhere were also rebelling in their own ways against the so-called Greg-Bowers-Tanselle school of editing. Herschel Parker's objections were, perhaps, the most colorful of these rebellions; the most successful was waged by Jerome McGann; my own rebellion followed different lines. Eggert, with whom I agree more often than with anyone else, rebelled in his own way.

When I reviewed for *Text* 12, the Academy Editions produced under Eggert's direction, I discovered that no two of the volumes were edited according to the same set of editorial principles. The principles followed did not adhere strictly to standards set by the so-called Greg-Bowers-Tanselle school, nor the McGann school, nor the British versions of these schools, nor the German historical critical school, nor the French *critique génétique*. Instead, each volume of the Academy Editions narrated the textual history in an orderly fashion, identified those aspects of the history that were ambiguous, fixed its eyes on the kind of text it wished to produce, and produced it. There is no claim that these editions are correct nor that their thoughtful and clearly elaborated methodologies were inevitable. They are solid works of editorial scholarship that leave the user with a clear sense of developing versions. They are edited by scholars who acknowledged the inevitable critical implications of their editorial choices. They also leave one with a clear sense of what the edition does not, nor ever tried to, accomplish. Fredson Bowers could have said "That isn't the way I would have done it, but at least they had the boldness to edit the work." The volumes appear to me to fulfill the goals for which they were designed. They represent the application of thought to textual criticism.

John Gouws invited me in 2003 to give a two-day workshop on scholarly editing at Rhodes University in Grahamstown, South Africa. At the time, I was working on the idea of script acts, now the subject of chapter 3 of *From Gutenberg to Google*. The idea begins with the proposition that every form of communication takes certain things for granted because they go without saying. Consequently, these things do not get said or written, even though for successful communication they are essential. This nontext aspect of communication can be assumed by both sides of a communication if the frame of reference is shared. Some communication failures are easy to observe in ordinary speech because rapid give-and-take quickly reveals mistakes. Other miscommunications can go undetected if the frame of reference assumed by a speaker is misidentified by a listener but makes sense of some sort. Both speaker and listener are satisfied with the communication, even though each has a different understanding of what was communicated. In written texts, writer and reader are not present together. There is no rapid give-and-take— no give-and-take at all. When a reader has questions about what exactly went without saying in the text, there is no way to ask the author for clarification. Any dialogue that ensues is in the mind of the reader.

That being the case, authors sometimes try to say all that is required, leaving little to be assumed. No author can, however, completely succeed. The tricky thing about the things that go without saying is that they do so because they are common and unnoticed. The passage of time and movement from one region to another causes the erosion of these crucial, commonly known, unnoticed nontexts that had once been taken for granted. New assumptions take their place and texts take on new, perfectly reasonable meanings, different from those that operated for the author and original audience. This condition has been frequently celebrated by literary criticism as the richness of textual meaning.

A significant part of South African literature is in English—reflecting a particular and, for non-South Africans, foreign culture. Further, South Africa is a country with twelve official languages, offering a perspective on editing that is not encountered in countries with one official language. If the passage of time can change what goes without saying within a country and culture, it is an even greater difficulty when that literature travels to other countries and cultures. These difficulties were uppermost on our minds as we contemplated the idea of developing scholarly editing in South Africa. We quickly focused on what we knew—English. As in Australia, the shift of editorial attention from the literature of the so-called mother country to that of the emerging nation entailed a shift to writers previously neglected though they wrote in English. Editors wished also to address neglected native writers— those for whom editors limited to English could do nothing.

Again, the first focus of attention was bibliography. Before editorial work can start, one needs to know what had been written, where it had been published, where, if at all, it had been republished. It is not an easy task for a country turning serious scholarly attention on itself in a climate of new openness to discover which of the many neglected texts from its past are most worthy of new scholarly attention. Which among these works should be fully edited on a par with scholarly editions in other countries? Which works should be edited to a reasonable level of respectability, at a reasonable cost, in a reasonably short amount of time? These are difficult questions. It is notable that scholarly attention being paid in South Africa to its literary past has focused first on book history and bibliography rather than on scholarly editing.

Next, I turn to India, where in 2009 I spent ten days at Visva Bharati University in Santiniketan, Bengal, meeting with twelve scholars interested in organizing an eighty-two-volume scholarly edition of the works of India's Nobel Prize laureate Rabindranath Tagore (1861–1941). Tagore wrote in both Bengali and English. He wrote poetry, short stories, novels, textbooks, philosophy, plays, and histories. Much, but not all, of his writing was published from printing presses and a publishing house that he himself had founded and over which he had control. He was an active reviser and translator of his own works. To complicate matters, he also put his name to translations of his work that were actually done by others.

Although I know not one word of Bengali, Sukanta Chaudhuri persuaded Swapan Mujamdar, the director of the Tagore museum and library at Visva Bharati, that I could be useful in their organization of a major edition of a Bengali writer.

We started with questions. Why this project? Why at this time? The year 2011 would be the one hundred fiftieth year of Tagore's birth. What should the new edition accomplish? Could they create a comprehensive scholarly edition on a tight schedule, delicately reshaping the author's reputation and issued cheaply for the common reader—and still be a scholarly edition? There are more literate Bengali people than there are people who know how to read or speak Dutch anywhere. Yet, Dutch literature is far better served by scholarly editors than Bengali literature. If the Tagore edition fulfilled the prospectus that we drew up for it, it would be the first major scholarly edition of an Indian writer ever undertaken. It would stand in the history of textual scholarship for India in much the same position that Goethe stands for Germany and Shakespeare stands for England.

The enormous cost of the project dictated that the edition be shaped by a number of conflicting forces. The first was academic and intellectual, representing textual scholarship. Textual scholars were determined to identify all the significant forms of each work, to collate and record the relationships among the surviving texts, and to present each work in the context of its composition, revision, and production history. A second important force was nationalistic, representing a desire to create a monument to the memory and achievements of Rabindranath Tagore, Nobel laureate of Bengal and India. The edition was to make a timely appearance at the sesquicentennial celebrations in a form that does the writer honor. Furthermore, the edition was to be priced within the financial grasp not only of libraries but of people who wish to read and venerate the man by showing his works on their bookshelves at home. What would the editorial principles be that could fulfill each of these desired goals and serve as a model for scholarly editing?

Four days of discussion produced a plan. The basic organization of the Tagore edition would be chronological by date of publication, each work edited to reflect its development at the point of first publication, each accompanied by a textual history. Heavily revised works would be published again in the chronological place of revised republication. With regard to each work, each volume editor would answer the questions "How does your proposed method make sense in view of the surviving evidence?" and "What alternatives to your chosen method were considered?" As always, practicalities arose: to edit eighty-two volumes, how many technical assistants, how many editorial and clerical assistants, how many volume editor scholars, how many years, how many volumes per year? How many millions of rupees? Would this project ever be finished if ever begun? These questions remain for the new print edition. An accompanying electronic archive of the raw materials for the edition—representations in image and transcription of all the works in all the extant authoritative forms—was planned to make the project complete. As it turned out, *Bichitra: Online Tagore Variorum* was begun and completed first.[14]

In Japan, a good deal of attention has been paid by scholars to the textual and editorial history of English and German literature. There are also substantial projects for the recovery and re-presentation of ancient Chinese and classical Japanese texts, both of which show the influence of European editorial principles. There seems to have been little carryover, however, of American and European textual methodology to the editing of modern Japanese literature. I was invited to a two-day conference in Tokyo and Saitama in 2010 organized by Christian Wittern and Kiyoko Myojo. I understood this to be the first international conference in Japan devoted to textual studies. If there were a tradition of scholarly editing in Japan, focused on modern Japanese literature, it was too small to be noticed. Wittern works on ancient Buddhist texts in Chinese, and Myojo works on Franz Kafka in German and

---

14. See http://bichitra.jdvu.ac.in/index.php (at the School for Cultural Texts and Records, Jadavpur University). See also Sukanta Chaudhuri, ed., *Bichitra: The Making of the Online Tagore Variorum* (Cham, Switzerland: Springer, 2015).

is also the translator into Japanese of several works on textual studies, including my own *From Gutenberg to Google*. Already uppermost in my mind at the time—aside from my own contribution (a presentation of the HRIT project, i.e., Humanities Research Infrastructure and Tools)—was the question about the cultural influences on textual studies. It is, probably, inappropriate for a person who does not speak or read Japanese to take up the subject of what cultural influences are or should be at work on what is or will become regarded as the Japanese approach to scholarly editing. Following the conference, I had two days of peripatetic seminars on editing with Wittern, Myojo, and John Gouws, which in some ways was more revealing about editing in Japan than the conference itself. Whatever develops as a Japanese textual school, it will have to address the questions common to all scholarly editing, regardless of culture or language:

1. What are the material forms bearing texts that represent the work to be edited?
2. What are the relationships among these forms of the work?
3. What were the conditions under which these forms came into being?
4. What evidence is there of individual intervention in the production of each text?
5. How should the basic evidence, once collected and analyzed, be stored?
6. How should the basic evidence be made accessible?
7. For print editions, who is the audience? What compromises or design features of the edition will be dictated by the editor's understanding of that audience?
8. How much will the edition cost to produce? Where will the money come from?

In 2015, I returned to Tokyo for another conference on editing Japanese literature. The effect was to show the truth of my premise, that the discipline and intellect of textual studies is universal but the methods and goals of editing are not. It is inevitable that the customs of a country will have a bearing on how these questions are answered. The experiences of scholarly editors everywhere show, furthermore, that the individual demands of particular authors or particular forms of a work will have a bearing. The particular values and goals of the individual editor or editorial team will influence the answers. Funding agencies and publishers will also have a say. The result from project to project and country to country will be a range of answers that amount to disagreements. Disagreement does not mean that some answers are wrong, or that one method is right. Do not mistake me; there are wrong answers, inappropriate answers, and answers that do not serve the purposes of those proposing them. Inept editors, unfortunately, like the poor, are with us always. The crucial questions are, however: Are the answers appropriate for the goals and conditions of the edition? Does the edition place itself in the global range of potential goals, such that its raison d'être and processes are clearly articulated and understood? If, or when, the work is done, will it have been done accurately and clearly? No edition is the final word; every good edition brings something important to the attention of readers—something not visible in other good editions.

Work and Text in Nonliterary Text-Based Disciplines

In *Scholarly Editing in the Computer Age* and *Resisting Texts*, I examined concepts of *work* and *text* in discussions among scholarly editors. Their ideas ranged from the idealist concepts of final authorial intentions to a variety of materialist concepts that emphasize historical accuracy, strict adherence to documents, attention to sociopolitical and industrial relationships, or Marxist ideology.[1] Having surveyed the question within my own discipline, I thought I might learn something from seeing how scholars handle these concepts in other fields in which texts and their uses are also central concerns.

Other text-based disciplines investigate sacred texts, historical records, policy statements, or legal documents.[2] Concerns and questions about professional archival preservation, conservation, and editorial and interpretive conventions have developed separately in each discipline. Close connections already exist between literature and religion. Other textual principles and practices are known in historiography. Cognitive studies and linguistics provide complementary investigations into how language works and how the brain or consciousness processes language. Politics and the law seem to man-

Previously presented to the Society for Textual Scholarship, New York, 1999; revised for presentation at the Humanities Research Center, Australia, 2002; revised for presentation at the University of Washington, March 2003; and revised for presentation at Rhodes University, Grahamstown, South Africa, May 2003.

1. Internal divisions among scholarly editors are explored in my "On Being Textually Aware," *Studies in American Naturalism* 1 (Summer and Winter 2006): 170–95; and in the introduction to *Anglo-American Scholarly Editing, 1980–2005*, co-edited with Paul Eggert and Kevin Caliendo, published as a special issue of *Ecdotica*, an Italian and Spanish journal of textual studies (2010; dated 2009).

2. The list is not exhaustive, for music, dance, medicine, mathematics, archeology, and other fields of knowledge also examine writings from the past as primary objects of study. I chose only those with which I was most familiar—even though still at an amateur's level.

age textuality on the fly, with disputes adjudicated by convention and the exercise of empowered judgment and arbitration rather than by textual studies and the disciplines of preservation and transmission of textual integrity.

Some background will put these concerns into a context. There was a time when literary scholars conceived of works of literary art to be solid and stable entities, such that *Moby-Dick* or *Hamlet* were works of art about which we could be or should be confident that we shared access by means of the copies we held in our hands. A prime purpose of scholarly editing was to ensure that we all had the same text—presumably the *right* text. Many still believe that the business of editing is to find and weed out errors from what is otherwise a stable, durable whole. There was once a widespread assumption that a text could be edited "definitively." A single text was expected to represent the best or final work of an author, who was the ultimate authority over the text. Among editors, it is seldom now expected that a single text can serve all people for all purposes.

Two important developments in concepts about literary works and the function of texts help to explain this change in editorial expectations. First, the roles of *production* and *consumption* of literature have assumed equal prominence with the role of *authoring*. What texts became as a result of production is just as important as how texts could be made to better fulfill authorial intentions. Textual or verbal works as cultural documents tell a tale of human behavior and social being; texts as works of art are monuments to artistic genius. The difference has significant editorial consequences. As cultural history displaced new criticism at the center of the college curriculum, the text as index of culture began to overshadow the text as work of art in editorial circles. Interest in the history of text reception is not well served by eclectic editions. Eclectic editions were designed for a different purpose— to restore authorial purpose, not to record text production and reception.

The second relevant change is probably a result of the first. It consists of the acknowledgment that works are unstable—not all variant forms are errors. A single work can take multiple forms that result not only from authorial revisions and production interventions but also from readerly appropriations. These changes in critical and editorial views of literary documents highlighted the narrowness of editing to produce definitive editions of authorial final intentions. There persists, however, a tendency among critics and general readers to act as if all texts of a work are identical, or as if their differences are insignificant. To many readers, the text in hand *is* the work. That myth is dispelled by looking at the relations between the terms *work, text,* and *document*. Even some editors cling to the notion that the author's intentions are the only worthwhile object of editorial work, while some others believe that an interest in production and reception completely supplants interests in authorial achievements. Tunnel vision is what it is, regardless of the tunnel of choice.

These concepts are old and familiar enough. That they are vexed might not, however, be generally acknowledged. The relations between *text* and *work* or between *text* and *document* are not simple, nor do they seem to hold still long enough to give us steady pleasure or unshaken confidence. These words refer to concepts that stand in the same kind of relationships that exist between thought and action, between concept and proof, between inspiration and accomplishment, and between intention and fulfillment. Between such terms, there is slippery ground. If a "work" can exist in multiple texts that vary among themselves, then a "work" is not the same as any particular text of it, nor can it be coeval with any particular document. To fully represent a "work" in the text and apparatus of a new edition is, therefore, complicated, if not impossible. If one views the material documents as evidence of cultural history, what, then, becomes of the text that the author wished for but failed to produce because others altered it, either intentionally or accidentally?

Just as there can be a slip between the cup and the lip in the process of creating documentary texts, there can also be slips in the readerly uptake of texts. We interpret what we see in the document. We may come away from the document with the sense that we have encountered and read a text about which we now know something. That something in the first instance is only the meaning of our perception. It might or might not also be the meaning that the author had in mind for the text. Whatever that something is, it has an abstract, insubstantial, nonconcrete existence somewhere in the reader's consciousness. When we try to pin down exactly what has happened, we find ourselves in difficulties. Reading is an interpretive process, converting the material object by means of symbols into the reader's ordering consciousness. Reading is not an unmediated assimilation of what we see in the document. Our understanding of text is what we make of our reading over time. Presumably, the author had a meaning; the publisher may have had the same or a different meaning in production. Readers develop their own meanings without a sure way to determine if their newly constructed meanings are what the author meant. It is patent nonsense to speak of the meaning of the text as if inanimate paper and ink could have meaning or understanding. A text means either what was meant by the author, the production staff, or the reader. Each person's engagement with a documentary text has a conceptual and temporal existence that is difficult to pin down. Unlike spoken conversation, written texts do not offer give-and-take between writer and reader to sort out misunderstandings.

Textual studies and editing is not primarily about meaning (though it is unavoidable); it is primarily about the symbols preserved in material forms. It is *textual* instability, not *meaning* instability, that is the focus of editorial concern. The fact that meaning instability is behind much of the textual instability does not alter this distinction. If what David Greetham wrote ("Any text will do, but not all texts will do the same thing.") applies, the next step is to ask why and how the texts are different. That is not easy, but it can be fascinating.

This state of affairs is not a problem if we are content to remain in uncertainties or if we are content to remain only in the certainties that our own consciousness provides. We might, in fact, revel in the fact that reading is an experience to be shared in debates and arguments and in friendly or unfriendly disputes. When one compares how texts work in other disciplines and in "real life," as opposed to how they work in the hermetic atmosphere of academic discussions of novels and poems, two very important things stand out: first, stable texts and stable meanings are often very important to people who use texts in ordinary life, and, second, texts work differently in disciplines other than English departments.

Examining situations in which a reader's license to create meaning is not tolerated will help us to think again about the importance of understanding script acts.[3] Several religions take as their foundation a sacred script thought to be the word of God—sometimes claimed to be inerrant. Devotees wish to know first that the words inscribed on the page are, in fact, the words of God, and they want to know that their interpretation of those words is the right interpretation. Uncertainties about text and document and work, when it comes to sacred texts, is intolerable to devotees. They need to know for certain. A long tradition of biblical textual criticism and scholarly translation attests to the fact that many people worry about these things and hope for resolutions. Textual histories often thwart that hope. Ancient works often lack urtexts. The surviving facts leave gaps, preventing sure knowledge. Priesthoods and

---

3. A full elaboration of "script acts" (as opposed to speech acts) is in my *From Gutenberg to Google: Electronic Representations of Literary Texts* (Cambridge: Cambridge University Press, 2006), particularly chapter 3.

dogmas tend to assert a stable textual foundation and codified hermeneutics to mitigate or hide the uncertainties.

There are a variety of scholarly traditions, not only within the biblical textual experience of the Judeo-Christian community but in the history of scholarship on sacred texts of other religions as well. Both priests and scholars of sacred texts are well acquainted with conflicts between the forces that impel participants toward the Truth with a capital *T* of the teachings and dogmas of the religion and the forces that impel them toward the truth with a lowercase *t* of the material evidence of texts, textual transmission, and explanations for textual variation. Ideally, there is no conflict because textual scholarship on sacred texts should perfect the textual rendition of the original work: the *Truth* and the *truth* should be the same. Tension arises when lowercase *truth* undermines preconceived or established capital *Truth*. In literary study, the ideal of pursuing authorial intentions may have been built on analogy with textual scholarship on sacred texts. The divine originator of all things and ultimate authority is like the human author, the originator of the work of art. Unlike devotees, modern textual scholars, whether biblical or literary, are usually not among those for whom absolute certainty about texts and meaning is fundamental to their beliefs. The evidence for instability of texts tends to undermine such hopes. In their place is the satisfaction of revealing lowercase, verifiable truths.

The conflicts between cautious, careful respect for the evidence, on one side, and passionate, enthusiastic beliefs in a larger truth and beauty, on the other, are, nevertheless, far from resolution. This tension energizes conflicts in other fields as well. In contemplating them, however, one might consider the possibility that the two sides in this tug-of-war serve a common cause: caution helps to correct the faults of enthusiasm and devotion and passion help to correct the sterility of details and pedantry.

Business contracts also require stable meanings. Written agreements between consumers and providers of goods or services, or contracts by which houses are built, altered, and purchased, or by which landlords exercise the right to evict, and by which all kinds of business is conducted—all signed contracts have standing as scripts with power. When there is a dispute about a contract, the concepts of work and text have bearing. The questions are: Is this an authentic copy of the contract? Are these the words to which the contracting parties affixed their names? Have the words been altered? What is the meaning of the contract? At this point, no one is happy to allow each reader a personal rendering of meaning. Each reader *does* have a personal interpretation, but in the end only one interpretation is allowed. Does it matter what the contract meant when it was signed? Can that meaning change through time? A system of laws, courts, judges, and, perhaps most important, lawyers has been developed to curtail the spread of individual renderings of contracts. Perhaps the hope is vain, but considerable effort goes into making contract language determinate and arbitrary. The arbitration system provides tacit acknowledgment that texts do not have or convey stable meanings. Arbiters establish stability.

Closely related to contracts are treaties and the laws of the land. Is the law as agreed in parliament or congress adequately and fully represented in the text that records the agreement? The "intention of the law makers" might or might not be "adequately or fully" represented in the text of the law. It is what the law says, the letter of the law, that matters. If that were so, then it is what the *law means* and not what the *legislature meant* that matters. But is that so? Suppose the printer preparing the text of the law for publication made an inadvertent, or a malicious, or a well-intentioned but misguided alteration in the text? Does the printer have the right to establish what the letter of the law says? Who proofreads? At what level of accuracy? Are reprinted laws identical to originally printed ones? If one thinks that it is the sacrosanct letter of the law that matters, why is it that judges and their attending clerks are interested in the accumulated parliamentary debates and rejected readings of the laws in their attempts to determine what the law means? In the practical situation of a dispute at law, it is the judge who judges what the law means. Presumably, judges, like other readers, can deal with obvious typos in the law, but what do they do when the text of the law is indecipherable or when the composition error or mischief makes plausible sense?[4]

Secure textual confidence is challenged by the slippery, recalcitrant relations among the *document* as a physical object, the *text* as a semantic item in a symbolic system, and the *work* as a concept or understanding witnessed by the documents and texts. Furthermore, tension persists between rational analyses of evidence and enthusiastic support for ideals.

4. An Internet search for "typos in laws" generates many journalistic accounts with sentences such as "The controversial comma sent lawyers and telecommunications regulators scrambling for their English textbooks in a bitter 18-month dispute that serves as an expensive reminder of the importance of punctuation." Grant Robertson, "Comma Quirk Irks Rogers," *Globe and Mail*, August 6, 2006, http://www.theglobeandmail.com/report-on-business/comma-quirk-irks-rogers/article1101686/

In the Law, the passionate ideals go by the names of Justice, Truth, and Equity (all capitalized). Careful adherence to details goes by the names of codes, rules, precedents, and forms (in lowercase). Students of the texts of law also attend to matters familiar in textual criticism. Studies of double sayings in law such as "heirs and assignees," "goods and chattels," "executors and administrators," "belonging to or in possession of the owner," "claim, privilege, lien, or encumbrance," "lost or impaired by any neglect, omission, or error" "grant, bargain, sell, and convey," or " give, grant, bargain, sell, remise, release, alien, convey, and confirm" are said to have their origin explained at least in part by the Saxon and Norman bilingual days, when such dual or multiple statements ensured that most persons affected, regardless of their native language, would have some notion of what the law was about. Redundant legalese is said by others to have originated in attempts to prevent misunderstanding by the strategy of saying the same thing in several ways, the interpretation of each of which must be compatible with the interpretations of the others—thus achieving precision through a form of verbal triangulation. Conversely, there are others, naysayers, who claim legalese is designed to prevent any interpretation from being very clear or determinate in order that lawyers might make the text mean whatever they want. In this regard, there is, perhaps, little difference between lawyers and literary critics, except that in law, there is a judge to act as arbiter. The rhetoric of interrogations, examinations, cross-examinations, and negotiations have prompted a concern in the law profession for the practical effects of textual matters on the outcome of legal disputes. Studies show, for example, that since the shift of divorce proceedings from the adversarial courtroom to the friendlier atmosphere of negotiated settlements, the economic fate of women and children has, surprisingly, suffered. Some observers would say that such was not the "intent of the law." This phrase raises another concept of interest to textual scholars: the idea that *intentions* could be asserted somehow by a conceptual entity rather than by a person or persons. The *law*, in some abstract, disembodied, or ideal sense, manages to have an intention of its own. It seems easier to conceive of God as having had an intention in a sacred text than it is to conceive of the Law as having an intention in a statute. Perhaps the concepts are not that far apart.

That the texts of laws are themselves incapable of ensuring Justice was illustrated in *The Star Chamber*, a movie in which a young judge played by Michael Douglas has just had his idealism shaken by the release of two hooligans accused of murder. The young judge had played the law straight and disallowed damning but illegally obtained evidence. He stands before a bookshelf full of beautifully bound law books, pulls one down, and reminisces to his wife about his first love for the law. The *law* was embodied (so to speak) in shelves full of beautiful books with red-and-black bindings and gold-lettered spines arranged in substantial, organized space. Metaphorically, a wall of books stands against crime and evil. The judge seemed not to know how he had been betrayed. Hooligans released on technicalities strike again. "The letter of the law," it turns out, does not by itself manage to save justice or persons. Rather, it had ground up and discarded the innocent without regard to the truth. It seems closer to the truth that the law is embodied not by books and texts but by the lawyers, judges, and juries who are the arbiters of the law. That is to say, the law is what readers, vested with authority to have an opinion, say it is. This idea is, however, flatly denied by a remark made by Mr. Justice Brewer in 1905 in a United States Supreme Court opinion regarding *South Carolina v. United States* (199 n.s. 437, 448, 50L. Ed. 261, 264): "The Constitution is a written instrument. As such its meaning does not alter. That which it meant when adopted, it means now." With all due respect to Justice Brewer, the "it" used twice in his sentence refers to "text," which, more's the pity, does not have a fixed meaning. The meaning of "it" is determined by authors, compositors, publishers, and readers. Judges are readers who in their official roles have special powers to determine meaning.

A remarkable thing about the law is its element of human frailty. It is never enough for a litigant to point out what a law says. It is incumbent on him or her to demonstrate to the satisfaction of a jury or judges that what the law says means a certain thing in relation to the issue at hand. Interpretation is everything. When persons who disagree on legal matters cannot reach a satisfactory accommodation among themselves, they turn to the courts, which have an elaborate system of "arbitration" by which the dispute is turned and probed and examined. In the end, a jury or judge determines a conclusion, and that is the end of it. The conclusion is called "a finding," as if it preexisted and the arbitration system hunted it down. Appeals to higher courts for new or different findings tend to discredit that notion. The system determines a conclusion that its players hope will not be discredited by anyone with the power to "vacate the finding."

It is not just interpretation of the law that is in the hands of fallible humans. The documentation itself is a matter of arbitrary definition. I was amazed to discover in a legal transaction of my own that I was asked to sign a document of which there were two copies, each bearing the statement

"Each of these two copies are the original." The grammar alone gave me pause. Reflection simply deepened the mystical dimensions of the concept. In contracts, declarations of independence, and treaties, only the original counts before the law. One can scarcely introduce a carbon copied or photocopied contract as evidence in a contractual dispute. Which was the "real original" of the documents I signed? Each of the two copies was produced from a computer that could spit out an endless number of identical copies. If "original" has something to do with "origins," then perhaps the computer contained the original and could only ever produce "copies." Despite Tron, computers are "dumb machines." They do the bidding of the originators who use them. Was the computer operated by a copyist or by the author? Am I confusing author and originator with the original? Probably. Let's back up and have another go. The two copies perhaps "are the original" by virtue of my signature on each and the signature of the person with whom I was contracting the agreement. By signing the documents, we authenticated each of them as the original (i.e., we declared them to be the original by virtue of our authority to do so). This is an extension of the concept of "certified copy." Original in this context must mean something like authentic or authorized. Is it not interesting in this case that "authorization" is accomplished by signing a document that was actually "authored" by someone else? So, we see, what constitutes the texts for the purposes of law is arbitrary, a thing determined by convention, by definition, or by arbiter, just as are the conclusions or findings or verdicts of juries and judges. Truth and Justice depend on the detail—but *only* by way of critical interpretation and judgment. Perhaps that is why the concept of intention is so important in law: what is the "intent of the law" or even "the full intent of the law," or "what did the founding fathers intend" or what did the "framers of the Constitution have in mind"? The conflicts between the cautious literalists and the passionate idealists rage on.

Scholars of the law have been known to turn to the draft versions of the law during its composition, and to the debates and comments of the legislators formulating the law, to help determine the intention of the framers—what they meant to mean by the finished law. When a law is determined to be flawed, it is emended by an elaborate process conducted only by those with the legal authority to do so—a legislative body empowered to write new law or a judicial body empowered to render one interpretation of the law the operative one—or to declare a law unconstitutional. Scholarly literary editing does not have comparable legislative and judicial bodies.

The textual conditions of literature provide difficulties similar to those of applying law to specific cases. Even in literature a text alone, or even an array of variant texts, is not enough for students and readers. Individuals can, of course, go their own way, but "schools of thought" or "interpretive communities" develop by adding traditions of commentary to the texts. The functional value of documentary texts depends on more than the physical and symbolic existence of documents. Each text must be lifted or extracted from the page by acts of interpretation. Functionally, we are interested in the interpretive consequences of texts and their potential for conceptual beauty or truth. Textual and literary critics have found what judges and lawyers have found: that the "finished" text can be better understood in the light of its compositional history than it can as a single text taken alone. Collectors and historians might, nevertheless, be interested in a document or array of documents for the mere physical existence and for the material or cultural artifactual value.

The field of psychology also has a broad interest in textuality. Of potential interest to us are studies of intention and self-knowledge. Some philosophers of cognitive science have abandoned intentionality altogether. Others, as Alison Gopnik suggests, still hold to the commonsense notion that "intentionality involves a special relation between psychological states and the world."[5] They endorse the view that "intentionality is a theory that explains experience and behavior" (2–3). In explaining the sources and functions of intentionality, some researchers suggest that it is a "stance that we adopt toward ourselves and others," or that it is a matter of "convention or language." Yet others consider intentionality an essential element that "is a consequence of certain distinctive features of the human brain" (3). In psychology, a range of opinions on intentionality is still operative. In the humanities, and in literary criticism particularly, theorists spin arguments—more or less as I am doing here. In the social sciences, by contrast, empirical experiments are conducted to test the viability of theories. For psychologists, it is not just a battle of theorists seeing who can provide the most coherent or the safest or the most exciting idea. Questions about how children perceive or learn to perceive (the difference was not unknown to Wordsworth) and whether one's knowledge of one's own motives and intentions is qualitatively different from one's knowledge of the motives or intentions of others are

5. Alison Gopnik, "How We Know Our Minds: The Illusion of First-Person Knowledge of Intentionality," *Behavioral and Brain Sciences* 16, no. 1 (1993): 2.

subjects of empirical studies that occasionally suggest counterintuitive answers unsupportive of commonsense notions. Much of the work on intention is about the ability of individuals to recall their intentions for past actions rather than about the functionality of intention before action. These studies suggest, furthermore, that certain positions, such as the abandonment of the concept of intention, tend to push one by implication toward acceptance of other beliefs, such as behavioral determinism.

Psychologists are also interested in rhetorical studies, exploring the way in which things are said. The words used to convey news or decisions can have psychological effects. Cognitive science, which draws from philosophy, linguistics, computer science, neurology, and psychology, includes attention to how texts are processed and generated (spoken and written), and how they are received and processed in the brain (heard, interpreted, and remembered). The conflict I found in religion and law (between large ideal, passionately held beliefs and careful, cautious adherence to the evidence) manifests itself also in psychology as a passion for Understanding, on the one hand, and the cautious concern with the details of physical stimuli, synapses, location of certain processes in the brain, and measurable chemical and electrical activities that trigger or are triggered by communicative acts, on the other. Cognitive scientists, like poets, are interested in why two ways of saying the same thing can have different effects. The conclusions drawn in cognition studies could influence how editors value variants in texts. More attention might be paid to intonation or cadence, which in writing are often only roughly indicated by punctuation. When written works are performed orally, the subtlety of such variations become more palpable. For psychologists, such differences are not merely an array of historical facts. They have consequences in the responses triggered by the particular forms of the text.

Other variants in texts indicate a change of mind about what to say, not just how to say it. Most scholarly editors have already agreed with the notion, perhaps suggested more by linguists than by cognitive scientists, that one's understanding of a text can be modified or even determined by knowledge of a specific alternative that was rejected or used in a different rendition of the text. Psychologists are constantly probing the effects of encountering texts in different contexts or in different associations. Studies of advertisements analyze the effects on the public after publication. They also examine the effects of variant forms of the ads before publication, looking for effects of contexts on viewers' uptake. Does the ad mean the same on a billboard, on TV, or on the barriers around a soccer field? Furthermore, psychologists study the ways in which responses to identical textual stimuli are generated in persons in different cultural groups—how one's ethnic, cultural, economic, or national background affects one's responses. Economic forces being what they are, the psychologist's insights in this matter might be of greater importance to admen than to scholarly editors, but in view of the insight, does it still seem reasonable to believe that one edition should do for all persons in all places? Or can editors focus solely on authors and producers without taking audience and contexts or formats into account?

I will not touch here the problem of text and work as it might be seen in the fields of politics or history, though I am familiar with much of the discussion among American historians relating to documentary editions.[6] I believe that the conflicts between the cautious adherents to already-extant texts, on the one hand, and the passionate advocates for the restoration of Truth, Justice, or Beauty, on the other, will continue to be productive. Like William Blake, the possibly mad poet who saw the whole world as sustained in the tensions created by conflicts and contraries, I think that neither side of these contraries ever wins. The godly tyranny of factual detail threatens to stifle the life out of the texts that scholars edit, just as the devilish wildness of editorial vanity threatens to play fast and loose with the facts in the pursuit of truth and beauty.

6. See multiple discussions listed in Beth Luey's *Editing Documents and Texts: An Annotated Bibliography* (Madison: Madison House, 1999).

Publishers' Records and the History of Book Production

An incident in the bibliography of Thackeray's works and the archival survival of apparently redundant books perhaps should be expressed in surroundings other than a research library at a major university, where these issues are not such a problem. Major libraries often collect multiple editions, and even multiple copies of editions. In other libraries, the preservation of material books is too often at risk in an age of digital information and information access. Digitization promises to save space and money, and to increase the dissemination of knowledge, but it also threatens the existence of the material evidence on which knowledge is built.

This Thackeray incident is but a small drop in the ocean of English book production. It dates at the most from 1832 to 1863—the years in which Thackeray had active relations with his publishers. My scope here is even narrower, for I focus on one example of how publisher's records can reveal those relationships and help preserve dark corners of book history. The manuscript record of Thackeray's relations with his publishers is shared by several archives: Houghton Library at Harvard University, the National Library of Scotland, the John Murray publishing company, and *Punch Magazine* (still in the possession of Bradbury Agnew when I examined them), the latter having inherited records from the Bradbury and Evans printing and publishing house. Bradbury and Evans, publisher of *Punch Magazine*, had produced *Vanity Fair*

Originally presented at the Houghton Library, Harvard, for Thackeray's two hundredth birthday celebration, October 6, 2011. The summary of Thackeray's life and the bibliographical details for *Samuel Titmarsh* are taken with slight revisions from two books by me: *Pegasus in Harness: Victorian Publishing and W. M. Thackeray* (Charlottesville: University of Virginia Press, 1992), and *William Makepeace Thackeray: A Literary Life* (London: Palgrave, 2001).

(1847–48) in serial and volume formats just before the main part of the present story.

I begin with a brief picture of who Thackeray was as a man and writer, and an account of how he has been perceived. My view of Thackeray is contrary to the image of Thackeray that he (in jest) cultivated himself and that was further created by some of his early readers and biographers—a view I consider to be a fiction that is not borne out by the surviving evidence. That somewhat negative and erroneous view nevertheless undergirds the perception of many subsequent commentators on the man and his work. The alternative view presented here is built on an investigation of the publishers' archives, including production and financial records, and particularly on the correspondence between the author and his publishers, most of which lay unexamined before the 1970s. Much of it was unpublished until recent collections of letters and papers edited by Edgar Harden and John Aplin.[1] These collections fill gaps in Thackeray's collected letters, compiled and edited by Gordon Ray.[2]

Born in Calcutta in 1811, Thackeray was sent to England at age five for his health and education, as was typical of the children of Anglo-Indian families. Richmond Thackeray, his father, had been an East India employee. His recent death had left mother and son with a fortune of £18,000[3] or so, in trust for William until his twenty-first birthday with lifetime annuities to his mother and to his father's Indian mistress and his half-Indian daughter, William Thackeray's half-sister. Thackeray was raised with a gentleman's education to no particular trade, anticipating a healthy inheritance, and free to follow his inclinations as to avocation. Readers of *The History of Pendennis* will get a not too distorted, though slightly sanitized, sketch of the young man Thackeray himself was: a romantic lad, with aspirations as a writer of love poems, enrolled with small ambitions and a love of fun at Cambridge, who drank too much, lost too much money at play, contracted a debilitating

---

1. *The Letters and Private Papers of William Makepeace Thackeray: A Supplement*, 2 vols., ed. Edgar F. Harden (New York: Garland Publishing, 1994); John Aplin, *Inheritance of Genius: A Thackeray Family Biography, 1798–1875* (Cambridge: Lutterworth Press, 2011); and Aplin, ed., *The Correspondence and Journals of the Thackeray Family*, 5 vols. (London: Pickering & Chatto, 2011).

2. Gordon N. Ray, ed., *The Letters and Private Papers of William Makepeace Thackeray*, 4 vols. (Cambridge, Mass.: Harvard University Press, 1944).

3. That amount, invested in Indian banks, represented an annual income of between 3 and 5 percent, or 540 to 900 pounds per annum. That compared favorably with the incomes of successful upper-middle-class London merchants.

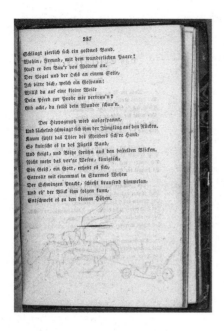

FIG. 12.1   Thackeray's sketch
of Pegasus pulling a cart in Schiller's
Poems. Image from the Harry Ransom
Center, The University of Texas at Austin.
Reproduced with the permission of
Al Murray.

venereal disease, either in Cambridge or on a long vacation in Paris, and left university after eighteen months without a degree.

Thackeray spent time in 1832 in Germany, at Weimar, where he met Goethe and purchased a copy of poems by Friedrich Schiller, including his poem about Pegasus being sold to a farmer who harnesses him unsuccessfully to various coaches and plows. In Schiller's poem, Pegasus will not behave as a proper horse while in harness, though Thackeray drew a relatively docile picture of a winged horse and cart in his own copy of the book.

In 1850, in *The History of Pendennis* Thackeray referred to the professional writer as a Pegasus in harness, the relevance of which will, I trust, emerge.

On his return to England, Thackeray made a brief attempt to study law in London, which did not prevent him from spending most of his time with Edward Fitzgerald studying London theaters. He made an equally brief attempt to study painting in Paris, which seemed not to have interfered with a life of dissipation, from which, however, love appears to have rescued him in the person of Isabella Shaw, for whom he reformed himself. With his stepfather's assistance, he became a journalist, first with *The Constitutional* as a writer/owner/editor, and then as Paris correspondent on *The National Standard*, which he believed would give him the stability needed to marry Isabella. She thought so, too; they married and produced a child, and then an Indian bank failure and the demise of *The National Standard* dashed all hopes Thackeray had of being a gentleman and turned him into a tradesman, a hack, writing for his life and family—a hand-to-mouth existence that lasted from 1837 to 1847 and the publication of *Vanity Fair*. Skipping for now Thackeray's rise to success and descent into more and more frequent bouts of illness relating primarily to what he referred to as his waterworks, he became a professional writer, rewarded by success but dying suddenly and unexpectedly at age 52, in 1863, leaving his daughters with about £10,000 apiece, which was his stated goal.

This is the man who, unfortunately I think, is known to many from his own day to ours as a proud, sensitive, prickly man who disdained his fellow writers, who kowtowed to the aristocracy, and who toned down his criticism of the wealthy once he also became wealthy. This view of Thackeray was boosted by his good friend but effective detractor Anthony Trollope, who wrote of him after his death:

> Unsteadfast, idle, changeable of purpose, aware of his intellect but not trusting it, no man ever failed more generally than he to put his best foot foremost. Full as his works are of pathos, full of humour, full of love and charity, tending, as they always do, to truth and honour and manly worth and womanly modesty, excelling, as they seem to me to do, most other written precepts that I know, they always seem to lack something that might have been there. There is a touch of vagueness which indicates that his pen was not firm while he was using it. He seems to me to have been dreaming ever of some high flight, and then to have told himself, with a half-broken heart, that it was beyond his power to soar up into those bright regions.[4]

With friends like that, who needs enemies? I suppose one could expect that kind of judgment from the author of Trollope's *Autobiography*, where steadfastness, undeviating purpose, and careful placement of the next foot is so assiduously mapped. The record of Thackeray's business dealings with publishers,

4. Anthony Trollope, *Thackeray* (London: Macmillan, 1879), 20.

found in the ledgers, contracts, letters, and in his professionally fulfilled writing assignments, reveals a different man—one whom Trollope apparently did not know, or, knowing, was unable to understand. Thackeray missed only three writing deadlines in his life, one during the writing of *Barry Lyndon*, while on his trip to Egypt, and which might have been the fault of the post office as much as of the writer; one during the writing of *Pendennis*, caused by an attack of what was probably cholera, which nearly killed him and that interrupted the serial novel for three months; and one just as he was finishing *The Virginians*, caused by illness and resulting in the serial text ending not in a single-double number 23/24, as was the normal practice, but in two separate numbers: 23, followed the next month by 24. He was not lazy or unreliable, but did he make other missteps?

His correspondence with his publishers shows a range of emotions: anger over unfulfilled promises, pleading for work or for payments, demands for higher rates of payment, inquiries about the health of the publishers' wives and children, and invitations to dinners or family celebrations. In one letter, Thackeray makes arrangements to nominate his then-publisher, George Smith, to become a member of the Reform Club.[5] In another, he directs a watchmaker to inscribe a watch to his servant, James S., who was about to embark for a new life in Australia. The allegedly arrogant, aloof, self-important wannabe aristocrat does not show up anywhere in Thackeray's correspondence with his publishers. The records cover thirty years in the life of a professional writer who appears to have lost his temper with only one publisher—Richard Bentley, who had accepted but then did not publish or pay for a substantial story at a time when Thackeray was desperate for cash. That story is an anomaly in Thackeray's long record of reliability and friendly relations with his publishers. Even of American "pirate" publishers, the Harpers of New York, he once said with a shrug, "A half loaf is better than no loaf at all." That long record is set over against two events, rather famous semi-public and public controversies, in which Thackeray was involved and that form the basis for much negative writing about his supposed prickly, sensitive, arrogant personality. The first episode, in 1849–50, was a public argument, usually referred to as the "dignity of literature" debate, pitting Thackeray against John Forster and Charles Dickens concerning the Guild for Literature. The other combined the results of an unfortunate remark Thackeray had made in 1858 about Dickens's affair with Ellen Ternan and the almost-

5. Harden, *Letters and Private Papers, Supplement*, 2:1026.

simultaneous objections that Thackeray made to Edmund Yates's published satirical portrayal of him—both of which have been the subject of scholarly and other gossip for a hundred and fifty years.

What I focus on instead is the bibliographical, book production, and textual issues that have been illuminated by the publishers' records, ledgers recording production costs, contracts, and letters between the author and the publishers.

The list of Thackeray's book publishers includes Chapman and Hall, Hugh Cunningham, John Macrone, David Bouge, Bradbury and Evans, and George Smith in England, and Harper and Brothers of New York, Appletons of New York, and Ticknor and Fields of Boston. Carey and Lea of Philadelphia made him an offer, but he declined, having already come to terms with the Harpers. He contributed shorter pieces and serials to dozens of periodicals, including most famously *Punch, Fraser's Magazine, The Westminster Review, Blackwoods, The Quarterly Review, The British and Foreign Review, The Times,* and *Britannia,* among dozens of others. He illustrated most of his own works and some works by others.[6] In sum, regardless of multiple disparaging accounts of him, Thackeray was a successful professional writer who honored his reading public as the true (in fact only) patron for whom he worked. Addressing the Royal Literary Society at the height of the dignity of literature controversy he said:

> Literary men are not by any means, at this present time, the most unfortunate and most degraded set of people whom they are sometimes represented to be. . . . [C]ertain persons are constantly apt to bring forward or to believe in the existence, at this moment, of the miserable old literary hack of the time of George the Second, and bring him before us as the literary man of this day. I say that that disreputable old phantom ought to be hissed out of society. I don't believe in the literary man being obliged to resort to ignoble artifices and mean flatteries to get places at the tables of the great, and to enter into society upon sufferance. . . . As for pity being employed upon authors, especially in my branch of the profession, if you will but look at the novelists of the present day, I think you will see it is altogether out of the question to pity them. . . . Of course

6. Details and documentation for these statements are in my *Pegasus in Harness.* See also Edgar F. Harden, *A Checklist of Contributions by William Makepeace Thackeray to Newspapers, Periodicals, Books, and Serial Part Issues, 1828–1864* (Victoria: University of Victoria University Press, 1996).

it is impossible for us to settle the mere prices by which the works of those who amuse the public are to be paid. I am perfectly aware that Signore Twankeydillo, of the Italian Opera, and Mademoiselle Petupas of the Haymarket, will get a great deal more money in a week for the skilful exercise of their chest and toes than I, or you, or any gentleman here present, should be able to get by our brains and by weeks of hard labour. We cannot help these differences in payment; we know there must be high and low payments in our trade, as in all trades; that there must be gluts of the market and over-production; and there must be successful machinery, and rivals, and brilliant importations from foreign countries; that there must be hands out of employ, and tribulation of workmen. But these ill-winds which afflict us blow fortunes to our successors. They are natural evils. It is the progress of the world, rather than any evil which we can remedy; and that is why I say this society acts most wisely and justly, in endeavouring to remedy, not the chronic distress, but the temporary evil; that it finds a man at the moment of the pinch of necessity, helps him a little, and gives him a "God-speed," and sends him on his way. For my own part, I have felt that necessity, and bent under that calamity; and it is because I have found friends who have nobly, with God's blessing, helped me at that moment of distress that I feel deeply interested in the ends of a Society which has for its object to help my brother in similar need.[7]

This does not mean Thackeray thought authors should endure whatever publishers sent their way. My next anecdote might be titled "On Learning Not to be a Publisher's Whatdyacallum." This is the story alluded to earlier as the one instance we know in which Thackeray lost his temper with a publisher. It also is the main contribution of this essay.

In 1841, Thackeray was in rather desperate straits. His second daughter, Jane, had recently died at eight months of age; his wife had not and would never recover from depression after the birth of their third daughter, Harriet Marian, better known as Minny. He was writing as much as he could for as many different magazines as he could. He wrote a long short story, a novella really, called *The History of Samuel Titmarsh and the Great Hoggarty Dia-*

7. Lewis Melville [pseud. of Lewis Saul Benjamin], *William Makepeace Thackeray: A Biography Including Hitherto Uncollected Letters and Speeches and a Bibliography of 1,300 Items*, 2 vols. (London: John Lane, 1910), 2:71–75.

mond—a story that Gordon Ray, in *The Buried Life*, suggests is more than a little bit autobiographical and that perhaps was also more than just a bit therapeutic. The manuscript was submitted to Richard Bentley on February 25 and was accepted immediately but was neither paid for nor published by the first of June, when Thackeray wrote angrily to have the manuscript turned over to another publisher, one named Hugh Cunningham. It was unusual for a publisher to take three months to act on a working journalist's writings, and Thackeray, in 1841, didn't have three months. He owed Chapman and Hall the manuscript of the still-unwritten *Irish Sketch-Book*. Chapman and Hall had advanced Thackeray a substantial amount of cash for a book on Ireland but had taken in surety Thackeray's chest of plate and made him sign a promissory note, co-signed by his cousin. Furthermore, Thackeray had just placed his mentally ailing wife in a French *maison de santé*, for which he needed money. Although Thackeray had published only twenty-five magazine pieces a year in the two years previous, he had in 1840 successfully published his first book, *The Paris Sketch Book*.[8] Thackeray's exasperated letter to Bentley, who was dragging his heels over *The History of Samuel Titmarsh*, is a notable one revealing both frustration and a new confidence in his status as an author who did not mind offending a publisher. He finished his letter saying: "& next time your obedient Servant sends you an article you may set him down without fail to be you understand what [sketch of a donkey] yours & whatdyecallem W M Thackeray."[9] As luck would have it, the work's next projected publisher, Hugh Cunningham, was having troubles of his own and also did not publish the story. So, Thackeray turned to *Fraser's Magazine*, where *Titmarsh* finally began serialization in September 1841, eight months after he first submitted it to Bentley.

Over the next seven years, Thackeray published *The Irish Sketch-Book*, *Notes on a Journey from Cornhill to Grand Cairo*, *The Book of Snobs*, *Novels by Eminent Hands*, and *Vanity Fair*. In addition, from 1845 to 1847 he was also publishing short sketches, articles, poems, and stories at an average rate of one hundred per year. That brings us to the story in hand.

Thackeray's struggle to become a professional and successful writer, rising above the run of hacks and penny-a-liners, took a turn for the better in 1847

8. Actually, Thackeray's first published book was *The Yellowplush Papers*, but it was pirated and published as a book in America without his knowledge or permission. *The Paris Sketch Book*, in 1841, was the first work published in book form for which he received payment.

9. Gordon N. Ray, *Thackeray: The Uses of Adversity* (New York: McGraw-Hill, 1955), 478.

THE HISTORY

OF

SAMUEL TITMARSH

AND

THE GREAT HOGGARTY DIAMOND.

BY

W. M. THACKERAY,

AUTHOR OF "PENDENNIS," "VANITY FAIR," &C. &C.

LONDON:

BRADBURY & EVANS, 11, BOUVERIE STREET.

MDCCCXLIX.

FIG. 12.2   Title page of the
first edition of Thackeray's
History of Samuel Titmarsh
(London: Bradbury and Evans,
1849), also used for the second
edition, first issue, 1849.

and 1848 with the publication of *Vanity Fair*. He suggested to his publisher,
Bradbury and Evans, that the firm reprint in book form *The History of
Samuel Titmarsh and the Great Hoggarty Diamond*. He wrote his mother the
same month that he was to receive £100 for the reprint.[10] The first English
edition of *Titmarsh*, published by Bradbury and Evans, appeared in January
1849 and was followed immediately in February by a second edition from the
same firm.

That the title page illustrated in figure 12.2 represents both the first and
the second edition requires some explanation. The story of these two editions
illustrates, first, a strong turning point in how publishers thought of Thackeray
and, second, the importance of archival preservation.

These two editions have always been referred to as one edition in book
form because, before I looked at the publisher's ledgers in 1970, no published

---

10. Ray, ed., *The Letters and Private Papers of William Makepeace Thackeray*, 2:382.

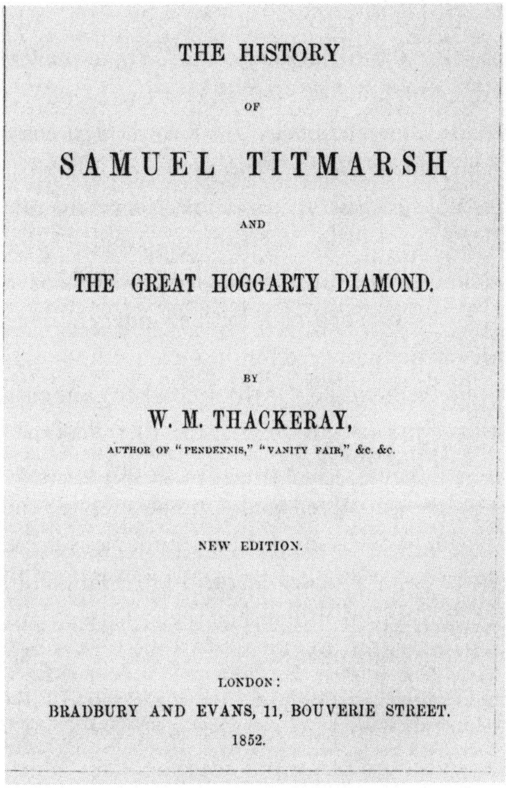

THE HISTORY

OF

SAMUEL TITMARSH

AND

THE GREAT HOGGARTY DIAMOND.

BY

W. M. THACKERAY,

AUTHOR OF "PENDENNIS," "VANITY FAIR," &c. &c.

NEW EDITION.

LONDON:

BRADBURY AND EVANS, 11, BOUVERIE STREET.

1852.

FIG. 12.3   Title page of the second edition, second issue, of Thackeray's *History of Samuel Titmarsh* (London: Bradbury and Evans, 1852).

account or bibliography recorded that there had been two editions. The ledger records payment for composing and printing two thousand initial copies. Most of the metal type used in that printing was immediately distributed. Extraordinarily and unexpectedly, the first edition sold out immediately. A second edition required that the type be reset, but the new edition, also printed in two thousand copies, did not sell well, and sheets from that edition were reissued with new title pages and slightly altered preliminaries by Bradbury and Evans in 1852, and then again in 1857, and finally again by Smith, Elder, and Company without a date but noted in the ledgers as 1872 (no copy has been found). In short, although there was only one printing of each of these two editions, some copies of the second edition have the same title page as that used for the first edition; other copies (reissues) of the second edition have one of three additional different title pages (see fig. 12.3).

Without the publisher's records, it is unlikely that the existence of the second edition would ever have been discovered. No bibliography and no library catalogue anywhere in the world recorded its existence. The publisher's records, however, show that the first two thousand copies of *The History of Samuel Titmarsh*, printed on January 27, 1849, cost £40 5s. 6d. for typesetting but have no entry for stereotyped plates. The record's next entry shows a printing of two thousand more copies on February 17, referred to as the second edition, entered this time at the cost of £36 for "composing and working"—a figure more than £4 less than the original composition costs. The ledger then records charges for stereotyping. The obvious conclusions to draw are that, first, stereotyped plates were not made for the January edition; second, redistribution of type began before a need for the second edition was recognized; third, type had to be recomposed for the second edition only twenty-one days after the printing of the first edition; and fourth, stereotyped plates were cast of the second edition, and, not especially obvious from the ledgers alone, the stereotyped plates were never used. Composition for the second edition was less expensive for two reasons that became obvious to me only after examining the two editions side by side. That task proved difficult, since no bibliography or library catalogue distinguished them. I would just have to go looking and hoping I could find one.

When I was young and had little money, I did have a Volkswagen camper and a Xeroxed photocopy of what purported to be a first edition of *Samuel Titmarsh*. I also had access to a Lindstrand Comparator (see fig. 12.4), which is a more or less portable optical instrument for comparing books and detecting variants. I began my hunt for a second edition at Mississippi State University, where I worked at the time, and where Special Collections had one copy of *Titmarsh*. My first stop was the University of Alabama, Tuscaloosa, where they also had one copy of *Titmarsh*, identical to the one I had photocopied. My second stop was the University of South Carolina, where they had two more identical copies, then on to Duke University, University of North Carolina, Virginia Polytechnic Institute and State University, the University of Virginia, New York Public Library, and the Pierpont Morgan Library—all of which had single or multiple copies identical to the one I already had. This took two weeks and two visits to laundromats. There was one glimmer of light on that trip. In the North Carolina Room at UNC, I had found a copy of *Titmarsh* published by Smith, Elder, and Company with no date. The title page made it look like a new edition, but it also looked suspiciously like the first edition in size and shape. The line breaks throughout the book corresponded to those in the first edition. Using the Lindstrand

FIG. 12.4   The Lindstrand Comparator. Photo: David L. Vander Meulen.

Comparator, I determined that the last gathering in the book was identical to the edition I had. At the time, however, I did not know what I was looking at, and I thought that what I wanted was a copy with a Bradbury and Evans title page dated 1849 but with a reset text, as indicated in the ledgers. What I found in North Carolina was a book with gatherings B through M reset and gathering N, the last one, identical to my copy. It was an important clue but not what I was expecting. By the way, the reason the North Carolina collection had the book is that it had been owned by and bore the signature of Zebulon Vance, twice governor of the state. So much for institutional interest in Thackeray. Discouraged in a hot New York summer, I gave up and headed home.

On a whim, I stopped in Philadelphia at the Library Company, the library founded by Benjamin Franklin. There, I found two copies of the second edition, looking, initially, exactly like the first edition, with Bradbury and Evans, 1849, title pages. The reading room protocols for acceptable behavior at the Library Company required me to go outside for a few minutes.

The two reasons that explain the reduced cost for composing the second edition became clear. Preliminaries and signature N in both the first and second edition were identical. These two gatherings were the last two gatherings of the book to go through the press. The reason the preliminaries of a book are printed last is so that the table of contents can refer to the page numbers in the already-typeset-and-printed body of the book. It stands to reason that they were also the last to be slated for type redistribution. Obviously, they were still in standing type when the order for the second edition came. The type set initially for gathering N and the preliminaries was salvaged. Gatherings B through M, however, had to be reset, a task made somewhat easier and faster than the first typesetting because (1) compositors reset from print, not from manuscript, (2) compositors reset line for line (with a few exceptions) without having to determine appropriate line breaks and right-margin justification, and (3) compositors had two sheets fewer to reset. Line-for-line resetting insured that the salvaged last gathering of type would mesh perfectly with the newly reset first part. The new typesetting introduced approximately eighty-five variants, none that would suggest an author's attempt to revise—a few of them new errors, others corrections of obvious errors, and a few introducing alternatives that made little difference, such as adjusting line breaks to avoid a tight line or end-line hyphenation. I have now seen a total of five copies of the second edition issued in 1849 (Fales, Library Co.[2], British Library, and Huntington). As already noted, the second edition did not sell well, and so leftover printed sheets were warehoused and reissued with new title pages in small batches in 1852, 1857, and 1872. Needless to say, the bindings also show minor variations. The Zebulon Vance copy in North Carolina, though undated, corresponds to the ledger's notes for the third reissue of second edition sheets, this time by Smith, Elder, and Company, who, in 1865, about eighteen months after Thackeray's death, had purchased from Bradbury and Evans Thackeray's copyrights and all remaining stock of printed sheets and books.

Incidentally, the enthusiasm for Thackeray's rising popularity, evidenced by the immediate selling of the entire first-edition print run of *Titmarsh* and the brisk sales of the serialization of *The History of Pendennis*, caused Bradbury and Evans to order not only the resetting of type (costing £36) but also stereotyped plates (costing £15.18.9) for the second edition, even though the first and only printing of the second edition was printed from the standing type before stereotypes were cast.[11] In the aftermath, those plates were never used

---

11. The process of plaster-cast stereotyping causes a slight shrinkage in the size of the page. The page size of the second edition is identical to that of the first edition.

and ultimately were sold by Smith, Elder, and Company as surplus metal in the 1870s.

The publisher's records and an analysis of copies of the two 1849 editions of *Samuel Titmarsh* (1) show how the books were produced, (2) explain the carryover of the first-edition typesetting of the preliminaries and last gathering, (3) expose the odd alterations made by Bradbury and Evans in 1852 and 1857 for the second and third issues of the second edition, and (4) demonstrate how Smith, Elder, and Company altered the remaining sheets for reissue in 1872.[12]

Several conclusions can be drawn from this bibliographical analysis of the material books and of the publisher's ledgers and the correspondence between author and publisher. The study contributes to a correction of biographical accounts of Thackeray. The study also recovered a lost edition—lost in the sense that no one any longer knew about it, so that any user of the second edition was under the mistaken belief that it was a copy of the first edition. In relation to the general concerns explored in this book as a whole, the study demonstrates the importance of collecting and preserving multiple editions and multiple copies of editions in libraries. Most important, however, the study points to desiderata, or "desirables," in digital archives. First, that digital archives, no less than material archives, should contain multiple editions of the same work and multiple copies of each edition—new images carefully made from different material copies, not images duplicated from other images. Second, that detailed and accurate metadata for each image be provided after careful and extensive examination of the material originals. It seems an obvious but often-neglected truth that misidentified or underidentified information on the Internet is not information at all but "false facts." Perhaps textual scholarship will have no better recourse than that optimistically proposed by Thomas Jefferson, in his second inaugural address, in 1805, to curb false opinions:

> Since truth and reason have maintained their ground against false opinions in league with false facts, the press confined to truth needs no other legal restraint. The public judgment will correct false reasonings and opinions on a full hearing of all parties, and no other definite line can be drawn between the inestimable liberty of the press and its

12. A detailed technical analysis of the ledger entries, leading to the conclusions narrated here, is in my *Pegasus in Harness*, 170–86.

demoralizing licentiousness. If there be still improprieties which this rule would not restrain, its supplement must be sought in the censorship of public opinion.[13]

If we cannot police ourselves, perhaps the public will.

13. Thomas Jefferson, *The Writings of Thomas Jefferson*, Memorial Edition, ed. Andrew A. Lipscomb and Albert Allery Bergh, 20 vols. (Washington, D.C.: The Thomas Jefferson Memorial Association, 1903–4), 3:381 (quoted in "Thomas Jefferson on Politics & Government," http://famguardian.org/Subjects/Politics/thomasjefferson/jeff1600.htm).

Cultural Heritage, Textuality, and Social Justice

The English department at Loyola University Chicago, in 2008, named me to the Martin J. Svaglic chair in textual studies, which this essay commemorates. I used the occasion to review how textual studies contributes to the broader comprehensive goals of higher education. I also focused some attention on the role of digital technology in textual studies.

Martin J. Svaglic, for whom the chair in textual studies was named, was professor of English at Loyola University Chicago, a scholar whom I never met. His primary interests in Victorian literature overlapped rather than coincided with mine. He influenced my understanding of John Henry Newman, although my interest in Newman as a religious and philosophical writer has been an amateur's admiration for his lucidity, his gentleness, and his subtlety of thought. I do not pretend to have fathomed the quality of Svaglic's interest in Newman, or in other Catholic writers of the period. However, the following comment on Tennyson in Svaglic's 1952 essay on the revisions in Newman's *Apologia Pro Vita Sua* resonates with my own experiences in textual study. They offer one answer to the questions "Is it important to know textual sources when teaching?" and "Does knowledge of textual variation yield food for thought and knowledge?" Svaglic wrote,

There is little that is so transparently rewarding for close study as the comparison between, say, Tennyson's very uneven classical poems of 1832 and the superb revisions of the next decade. Yet, slight as most of the changes are, anyone interested in the nuances of writing will find much of interest and value in the process whereby the writer, always given to

Revised from my inaugural lecture delivered as the Svaglic Chair in Textual Studies, Loyola University Chicago, September 23, 2009.

the most painstaking revisions and now no longer pressed for time, made what had already been acclaimed a masterpiece into the clearer, more vivid, and dramatic story of a still more engaging figure.[1]

Of the changes Svaglic went on to trace in the textual history of Newman's *Apologia*, perhaps the smallest and most interesting is the triad of variants revealing Newman's developing attempt to make the doctrine of eternal punishment less terrible. In 1864, he wrote: "less terrible to the 'reason'"; the next year, he changed it to "less terrible to the 'intellect'"; and, finally, in 1886 he wrote: "less terrible to the 'imagination.'" When one tries to identify the possible motives for such changes or tries to follow the differences these variants indicate about how the doctrine of eternal punishment appears to our reason, our intellect, or our imagination, it becomes clearer why an interest in textual histories is worth the effort.

Contrary to a common misconception, textual studies is not devoted to stabilizing texts. Textual instability is a fact of life and is not, in itself, an error. The error is in assuming that textual stability is either achievable or desirable. Textual studies is the study of the composition, revision, and production of texts; the analysis and identification of interventions in textual histories; and the exploration of the interpretive consequences of textual variation. We want to understand how texts are made and remade and by whom they are affected. We want to understand how the life of texts interacts with the life of culture. Regardless of how comforting it might be to think otherwise, texts are unstable and copies not self-identical. Some people believe that the constitution of the United States was written in stone and that what it meant to the founding fathers it means now and ever will, amen. Similarly, wishful thinkers believe that education and academic investigation is for the purpose of simplifying the world so that it can be understood once and for all. These things are not true. The object of academic investigation is not to simplify but to clarify. Texts and textual histories are complex and sometimes confusing. They are susceptible to clarification so that their complexities can be understood. They are also susceptible to simplification, but simplification is distortion. There may be arguments on behalf of distortion, but academic investigation is not in that business. It is impossible to verify absolutely any reconstruction of the past, and accuracy is not the only purpose for which

1. M. J. Svaglic, "The Revision of Newman's *Apologia*," *Modern Philology* 50, no. 1 (1952): 43.

texts from the past are brought again into the present. But as academics, textual scholars are committed to understanding the history of texts and to explaining with clarity the interpretive consequences of textual variation.

In that endeavor, the Internet now plays a primary role. The authority of print and of the manuscript signature has migrated through photocopies, to fax copies, to digital copies, and the odd concept of copies that are "multiple originals." Even as it provides us with sources of general information about the world, the Internet, curiously and disturbingly, thrives on the notion that texts are stable and identical. Most Internet postings of literary texts fail to say what specific material text was the source of the posted version. That bit of carelessness seems to be based on the false notion that a text is a text is a text, regardless of where it came from or where it goes. Even in the more staid world of book history, it has taken years of pecking away by numerous scholars to make a dent in Elizabeth Eisenstein's argument that the invention of the printing press and movable type introduced textual stability into a world of scribal texts in which every copy of a work was known to be different in some way from every other copy.[2] Somehow, the repetitive mechanisms of print lulled into complacency our alertness to textual instability.

These matters require further thought because, in the world of knowledge, for works created before film, audio recording, and digital technology, all expression of knowledge is by way of a documentary text. The record of knowledge was and is textual. In the humanities (philosophy, theology, literature, history, and music), the sources of knowledge, when one drills back to bedrock evidence, are mostly textual, mostly documentary. One could add that maps, architectural and landscape designs, dance notations, and the topographical grids and chronological slices drawn by archaeologists are also documentary texts. Furthermore, because textual issues arise with regard to film, recordings, and digital storage, it can be said that all humanities knowledge is textual.

A Question of Justice

Recently, Loyola University's president, Michael Garanzini, addressed the faculty, challenging them to step up and speak truths in support of social

2. Elizabeth Eisenstein, *The Printing Press as an Agent of Change: Communications and Cultural Transformations in Early Modern Europe*, 2 vols. (Cambridge: Cambridge University Press, 1979).

justice. If the truths thus presented were uncomfortable to some, the president seemed undisturbed. He would, perhaps, be pleased to see a bit more discomfort around the university. In fact, it could be argued that comfort in the face of social injustice, which must I am sure be understood as comfort induced by blindness to social injustice, is just the sort of thing that needs to be dislodged. Hesitatingly, I offer a small attempt to address social justice, restricting myself to my own field of expertise, textual studies. Attempts to do good in fields one knows little or nothing about are bound to go wrong. It can easily be argued that the world is plagued by injustices far more pressing and important than those I will speak about, but these are the ones I know.

Many aspects of culture, once tied in the imagination to the printing press, have gone digital. Transcriptions and digital images of documents surviving from times past are just a small part. Music, painting, films, and museum objects have become more digital than flesh and concrete. And life is pervaded with email, texting, tweeting, googling, and doodling. Past, present, and future cultural heritage is digital. Digital representation of the past is, however, restricted to *representations* of documentary and material objects from the past—not born digital and, therefore, at a remove from the material (actual) evidence of history. Grecian urns are as much the evidence of past culture as are poems about Grecian urns. Books and manuscripts are just as physical and material as the brick and stone ruins of ancient civilizations. As a professor of textual studies, my focus on culture is restricted to books and manuscripts and as a professor of literature, I shall also stick to literary culture, though much of what I have been thinking applies to the textual artifacts of music, history, philosophy, theology, and architecture.

The material archive of books, manuscripts, and maps in the library is becoming the virtual archive on the Internet at a faster rate than the rate of development of proper tools to make it happen. In these early, incunabular years of the Internet, it has been common to view the page on the screen as equivalent to the page in the book—even when the screen displays only a transcription of unknown origin and authenticity. Scholarly articles in print journals, also, are giving way to articles refereed, accepted, and published on the Internet. Likewise, newspaper articles in which journalistic content was once vouched for by at least two checked sources are being jostled by multiple amateur reports on Twitter from places where bona fide reporters cannot go.

The digital age is also having an impact on what stands for truth. In the Church, truth has traditionally been that which has the stamp of authority;

in the university, truth has traditionally been that which can be verified by reference to original sources or that which can be replicated in the lab. On the Internet in wiki environments, it appears now that truth is what most people believe to be true, whether or not vouched for by authorities or supported by verified evidence. The gossip fence has moved from the backyard to the desktop.

I am not railing against these developments. What *passes* for culture may, in fact, *be* culture. The character and essence of a people is accurately reflected by what they think and how they act. Clearly, active culture is not controlled by what we think people should be thinking and doing. Is that a standard that we wish to see applied to our knowledge of, or notions about, the past? We know that the past becomes what we make of it, either by ignoring it, distorting it, appropriating it, or manipulating it for many purposes—some of which might be admirable. Yet, by preserving the evidence and asking for its analysis, academe puts an important drag on the mad rush to use, or abuse, the past for present purposes. Museums and libraries preserve cultural objects that not only spur investigations but inspire imaginations. Curators arrange the artifacts in ways that tell stories and bring coherence to the accumulation of historical objects. Historians write stories that arrange the surviving evidence in plausible ways. Then, new curators and new historians rewrite to make the past either more plausible or more useful or more credible. Texts are perhaps the most prolific, rich, and complex artifacts of cultural history.

Textual scholarship examines the history of text creation and text transmission from copy to copy and from one medium to another. Every text that is copied is copied for a purpose, and the result is likely to fulfill that purpose to the extent that the copier can achieve it. Producing an *accurate* copy is just one of many potential purposes. Preservation is seldom the sole purpose for re-creating ancient texts. Even when preservation and accuracy do happen to be the central aim, every copy is always different from the original in some way or ways. Sometimes, these differences are ones we care about, and other times they are differences that make no difference to us. When they make a difference, however, they do so whether or not we notice.

The myth that any copy of a work represents that work "more or less well" seems good enough for many people, including those students and scholars for whom the nearest or cheapest copy is good enough. Bookstores and publishers and generous people who populate the Internet with free copies of books all conspire to suggest that a new edition is as good as or even better than an original, because it is no longer protected by copyright laws and is free. Any text will do. Yet, it is not the case that any text will do what any other text of the same work will do. Texts are not self-identical. Therefore, throwing any old text up on the Internet and thinking that one has given access to a work is one of the most prevalent deceptions of our age. This deception constitutes a blindness to social injustice. What does it say about your attitude toward students and toward knowledge that you think any text will do—the cheaper the better?

Who gets to look at the source materials for texts? Where are such materials preserved? For whom are they preserved? Who has the training and curiosity to examine and interpret primary materials? Professors, (some privileged) students, investigative journalists, detectives—is it just for these people that primary materials are saved? Is it just to them that access should be given? Most of us are comfortable with the notion that the man and woman and child "on the street" (nice phrase, that, "on the street," meaning belonging nowhere in particular)—do not need access to primary materials, would not know how to use such materials, and in any case are not curious about them. We assume these things to be the case, and we are comfortable in thinking that in any case *we* have access.

Or if we are not comfortable, it may be that it is because we do not yet have access, or not easy access. Before the age of digitization, we all knew that if we wanted to access primary materials we had to go where the materials were: The British Library; the Library of Congress; the Folger, Huntington, Newberry, or Morgan libraries; and so on. Primary materials were preserved for those with sufficient desire to overcome the obstacles of time, distance, and travel funds. The heroic efforts required to go, find, consult, analyze, and understand primary materials perhaps blinded us to how this situation might be described by one with an interest in social justice: these materials are restricted for use by the privileged few. That is tantamount to saying that only the privileged few need to be able to verify what, for them, passes as knowledge. The rest of the population must settle for secondhand reports, taken on trust or with a naive belief in the authority of others. One could, in predigital times, shrug off this implication as just a practical fact of life. Is the public's willingness to take its information at second hand an indication of their willful laziness, or does it show an elite of power, blind to social justice, maintaining its privileges?

The digital age is upon us. Surrogates for primary materials abound. Although most individuals cannot do so, libraries can purchase digital images of thousands of books, pamphlets, and newspapers dating from the beginning of writing to the recent (public domain) past at a fraction of the cost of the originals—were it even possible to find originals for sale. By way of these images, one can sense an immediate connection to the originals—nearly perfect surrogates—even though one cannot study the objects themselves. An individual's need to travel to some far-off depository of primary materials is radically reduced by the advent of digital images—supposing, of course, that the individual is allowed to use the library and supposing that the source of the images is accurately labeled. Thousands of people are given access to these surrogate primary materials by library purchases. This is true even if no one uses these materials for ten or fifteen years because twenty, fifty, and one hundred years from now libraries will (we hope) still be providing access to these images of primary materials to future generations. Thus, social justice in the pursuit of knowledge is advanced. Somewhat.

This story is not rare in most first-world countries. Electronic surrogates for material texts are widely available to students and investigators in the United Kingdom because public institutions of education share their electronic resources among themselves and because access to the British Library and its electronic resources is unrestricted; anyone can apply for and get a library pass.

The United States lags behind the United Kingdom and most countries in the European Union in this regard. Those countries rely more heavily on publicly supported libraries to support education than does the United States. Here, the limited access of poor universities contrasts sharply with that of the rich universities. Some people are comfortable with this state of affairs. We are used to the notion of the rich having more than the poor. We allow ourselves to be comfortable with the notion that education and welfare, while desirable for all, competes with the capitalistic notion of letting the devil take the hindmost.

This miscarriage of social justice in the pursuit of knowledge is nothing to what is happening worldwide to the pursuit of knowledge. As electronic access to primary materials grows in the United States and Europe, the gap between what is available to us and what is available in third-world countries is growing greater daily. That this matters (even if we are talking only about English-language materials) is evidenced by the fact that the country in which the greatest number of students sit down every day to read Shakespeare in English is India. English is the language of education in many third-world countries. While it is true that the quality of education depends in part on the distance between the point of learning and the primary materials that support knowledge, that distance is more often forbidding in third-world countries than in the so-called first world. That distance could be, but seldom is, bridged by access to digital surrogates for primary material.

Access to primary materials is largely owned by commercial companies. They have seen what academe seems blind to, or is unwilling to see, or unable to understand or do anything about: corporations have seen that primary materials are the fallow fields from which knowledge comes, and they have staked their claims and turned these resources to profit making. It is a wonder that in a world of electronic digital access to practically everything, including primary material, in a world where Google and other search engines extend the democracy of knowledge to the men, women, and children on the street—in such a world, it is a strange wonder that access to digital images of primary materials is largely restricted to persons with subscriptions or with membership in subscribing institutions. Institutions around the world, dedicated to bringing education to all who can benefit from instruction, are for the most part unable to subscribe to all the sources of digitized literary material. Culture has gone digital for the few, not for everyone.

Other facts of textual life reflect social injustice. Universities around the world pay researchers to investigate and report their findings and, having paid for the research, give the reports to commercial companies that are in the business of selling access to information. The universities then must purchase back what they originally paid to produce. Something has gone dreadfully wrong with the system. Employees of companies that benefit from research paid for by universities seem to be perfectly honest people who believe that they are adding value. The companies are doing what the universities seem not to know how to do—disseminate the knowledge that they produce. Some scholars, already aware of the problem, give copies of all their essays and research reports to their institutional repositories.

I have conflated two separate elements in the digitization of culture. The first is the digitization of primary materials (literary manuscripts and books) and the second is the digitization of new knowledge (scholarly treatises, monographs, journals). There are important differences: the former is timeless; the later should be timely. But, the principle is the same in both. Our cultural artifacts, collected by libraries and museums, are being bought (i.e., images of them are being bought) and resold to the rest of the world for profit. I say bought because when Google Books, Gale CENGAGE, ProQuest, Taylor & Francis, or Elsevier—to name the most aggressive—make deals with the British Library or other major repositories of antiquities and collectibles, and with the editors of learned journals, they pay those institutions for exclusive rights to images. Why not? If you owned unique materials, would you not accept money from a commercial operation prepared to pay for the privilege of selling images of your holdings? It could enhance the curation and growth of your collection. What's not to like? No one in the chain of the system seems to be doing anything wrong. It all seems comfortable, normal, and even good. The social injustice becomes apparent only when one looks beyond the immediate "good" being done locally. Academics might or might not have an economic interest in their pursuit of new knowledge. The effects of the current system, however, place the academic "commodity" in the hands of merchants, whose interests are not democratic or universal. The system does not conform to any notion of social justice known to me. Is there anything we can or should do about it? Do we have a social responsibility to make resources available to universities, students, and scholars—to the able-but-poor everywhere?

A Question of Ethics

It is not just that students and scholars in the third world lag further and further behind because electronic access to primary materials and new knowledge is so much slower in reaching them. Nor is it just that those of us in the education industry in the developed world often ignore the riches that are actually available to us by failing to examine primary materials (or images of them) for the works we teach and study. It is that we often encourage a "make do" attitude in ourselves and our students when we reach for the cheapest or closest copy of a copy of a copy of a work to study or teach.

It is not a crime to be ignorant. We would all be in jail if it were. We cannot know many things. We do not have time to investigate every text. We can, however, instill in ourselves and others a sense of curiosity and skepticism about sources, even when we cannot do anything about it in *every* case. We can and should "teach the ignorance," declaring when we did not investigate that which might, upon examination, require revisions in our thinking. Furthermore, in every case we can be honest about our sources. I give as an example something I was taught to do that I now know to be unethical and self-defeating, even though it is a practice followed by many. Respectability being occasionally more important than honesty, critics sometimes do their work relative to the most convenient text at hand, the one on the nearest shelf (one about whose provenance they know nothing), and to encourage students to get a text, any text, a cheap text, any text being better than no text at all. The dictates of respectability are such that, having studied this copy of a copy of a copy and written one's term paper or one's scholarly article, one then goes to the library, finds the rare original edition or the expensive and highly touted scholarly edition and checks the accuracy of the quotations, and cites as one's source the respectable text one did not actually use in studying the work.

The ethics are already questionable, but the consequences lie like hidden land mines; for anyone operating in this manner has no idea if the primary work or the scholarly edition said something different in some other passage, not quoted, that would have affected the argument. So, even if one is too lazy (strike that, I meant to say, "too pressed for time") to find out if the text in hand has been revised, censored, or badly printed, at least one can have the honesty to cite the text actually used.

There is another, better reason to be textually aware—to determine what text one is using and how it differs, if it does, from others. It is that texts are always understood in relation to the events contingent to their creation and that are silently evinced in the particular book one is using. Books are seldom manufactured by authors. They are not even manufactured by publishers. There are book designers, copy-editors, compositors, pressmen, correctors, and binders who do that. Authors just write or type; sometimes their work passes through the hands of secretaries before reaching the publisher. Publishers don't do anything but agree to publish or reject, and they pay the bills. In short, the book one uses is a composite of capital and labor by a community of persons who influence what the text says and what it looks and feels like. Social, political, and economic events of the day influence the writing, editing, and production. One's interaction with the resulting book is influenced by the things that influenced the production of the copy in hand, whether it is a first edition, an image of a first edition, a printout of a first edition, a revised or pirated edition, or a modern paperback edition. Each will be different from other copies. Each is witness to the conditions of its own manufacture.

A Question of Consequences

Nadine Gordimer, the 1991 Nobel Prize–winning South African writer, wrote: "The creative act is not pure. History evidences it. Sociology extracts it. The writer loses Eden, writes to be read and comes to realize that he is answerable."[3] Literary art is embedded in history, politics, and social milieus. The artistic ideals of the writer's Eden are exchanged for the practicalities of survival in the marketplace. Gordimer was a white woman writing about being white and being black under the conditions of South African apartheid. This quotation might suggest that she was aware that her writing was dangerously close to the ethical bone of race relations, and that, therefore, she was constrained to exercise self-censorship. She claimed, however, that she never thought about censorship while writing; and, indeed, several of her books were banned in South Africa. The point is that whether a writer responds self-protectively or recklessly, the writing has a context and the writer is answerable. Is the reader answerable or responsible, also? If history, sociology, and politics impinge on the creative act, it follows that a reader unaware of these contexts of creative acts is not going to understand the literary work as the author expected it to be. There is, of course, no law requiring readers to understand what authors wanted or expected them to understand, and the appropriation of texts for current uses is as respectable an approach to literature as those that pay homage to historical, social, and political events and uses for texts. Gordimer's remark challenges us to see how the writer and the writings have been affected by history, for that is a way of trying to understand what was expected and to appreciate what was achieved in the circumstances. Historical reading, as a methodology, is a way of reaching across the communicative gulf to the Other, although reading inevitably always draws the Other in to the Self. Knowing that is the first step in resisting it.

Understanding what an author intended is, of course, never a sure thing, and that fact can be illustrated by almost any text. Take Robert Browning's "Soliloquy of the Spanish Cloister," in which the speaker is an envious monk muttering his disapproval of and hatred for his fellow monk, Brother Lawrence, who does not, at the end of meals, cross his knife and fork as a sign of reverence for Christ's death, and who dispatches his orange juice in one gulp instead of illustrating the Trinity by taking three sips. Meanwhile, the envious one disregards charity, pays lascivious attention to Sanchicha's damp hair, and plots how to make Brother Lawrence commit a fatal sin just as he dies. Critics have pointed to the angry monk's attention to ceremonial ritual, as evidence of Browning's Protestant criticism of Catholics. Can we know that is what Browning meant for us to understand? The evidence could just as

3. Nadine Gordimer, *Something Out There* (New York: Viking, 1984).

easily be pointing to Browning's disapproval of any shallow appeal to form over substance and to any angry rationalization in any religion or none. These are human failings, the counterargument says, not attributable to any particular religion. Nothing in the poem requires an anti-Catholic reading. Indeed, Brother Lawrence is a Catholic portrayed in a very good light, though seen only through the hateful speech of his angry, envious brother monk. Brother Lawrence's attention to his garden and his obliviousness to temptation provides a counterweight to the poem's angry speaker. The fact that Browning lived in Italy and is on record associating many of the things he did not like about Italian culture with Catholicism allow the first interpretation, but Browning also loved life in Italy, and this poem could just as easily support the notion that Browning distinguished between the principles of the religion and its practice in the hands of a madman.

Or, take the well-known "Ulysses" by Alfred Lord Tennyson, in which the hero of the Trojan war, having been to Hades and back, having drunk with and slept with a goddess, and braved, suffered, and enjoyed many adventures, returns to Ithaca to reclaim his wife and throne. There, he falls into a depression of inaction and despair over his uneventful, boring, settled state. To himself, he says, "I cannot rest from travel; I will drink / Life to the lees." The poem ends famously with Ulysses's words to his fellows as they launch their long boat in pursuit of the horizon:

> Tho' much is taken, much abides; and tho'
> We are not now that strength which in old days
> Moved earth and heaven; that which we are, we are;
> One equal temper of heroic hearts,
> Made weak by time and fate, but strong in will
> To strive, to seek, to find, and not to yield.[4]

We hear these lines rousingly quoted on stately occasions. But questions arise: Has Ulysses found real meaning for his life? Has he chosen adventure as life's fulfillment to be stopped by nothing short of death? Or, is he an irresponsible husband, father, and king, abandoning his duty in favor of selfish pleasure? Two lines can illustrate the problem. In them, he claims, either straightforwardly or ironically, that his son Telemachus would be a

---

4. Alfred Tennyson, "Ulysses," written in 1833; first published in 1842. Quoted from *Poems*, 3 vols. (Boston: Ticknor & Co., 1859), 2:30–32.

better king and suggests, therefore, that quitting is a virtue, as other governors have done. Read these two lines first as if Ulysses were a proud papa, fully confident of his son's capacities and of the results of his joyful embrace of life's adventure, and then again as if Ulysses were the cynical and jaded king, yoked to an "aged wife" and ruling over "a savage race, / That hoard, and sleep, and feed, and know not me." Is he leaving his kingdom in the hands of a son he believes fit to be a great king, or just one who is fit to be king over a savage ungrateful race? Does he say with glowing heart and great pride:

> This is my son, mine own Telemachus,
> To whom I leave the sceptre and the isle,—
> Well-loved of me, discerning to fulfil
> This labour, by slow prudence to make mild
> A rugged people, and thro' soft degrees
> Subdue them to the useful and the good.

Or does he say with ill-concealed disdain and sarcasm:

> This is my son, mine own Telemachus,
> To whom I leave the sceptre and the isle,—
> Well-loved of me, . . .

When Ulysses adds:

> Most blameless is he

do we hear an echo of Marc Anthony's ironic

> Brutus is an honorable man?

There is nothing in the textual history of this poem or in authorial commentary on the poem to resolve definitively what the "correct" view is.[5] Let

5. Tennyson is on record saying he wrote the poem, upon hearing of his friend Arthur Hallam's death, to express "the need of going forward, and braving the struggle," which supports the positive view more than the negative, but, as they say, that is just the author's view (quoted in *Tennyson's Poetry*, ed. Robert W. Hill Jr. [New York: W. W. Norton, 1971], 82 n. 1).

the debates resume. One point to make is that—even when different forms and editions of a work accurately reprint an unchanged text—nevertheless, literary texts are not self-identical. This is not just because two people reading the same text can understand it differently. It is also because literary works almost always have multiple forms that look and feel different from one another and have different effects on what we think of the text, even when the words on the page are the same—which is not always the case. Far more frequently than is generally assumed, the text you are reading and the one I am reading may not say the same things, though they have the same author and title. The differences might be simple textual errors easily detected and corrected, but sometimes errors produce new words, and sometimes authors, editors, and censors introduce changes deliberately.

Primary materials, however, have always been just out of reach for most teachers and students. The habit of asking "Where did this come from?" and "Can I see the original?" is not bred into us from childhood. Too often instead, "Because I say so" or "Trust me, child, I know" are the phrases that instill in us our habits of mind. The principles of investigation are contrary to these appeals to authority and trust. One becomes socialized by bowing to authority and by trusting other people, but one does not learn anything new or break any moulds whatsoever by bowing to authority or trusting others. For individual knowledge, one must ask "Where did that come from?" and "Can I see the original?" Furthermore, as A. E. Housman, in his role as textual scholar, once said, one must have a head and not a pumpkin on one's shoulders and brains, not pudding, in that head.[6]

The story goes—an apocryphal one no doubt—that the head librarian of a great monastery was so protective of his manuscripts that he would not let anyone touch the originals and made everyone use copies that he prepared. He was, of course, doing a good thing, preserving the manuscripts, but at the same time he was condemning all users to rely on his copies. One day, however, a persistent researcher weaseled past the librarian into the library's vaults. Much later, he emerged with a pale face and, when confronted by the angry librarian, said, "Father, it says celebrate, not celibate."

---

6. A. E. Housman, "The Application of Thought to Textual Criticism," *Proceedings of the Classical Association* 18 (1922): 67–84; repr. in Housman, *Selected Prose*, ed. John Carter (Cambridge: Cambridge University Press, 1961), 131–50.

A Question of Practice

Now it remains to explain how questions of social justice relate to concern over how we engage with textual or lexical works and whether or not we actively pursue the question "Where did that come from?" It is true that many typos create nonsense that can be easily detected and corrected from context, but many also produce plausible false readings, as in the so-called Wicked Bible, where the word "not" was left out of one of the ten commandments— Thou shalt commit adultery. Well, perhaps "plausible" is too strong a word in that particular case. Hold in mind the notorious instability of texts and the dexterity with which humans manage sense making despite that instability.

Universities are charged with both the training and the education of students. As trainers, we socialize students, preparing them to interact successfully in the marketplace. Students come to us for the kinds of training that will make them marketable, and we have a responsibility to provide those kinds of skills. We should be training humanities students how to fare well in the digital world, for which we start professional MA programs in digital humanities. The university is, on the other hand, primarily a place of education, which is about living and thinking and changing, and that is different from training, which is about skills, conventions, and livelihoods. Education involves learning how to ask questions, how to question the status quo, how to discover what is not yet known, how to exercise critical inquiry in areas that might prove uncomfortable. For that process to occur, one must never think that the teacher knows and the student learns. If the only things students learn is what teachers teach, then there will be no education. If we do not make education, as well as training, possible, we have failed in promoting social justice; for we will have encouraged students to know only what they are told. Not worth doing, I think.

If we encourage students to ask "Where did that come from?," we will be promoting social justice. The best way to encourage this habit is to practice it ourselves. What is that book you have in your hand? What is that you have on your screen? How does it relate to the original? Were there revised or censored versions? Which one do you have? How do you know? Does your library allow you to seek the answers? Answers to those question will stand for naught unless we also provide access to the sources.

BIBLIOGRAPHY

Aplin, John, ed. *The Correspondence and Journals of the Thackeray Family.* 5 vols. London: Pickering & Chatto, 2011.

———. *Inheritance of Genius: A Thackeray Family Biography, 1798–1875.* Cambridge: Lutterworth Press, 2011.

Arnold, Matthew. *Culture and Anarchy.* 1867–69. Edited by J. Dover Wilson. Cambridge: Cambridge University Press, 1966.

———. "The Function of Criticism at the Present Time." 1865. Reprinted in *Selected Criticism of Matthew Arnold*, edited by Christopher Ricks, 92–117. New York: New American Library, 1972.

———. "Literature and Science." 1882. Reprinted in *The Norton Anthology of English Literature*, 3rd ed., vol. 2, edited by M. H. Abrams, 1446–462. New York: W. W. Norton, 1974.

Balderston, Daniel. *How Borges Wrote.* Charlottesville: University of Virginia Press, forthcoming.

Barthes, Roland. "The 'Death' of the Author." In *The Rustle of Language* (1968), translated by Richard Howard, 49–55. New York: Hill and Wang, 1986.

Blake, William. *The Complete Poetry and Prose of William Blake.* Edited by David V. Erdman. Berkeley: University of California Press, 1982.

Bordalejo, Barbara. "The Texts We See and the Works We Imagine: The Shift of Focus of Textual Scholarship in the Digital Age." *Ecdotica* 10 (2013): 64–75.

———, ed. "Work and Document." *Ecdotica* 10 (2013): 7–93. Essays by Peter Robinson, Hans Walter Gabler, Paul Eggert, Barbara Bordalejo, and Peter Shillingsburg.

Bornstein, George. "W. E. B. Du Bois and the Jews: Ethics, Editing, and The Souls of Black Folk." *Textual Cultures* 1, no. 1 (2006): 64–74.

———. "Yeats and Textual Reincarnation: 'When You Are Old' and 'September 1913.'" In *The Iconic Page in Manuscript, Print, and Digital Culture*, edited by George Bornstein and Theresa Tinkle, 223–48. Ann Arbor: University of Michigan Press, 1998.

Bowers, Fredson. "Authorial Intention and Editorial Problems." *Text* 5 (1991): 61.

———. *Bibliography and Textual Criticism.* Oxford: Clarendon Press, 1964.

———. *Essays in Bibliography, Text and Editing*. Charlottesville: University Press of Virginia, 1975.

———. "Established Texts and Definitive Editions." *Philological Quarterly* 41 (1962): 1–17.

———. "Multiple Authority: New Problems and Concepts of Copy-Text." *Library*, 5th ser., 27 (1972): 81–115.

———. "Practical Texts and Definitive Editions." In *Two Lectures on Editing: Shakespeare and Hawthorne*, 21–70. Columbus: Ohio State University Press, 1969.

———. *The Principles of Bibliographical Description*. Princeton: Princeton University Press, 1949.

———. "The Problem of the Variant Forme in a Facsimile Edition." *Library* 7, no. 4 (1952): 262–72.

———. *Textual and Literary Criticism*. Cambridge: Cambridge University Press, 1959.

———. "Transcription of Manuscripts: The Record of Variants." *Studies in Bibliography* 29 (1976): 212–64.

———. "The Yale Folio Facsimile and Scholarship." *Modern Philology* 53 (1955): 50–57.

Boydston, JoAnn. "In Praise of Apparatus." *Text* 5 (1991): 1–13.

Bucci, Richard. "Tanselle's 'Editing Without a Copy-Text': Genesis, Issues, Prospects." *Studies in Bibliography* 56 (2003): 1–44.

Büchner, Georg. *Leonce und Lena*. Vol. 6 of *Sämtliche Werke und Schriften: Historisch-kritische Ausgabe mit Quellendokumentation und Kommentar* (Marburger Ausgabe), edited by Burghard Dedner and Thomas Michael Mayer. Darmstadt: Wissenschaftliche Buchgesellschaft, 2003.

———. *Sämtliche Werke und Schriften: Historisch-kritische Ausgabe mit Quellendokumentation und Kommentar* (Marburger Ausgabe). Edited by Burghard Dedner and Thomas Michael Mayer. 10 vols. in 18 Teilbdn. Darmstadt: Wissenschaftliche Buchgesellschaft, 2000–2013.

Buzzetti, Dino. "Digital Representation and the Text Model." *New Literary History* 33 (2002): 61–88.

Caldwell, T. Price. "The Epistemologies of Linguistic Science: Reassessing Structuralism, Redefining the Sememe." *Meisei Review* 21 (2006): 27–39.

———. "The Molecular Sememe: A Model for Literary Interpretation." *Meisei Review* 15 (2000): 155–62.

———. "Molecular Sememics: A Progress Report." *Meisei Review* 4 (1989): 65–86.

———. "Topic-Comment Effects in English." *Meisei Review* 17 (2002): 49–69.

———. "Whorf, Orwell, and Mentalese." *Meisei Review* 19 (2004): 91–106.

Center for Editions of American Authors (CEAA). *Professional Standards and American Editions*. New York: MLA, 1969. Pamphlet.

Chaudhuri, Sukanta. *Bichitra: The Making of the Online Tagore Variorum*. Cham, Switzerland: Springer, 2015.

———. *The Metaphysics of Text*. Cambridge: Cambridge University Press, 2010.

Clare, John. *Poems of the Middle Period, 1822–1837*. Edited by Eric Robinson et al. Oxford: Clarendon Press, 1996.

Coetzee, J. M. *Elizabeth Costello*. London: Secker and Warburg, 2003.

———. *Elizabeth Costello*. New York: Viking, 2003.

———. *Elizabeth Costello*. London: Vintage, 2004.

———. "The Humanities in Africa." In *The Best Australian Stories 2002*, edited by Peter Craven, 101–99. Melbourne: Black, 2002.

———. "The Humanities in Africa." In *Resistance and Reconciliation: Writing in the Commonwealth*, edited by Bruce Bennett et al., 16–28. Canberra: ACLALS, 2003.

Coetzee, John M. [*sic*]. *The Humanities in Africa / Die Geisteswissenschaften in Afrika*. Munich: Carl Friedrich von Siemens Stiftung, 2001.

Collins, Thomas J. Review of the Ohio University Press Browning edition. *Victorian Studies* 13 (June 1970): 441–44.

Dedner, Burghard. "Editing Fragments as Fragments." *Text* 16 (2004): 97–111.

———. "The Editing Machine: Components, Tools and Goals." Conference Paper, Tokyo, March 2015.

Deppman, Jed, Daniel Ferrer, and Michael Groden, eds. *Genetic Criticism: Texts and Avant-Textes*. Philadelphia: University of Pennsylvania Press, 2004.

Dreiser, Theodore. *Sister Carrie*. The Pennsylvania Edition. Edited by Neda M. Westlake, James L. W. West, John C. Berkey, and Alice M. Winters. Philadelphia: University of Pennsylvania Press, 1981.

Eggert, Paul. "Autorität des Textes oder Autorisation: Die postkoloniale Adaptation herkömmlicher Editionsverfahren für *Robbery Under Arms*." *editio*, special issue, XXI (2004): 315–24.

———. *Biography of a Book: Henry Lawson's "While the Billy Boils."* University Park: Penn State University Press, 2013.

———. "Canonical Works, Complicity and Bibliography: A Case-Study." *Variants* 1 (2002): 159–73.

———. "Document and Text: The 'Life' of the Literary Work and the Capacities of Editing." *Text* 7 (1994): 1–24.

———. "Document or Process as the Site of Authority: Establishing Chronology of Revisions in Competing Typescripts of Lawrence's *The Boy in the Bush*." *Studies in Bibliography* 44 (1991): 364–76.

———. "The Editorial Position: Some Reflections on Editorial Orientations in Charlottesville, Cambridge and Canberra." *editio* 14 (2000): 104–16.

———. "General-Editing and Theory: Historical Version and Authorial Agency." In "Problems of Editing," special issue, *editio* 14 (1999): 42–58.

———. "The Importance of Scholarly Editing and the Question of Standards." In *Perspectives of Scholarly Editing*, edited by H. T. M. van Vliet and Bodo Plachta, 15–28. The Hague: Constantin Huyghens Institut, 2002.

———. "The Literary Work of a Readership: *The Boy in the Bush* in Australia, 1924–1926." *Bibliographical Society of Australia and New Zealand Bulletin* 12 (1988): 149–66.

———. "Recent Editorial Theory in the Anglophone World." *Anglia* 119 (2001): 351–74.

———. "Social Discourse or Authorial Agency? Bridging the Divide Between Editing and Theory." In *The Editorial Gaze*, edited by Paul Eggert and Margaret Sankey, 97–116. New York: Garland Publishing, 1998.

———. "Text as Algorithm and Process." In *Text and Genre in Reconstruction: Effects of Digitalization on*

Ideas, Behaviours, Products and Institutions, edited by Willard McCarty, 183–202. Cambridge: OpenBook, 2010.

———. "Textual Product or Textual Process: Procedures and Assumptions of Critical Editing." In *Editing in Australia,* edited by Paul Eggert, 19–40. Sydney: University of New South Wales Press, 1990. Reprinted in *Devils and Angels: Textual Editing and Literary Theory,* edited by Philip Cohen, 124–33. Charlottesville: University Press of Virginia, 1991.

———. "Version—Agency—Intention: The Cross-Fertilising of German and Anglo-American Editorial Tradition." *Variants* 4 (2005): 5–28.

———. "Version vs Documents: The Case of Joseph Conrad's *Under Western Eyes.*" In *Varianten— Variants—Variantes,* edited by Christa Jansohn and Bodo Plachta, 201–12. Tübingen: Max Niemeyer, 2005.

———. "Writing in a Language Not Your Own: Editions as Arguments About the Work—D. H. Lawrence, Joseph Conrad and Henry Lawson." *Variants* 9 (2012): 163–84.

Eggert, Paul, and Peter Shillingsburg, with Kevin Caliendo, eds. *Anglo-American Scholarly Editing, 1980–2005.* Special issue, *Ecdotica* 6 (2009).

Eisenstein, Elizabeth. *The Printing Press as an Agent of Change: Communications and Cultural Transformations in Early Modern Europe.* 2 vols. Cambridge: Cambridge University Press, 1979.

Eliot, George. *Middlemarch.* 1871–72. Edited by Bert G. Hornback. New York: W. W. Norton, 1977.

———. *Middlemarch.* 1871–72. Edited by David Carroll. Oxford: Clarendon Press, 1986.

Elliott, J. Keith. "Reflections on the Method: What Constitutes the Use of the Writings that Later Formed the New Testament in the Apostolic Fathers?" In *The Reception of the New Testament in the Apostolic Fathers,* edited by Andrew Gregory and Christopher M. Tuckett, 47–58. Oxford: Oxford University Press, 2005.

Erdman, David V., ed. *The Complete Poetry and Prose of William Blake.* Berkeley: University of California Press, 1982.

Ferguson, John Alexander. *Bibliography of Australia.* Sydney: Angus and Robertson, 1941–69.

Fielding, Henry. *Tom Jones.* Edited by Sheridan Baker. New York: W. W. Norton, 1973.

———. *Tom Jones.* Edited by Fredson Bowers. Oxford: Clarendon Press, 1974.

———. *Tom Jones.* Edited by Fredson Bowers. Middletown, Conn.: Wesleyan University Press, 1985.

Fish, Stanley. *Is There a Text in This Class? The Authority of Interpretive Communities.* Cambridge, Mass.: Harvard University Press, 1980.

Flanery, Patrick Denman. "(Re-)Marking Coetzee and Costello: The (Textual) *Lives of Animals.*" *English Studies in Africa* 47, no. 1 (2004): 61–84.

Foucault, Michel. "What Is an Author?" 1969. Translated by Josué Harari. In *The Critical Tradition,* edited by David H. Richter, 978–88. New York: St. Martin's Press, 1989.

Fowles, John. *The Magus.* Boston: Little, Brown, 1965.

———. *The Magus*. London: Jonathan Cape, 1966.

———. *The Magus*. Rev. ed. London: Jonathan Cape, 1977.

———. *The Magus*. Rev. ed. Boston: Little, Brown, 1978.

Frankel, Nicholas. *Oscar Wilde's Decorated Books*. Ann Arbor: University of Michigan Press, 2000.

Gabler, Hans Walter. "Editing Text—Editing Work." *Ecdotica* 10 (2013): 42–50.

———. "Joyce's Text in Progress." *Texte: Revue de Critique et de Théorie Littéraire* 7 (1988): 227–47.

———. "On Textual Criticism and Editing: The Case of Joyce's *Ulysses*." In *Palimpsest: Editorial Theory in the Humanities*, edited by George Bornstein and Ralph Williams, 195–224. Ann Arbor: University of Michigan Press, 1993.

———. "The Primacy of the Document in Editing." *Ecdotica* 4 (2007): 194–207.

———. "The Text as Process and the Problem of Intentionality." *Text* 3 (1987): 107–16.

———. "Textual Studies and Criticism." In *Editing in Australia*, edited by Paul Eggert, 1–17. Kensington: University of New South Wales Press, 1990.

———. "Unsought Encounters." In *Devils and Angels: Textual Editing and Literary Theory*, edited by Philip Cohen, 153–66. Charlottesville: University Press of Virginia, 1991.

Gabler, Hans Walter, George Bornstein, and Gillian Borland Pierce, eds. *Contemporary German Editorial Theory*. Ann Arbor: University of Michigan Press, 1995.

Gilbert, Penny. "Automatic Collation: A Technique for Medieval Texts." *Computers and the Humanities* 7 (1973): 139–47.

Gopnik, Alison. "How We Know Our Minds: The Illusion of First-Person Knowledge of Intentionality." *Behavioral and Brain Sciences* 16, no. 1 (1993): 1–14.

Gordimer, Nadine. *Something Out There*. New York: Viking, 1984.

Gottesman, Ronald, and Scott Bennett, eds. *Art and Error: Modern Textual Editing*. Bloomington: Indiana University Press, 1970. Reprinted by Oak Knoll Press. http://www.oakknoll.com/pages/books/61707/ronald-gottesman-scott-bennett/art-and-error-modern-textual-editing.

Greetham, D. C. "A Suspicion of Texts." *Thesis: The Magazine of the Graduate School and University Center* 2, no. 1 (1987): 18–25.

———. "[Textual] Criticism and Deconstruction." *Studies in Bibliography* 44 (1991): 1–30.

———. *Theories of the Text*. London: Oxford University Press, 1999.

———. "'"'"What Does It Matter Who Is Speaking," Someone Said, "What Does It Matter Who Is Speaking"?'"' (Greetham Version), or "'What Does It Matter Who Is Speaking?': Editorial Recuperation of the Estranged Author' (Eggert Version)." In *The Editorial Gaze*, edited by Paul Eggert and Margaret Sankey, 67–96. New York: Garland Publishing, 1998.

Greg, W. W. *A Calculus of Variants: An Essay on Textual Criticism*. Oxford: Clarendon Press, 1927.

———. "The Rationale of Copy-Text." *Studies in Bibliography* 3 (1950–51): 19–36.

Hancher, Michael. Review of the Ohio University Press Browning edition. *Yearbook of English Studies* 2 (1972): 312–14.

Harden, Edgar F. *A Checklist of Contributions by William Makepeace Thackeray to Newspapers, Periodicals, Books, and Serial Part Issues, 1828–1864.* Victoria: University of Victoria University Press, 1996.

———, ed. *The Letters and Private Papers of William Makepeace Thackeray: A Supplement.* 2 vols. New York: Garland Publishing, 1994.

Hardy, Thomas. *Tess of the d'Urbervilles.* Edited by Judith Grindle and Simon Gatrell. Oxford: Oxford University Press, 1983.

Hill, Speed. Review of *New Directions in Textual Studies. Text* 6 (1994): 370–81.

Hoover, David. "The End of the Irrelevant Text: Electronic Texts, Linguistics, and Literary Theory." *Digital Humanities Quarterly* 1, no. 2 (2007): n.p.

Housman, A. E. "The Application of Thought to Textual Criticism." *Proceedings of the Classical Association* 18 (1922): 67–84. Reprinted in Housman, *Selected Prose,* edited by John Carter, 131–50. Cambridge: Cambridge University Press, 1961.

———. "Introductory Lecture." In Housman, *Selected Prose,* edited by John Carter, 1–22. Cambridge: Cambridge University Press, 1961.

Howard-Hill, T. H. "Theory and Praxis in the Social Approach to Editing." *Text* 5 (1991): 31–48.

Hussey, Mark, and Peter Shillingsburg. "The Composition, Revision, Printing and Publications of *To the Lighthouse*." Woolf Online. http://www.woolfonline.com/?node=content/contextual/transcriptions&project=1&parent=45&taxa=47&content=6955&pos=3.

Iser, Wolfgang. *The Implied Reader: Patterns of Communication in Prose Fiction from Bunyan to Beckett.* Baltimore: Johns Hopkins University Press, 1974.

Jefferson, Thomas. *The Writings of Thomas Jefferson.* Memorial Edition. Edited by Andrew A. Lipscomb and Albert Allery Bergh. 20 vols. Washington, D.C.: The Thomas Jefferson Memorial Association, 1903–4.

Johnson, Samuel. "On the Character and Duty of an Academic." In David Fairer, "J. D. Fleeman: A Memoir." *Studies in Bibliography* 48 (1995): 1–24. http://etext.virginia.edu/bsuva/sb/.

Joyce, James. *Ulysses.* Edited by Hans Walter Gabler, Wolfhard Steppe, and Claus Melchior. With a preface by Richard Ellmann. New York: Random House, 1986.

Keats, John. *John Keats: Complete Poems.* Edited by Jack Stillinger. Cambridge, Mass.: Harvard Belknap Press, 1982.

Lawson, Henry. *"While the Billy Boils": The Original Newspaper Versions.* Edited by Paul Eggert. Explanatory notes by Elizabeth Webby. Sydney: Sydney University Press, 2013.

Luey, Beth. *Editing Documents and Texts: An Annotated Bibliography.* Madison: Madison House, 1999.

Martens, Gunter. "(De)Constructing Texts by Editing: Reflections on the Receptional Significance of Textual Apparatuses." 1975. Translated in *Contemporary German Editorial Theory,* edited by Hans Walter Gabler, George Bornstein, and Gillian Borland Pierce, 125–52. Ann Arbor: University of Michigan Press, 1995.

———. "What Is a Text? Attempts at Defining a Central Concept in Editorial Theory." In *Contemporary German Editorial Theory*, edited by Hans Walter Gabler, George Bornstein, and Gillian Borland Pierce, 209–31. Ann Arbor: University of Michigan Press, 1995.

Matthiessen, F. O. *American Renaissance*. New York: Oxford University Press, 1941.

McCarty, Willard. *Humanities Computing*. London: Palgrave Macmillan, 2005.

———, ed. *Text and Genre in Reconstruction: Effects of Digitalization on Ideas, Behaviours, Products and Institutions*. Cambridge: Open-Book Publishers, 2010.

McGann, Jerome J. *A Critique of Modern Textual Criticism*. Chicago: University of Chicago Press, 1983.

———. "From Text to Work: Digital Tools and the Emergence of the Social Text." *Variants* 4 (2005): 225–40.

———. "Literary History and Editorial Method." *New Literary History: A Journal of Theory and Interpretation* 40 (2009): 825–42.

———, ed. *Lord Byron: The Complete Poetical Works*. 7 vols. Oxford: Clarendon Press, 1980–93.

———. *The Textual Condition*. Princeton: Princeton University Press, 1991.

———. "Theory of Texts." *London Review* 18 (February 1988): 20–21.

———. "*Ulysses* as a Postmodernist Text: The Gabler Edition." *Criticism* 27 (Summer 1985): 283–305.

McKenzie, D. F. *Bibliography and the Sociology of Texts*. Panizzi Lectures, 1985. London: British Library, 1986.

———. "'What's Past Is Prologue': The Bibliographical Society and History of the Book." 1993.

Reprinted in *Making Meaning: "Printers of the Mind" and Other Essays*, edited by Peter D. McDonald and Michael F. Suarez, S.J., 259–75. Amherst: University of Massachusetts Press, 2002.

———, ed. *The Works of William Congreve*. 3 vols. Oxford: Oxford University Press, 2011.

McKerrow, R. B. *An Introduction to Bibliography for Students of Literature*. Oxford: Oxford University Press, 1927.

Melville, Herman. *White Jacket*. New York: Harper and Brothers, 1850.

———. *White Jacket*. London: Constable, 1922.

Melville, Lewis [pseud. of Lewis Saul Benjamin]. *William Makepeace Thackeray: A Biography Including Hitherto Uncollected Letters and Speeches and a Bibliography of 1,300 Items*. 2 vols. London: John Lane, 1910.

Meredith, George. *The Ordeal of Richard Feverel*. Introduction by Lionel Stevenson. New York: Random House, 1950.

———. *The Ordeal of Richard Feverel*. New York: Dover Publications, 1983.

Monod, Sylvère. "Between Two Worlds: Editing Dickens." In *Editing Nineteenth-Century Texts*, edited by Jane Millgate, 17–31. New York: Garland Publishing, 1978.

Neville, Sarah. "*Nihil biblicum a me alienum puto*: W. W. Greg, Bibliography, and the Sociology of Texts." *Variants* 11 (2014): 91–112.

Newman, John Henry. "The Idea of a University." 1852. Excerpts reprinted in *The Norton Anthology of English Literature*, 3rd ed., vol. 2, edited by M. H. Abrams, 1564–71. New York: W. W. Norton, 1974.

Nichol, John W. "Melville's 'Soiled' Fish of the Sea." *American Literature* 21 (November 1949): 338–39.

Nowell-Smith, Simon. "T. J. Wise as Bibliographer." *The Library*, 5th ser., 24, no. 2 (1969): 129–41.

Parker, Hershel. *Flawed Texts and Verbal Icons*. Evanston: Northwestern University Press, 1984.

———. Review of the Kent State University Press edition of Charles Brockden Brown's *Wieland*. *The Eighteenth Century: A Critical Bibliography*, n.s., 3 (1981): 177–79.

Peckham, Morse. "Thoughts on Editing *Sordello*." *Studies in Browning and His Circle* 5 (1977): 11–18.

Peckham, Morse, with David R. King. "The Editing of 19th-Century Texts." In *Language and Texts: The Nature of Linguistic Evidence*, edited by Herbert H. Paper, Gerald E. Else, Judith Goldin, and Albert H. Marchwardt, 123–46. Ann Arbor: Center for Coordination of Ancient and Modern Texts, University of Michigan, 1975.

Pettigrew, John. [Response to reviews of the Browning edition.] *Essays in Criticism* 22 (1972): 436–41.

Petty, George R., Jr., and William M. Gibson. *Project OCCULT: The Ordered Computer Collation of Unprepared Literary Text*. New York: New York University Press, 1970.

Pinker, Steven. *The Language Instinct*. New York: William Morrow & Co., 1994. The Penguin edition is available online at http://cirp-students.com/Research%20 Library/assets/the-language-instinct.pdf.

Plachta, Bodo. "In Between the 'Royal Way' of Philology and 'Occult Science': Some Remarks About German Discussion on Text Constitution in the Last Ten Years." *Text* 12 (1999): 31–47.

———. "Teaching Editing—Learning Editing." In *Problems of Editing*, biehefte zu *editio*, edited by Christa Jansohn, 18–32. Tübingen: Max Niemeyer, 1999.

"Practical Editions." Series edited by Joseph Katz. *Proof* 1–3 (1970–73).

Price, Kenneth. "Edition, Project, Database, Archive, Thematic Research Collection: What's in a Name?" *Digital Humanities Quarterly* 3, no. 3 (2009): http://www.digitalhumanities.org/dhq/vol/3/3/000053/000053.html.

Ray, Gordon N. *The Buried Life: A Study of the Relation Between Thackeray's Fiction and His Personal History*. London: Royal Society of Literature, 1952.

———. "The Importance of Original Editions." In *Nineteenth-Century English Books: Some Problems in Bibliography*, edited by Gordon Ray, Carl J. Weber, and John Carter, 1–24. Urbana: University of Illinois Press, 1952.

———. *The Letters and Private Papers of William Makepeace Thackeray*. 4 vols. Cambridge, Mass.: Harvard University Press, 1944.

———. *Thackeray: The Uses of Adversity*. New York: McGraw-Hill, 1955.

Reiman, Donald. "'Versioning': The Presentation of Multiple Texts." In *Romantic Texts and Contexts*, 167–80. Columbia: University of Missouri Press, 1987.

Reimer, Andrew. "Elizabeth Costello." *Sydney Morning Herald*. September 13, 2003. http://www.smh.com.au/articles/2003/09/12/1063341766203.html.

Robertson, Grant. "Comma Quirk Irks Rogers." *Globe and Mail*, August 6, 2006. http://www.theglo

beandmail.com/report-on-business/comma-quirk-irks-rogers/article1101686/.

Robinson, Peter. "Textual Communities." http://www.textualcommuni ties.usask.ca/.

Scheibe, Siegfried. "Theoretical Problems of Authorization and Constitutions of Texts." 1990–91. Translated in *Contemporary German Editorial Theory*, ed. Hans Walter Gabler, George Bornstein, and Gillian Borland Pierce, 171–91. Ann Arbor: University of Michigan Press, 1995.

Schulze, Robin, ed. *Becoming Marianne Moore: The Early Poems, 1907–1924*. Berkeley: University of California Press, 2002.

Shillingsburg, Peter. "Anglo-amerikanische Editionswissenschaft: Ein knapper Überblick." In *Text und Edition: Positionen und Perspektiven*, edited by Rüdiger Nutt-Kofoth, Bodo Plachta, H. T. M. van Vliet, and Hermann Zwerchina, 143–63. Berlin: Erich Schmidt, 2000.

———."Authority and Authorization in American Editing." In *Autor—Autorisation—Authentizität*, edited by Thomas Bein, Rüdiger Nutt-Kofoth, and Bodo Plachta, 73–81. Special issue of *editio*. Tübingen: Max Niemeyer, 2004.

———. "Editing Thackeray: A History." *Studies in the Novel* 27 (Fall 1995): 363–74.

———. *From Gutenberg to Google: Electronic Representations of Literary Texts*. Cambridge: Cambridge University Press, 2006.

———. "Hagiolatry, Cultural Engineering, Monument Building, and Other Functions of Scholarly Editing." In *Voice, Text, Hypertext: Emerging Practices in Textual Studies*, edited by

Raimonda Modiano, Leroy F. Searle, and Peter Shillingsburg, 412–23. Seattle: University of Washington Press, 2004. Reprinted in *From Gutenberg to Google*, 161–72.

———. "On Being Textually Aware." *Studies in American Naturalism* 1 (Summer and Winter 2006): 170–95.

———. "Orientations to Texts." *editio* 15 (2001): 1–16.

———. *Pegasus in Harness: Victorian Publishing and W. M. Thackeray*. Charlottesville: University of Virginia Press, 1992.

———. "Publications of Coetzee's 'The Humanities in Africa.'" *Script and Print* 28, no. 4 (2004): 105–12.

———. "A Resistance to Contemporary German Editorial Theory and Practice." *editio* 12 (1998): 138–50.

———. *Resisting Texts: Authority and Submission in Constructions of Meaning*. Ann Arbor: University of Michigan Press, 1997.

———. Review of George Eliot, *The Mill on the Floss*, edited by Gordon S. Haight. *Journal of English and Germanic Philology* 80 (1981): 590–92.

———. Review of Henry Kingsley, *The Recollections of Geoffrey Hamlyn*, edited by Stanton Mellick, Patrick Morgan, and Paul Eggert; Henry Handel Richardson, *Maurice Guest*, edited by Clive Probyn and Bruce Steele; *The Journal of Annie Baxter Dawbin 1858–1868*, edited by Lucy Frost; N. Walter Swan, *Luke Mivers' Harvest*, edited by Harry Heseltine; Catherine Martin, *The Silent Sea*, edited by Rosemary Foxton; and Ernest Favenc, *Tales of the Austral Tropics*, edited by Cheryl Taylor. *Text* 12 (1999): 264–73.

———. Review of Rolf Boldrewood, *Robbery Under Arms*, edited by Paul Eggert. *Script and Print* 31, no. 2 (2007): 118–22.

———. *Scholarly Editing in the Computer Age: Theory and Practice*. 3rd edition. Ann Arbor: University of Michigan Press, 1996.

———. "Textual Criticism, the Humanities, and J. Coetzee." *English Studies in Africa* 49 (2006): 13–27.

———. "Textual Variants, Performance Variants, and the Concept of Work." *Bulletin of the Bibliographical Society of Australia and New Zealand* 15 (1991): 60–71. Reprinted in *editio* 7 (1993): 221–34.

———. "The Three *Moby-Dicks*." *American Literary History* 2 (Spring 1990): 119–30.

———. *William Makepeace Thackeray: A Literary Life*. London: Palgrave, 2001.

Siemens, Ray. "Text Analysis and the Dynamic Edition? A Working Paper, Briefly Articulating Some Concerns with an Algorithmic Approach to the Electronic Scholarly Edition." *Text Technology* 14 (2005): 91–98. Also available at http://texttechnology.mcmaster.ca/pdf/vol14_1_09.pdf.

Stillinger, Jack, ed. *John Keats: Complete Poems*. Cambridge, Mass.: Harvard Belknap Press, 1982.

———. *Multiple Authorship and the Myth of Solitary Genius*. New York: Oxford University Press, 1991.

Subačius, Paulius. "Canonisation as Impediment to Textual Scholarship: Lithuanian Postcolonial Experiences." *Variants* 7 (2008): 23–35.

———. "The Problem of Polytext." *Literatûra* 49, no. 5 (2007): 133–37.

Svaglic, M. J. "The Revision of Newman's *Apologia*." *Modern Philology* 50, no. 1 (1952): 43–49.

Tanselle, G. Thomas. "The Editing of Historical Documents." *Studies in Bibliography* 31 (1978): 1–56.

———. "Editing Without a Copy-Text." *Studies in Bibliography* 47 (1994): 1–22. Reprinted in *Literature and Artifacts*, 236–57.

———. "The Editorial Problem of Final Authorial Intention." *Studies in Bibliography* 29 (1976): 167–211. Reprinted in G. Thomas Tanselle, *Selected Studies in Bibliography*, 309–53. Charlottesville: University Press of Virginia, 1979.

———. "Greg's Theory of Copy-Text and the Editing of American Literature." *Studies in Bibliography* 28 (1975): 167–229. Reprinted in *Selected Studies in Bibliography*, 245–307. Charlottesville: University Press of Virginia, 1979.

———. *Literature and Artifacts*. Charlottesville: Bibliographical Society of the University of Virginia, 1998.

———. "Part 5: Some Noteworthy Reviews of Scholarly Editions." Introduction to Scholarly Editing: Seminar Syllabus. Columbia University, 2002. http://www.rarebookschool.org/tanselle/syl-E-complete.090302.pdf.

———. "Reproductions and Scholarship." *Studies in Bibliography* 42 (1989): 25–54.

———. "Textual Criticism and Deconstruction." *Studies in Bibliography* 43 (1990): 1–33.

Tennyson, Alfred. *Poems*. 3 vols. Boston: Ticknor & Co., 1859.

———. *Tennyson's Poetry*. Edited by Robert W. Hill Jr. New York: W. W. Norton, 1971.

Thackeray, W. M. *The History of Henry Esmond*. Manuscript at the Trinity College Library. Cambridge, UK.

———. *The History of Henry Esmond*. Edited by Edgar Harden. New York: Garland Publishing, 1989.

———. *The History of Pendennis*. London: Bradbury and Evans, 1848–50.

———. *The History of Samuel Titmarsh and the Great Hoggarty Diamond*. London: Bradbury and Evans, 1849. New edition, 1849; reissued 1852 and 1857; reissued by Smith, Elder, and Company, n.d. (between 1864 and 1872).

———. *Letters and Private Papers of William Makepeace Thackeray*. 4 vols. Edited by Gordon Ray. Cambridge, Mass.: Harvard University Press, 1945.

———. *The Letters and Private Papers of William Makepeace Thackeray: A Supplement*. 2 vols. Edited by Edgar F. Harden. New York: Garland Publishing, 1994.

———. *The Newcomes*. Manuscript at the Charterhouse School, Godalming, England.

———. *The Newcomes*. London: Bradbury and Evans, 1847–48. Published serially; reissued in two-volume form, 1848; revised in one volume 1853.

———. *The Newcomes*. Edited by Peter Shillingsburg. Ann Arbor: University of Michigan Press, 1996.

———. *Vanity Fair*. Manuscript at the Pierpont Morgan Library, New York, N.Y.

———. *Vanity Fair*. Edited by George Saintsbury. London: Oxford University Press, 1908.

———. *Vanity Fair*. Edited by Peter Shillingsburg and R. D. McMaster. New York: Garland Publishing, 1989.

———. *Vanity Fair*. Edited by Peter Shillingsburg. New York: W. W. Norton, 1993.

Thoreau, H. D. "Economy." In *Walden Pond* (1854), edited by J. Lyndon Shanley, 3–79. Princeton: Princeton University Press, 1971.

Thorpe, James. "The Aesthetics of Textual Criticism." *PMLA* 80 (1965). Reprinted in *Principles of Textual Criticism*, 3–49. San Marino: Huntington Library, 1972.

———. *Watching the Ps & Qs: Editorial Treatment of Accidentals*. Library Series 38. Lawrence: University of Kansas Libraries, 1971.

Trollope, Anthony. *Thackeray*. London: Macmillan, 1879.

Vanhoutte, Edward. "Traditional Editorial Standards and the Digital Edition." In *Learned Love: Proceedings of the Emblem Project Utrecht Conference on Dutch Love Emblems and the Internet, November 2006*, 157–74. DANS Symposium Publications 1. The Hague: DANS, 2007.

Van Hulle, Dirk. "Compositional Variants in Modern Manuscripts." In *Digital Technology and Philological Disciplines*, edited by A. Bozzi, L. Cignoni, and J.-L. Lebrave, 513–27. Pisa and Rome: Istituti editoriali e poligrafici internazionali, 2004.

———. *Textual Awareness: A Genetic Study of Late Manuscripts by Joyce, Proust, and Mann*. Ann Arbor: University of Michigan Press, 2004.

Van Hulle, Dirk, and Peter Shillingsburg. "Orientations to Text, Revisited." *Studies in Bibliography* 59 (2015): 27–44.

Whitman, Walt. *The Original 1855 Edition of Leaves of Grass*. Edited by A.

S. Ash. Santa Barbara, Calif.: Bandanna Books, 1992.

Wimsatt, W. K., and Monroe Beardsley. "The Intentional Fallacy." *Sewanee Review* 54 (1946): 468–88. Reprinted in W. K. Wimsatt, *The Verbal Icon: Studies in the Meaning of Poetry*, 3–20. Lexington: University of Kentucky Press, 1954.

Woolf, Virginia. *To the Lighthouse*. London: Hogarth Press, 1927.

———. *To the Lighthouse*. New York: Harcourt Brace, 1927.

Yeats, William Butler. "September 1913." *Irish Times*, September 8, 1913.

Zeller, Hans. "A New Approach to the Critical Constitution of Literary Texts." *Studies in Bibliography* 28 (1975): 231–64.

———. "Record and Interpretation: Analysis and Documentation as Goal and Method of Editing." In *Contemporary German Editorial Theory*, edited by Hans Walter Gabler, George Bornstein, and Gillian Borland Pierce, 17–58. Ann Arbor: University of Michigan Press, 1995.

———. "Structure and Genesis in Editing: On German and Anglo-American Textual Criticism." In *Contemporary German Editorial Theory*, edited by Hans Walter Gabler, George Bornstein, and Gillian Borland Pierce, 95–123. Ann Arbor: University of Michigan Press, 1995.

INDEX

PREVIOUSLY PUBLISHED TITLES IN THE PENN STATE SERIES IN THE HISTORY OF THE BOOK

Peter Burke, *The Fortunes of the "Courtier": The European Reception of Castiglione's "Cortegiano"* (1996)

Roger Burlingame, *Of Making Many Books: A Hundred Years of Reading, Writing, and Publishing* (1996)

James M. Hutchisson, *The Rise of Sinclair Lewis, 1920–1930* (1996)

Julie Bates Dock, ed., *Charlotte Perkins Gilman's "The Yellow Wall-paper" and the History of Its Publication and Reception: A Critical Edition and Documentary Casebook* (1998)

John Williams, ed., *Imaging the Early Medieval Bible* (1998)

Ezra Greenspan, *George Palmer Putnam: Representative American Publisher* (2000)

James G. Nelson, *Publisher to the Decadents: Leonard Smithers in the Careers of Beardsley, Wilde, Dowson* (2000)

Pamela E. Selwyn, *Everyday Life in the German Book Trade: Friedrich Nicolai as Bookseller and Publisher in the Age of Enlightenment* (2000)

David R. Johnson, *Conrad Richter: A Writer's Life* (2001)

David Finkelstein, *The House of Blackwood: Author-Publisher Relations in the Victorian Era* (2002)

Rodger L. Tarr, ed., *As Ever Yours: The Letters of Max Perkins and Elizabeth Lemmon* (2003)

Randy Robertson, *Censorship and Conflict in Seventeenth-Century England: The Subtle Art of Division* (2009)

Catherine M. Parisian, ed., *The First White House Library: A History and Annotated Catalogue* (2010)

Jane McLeod, *Licensing Loyalty: Printers, Patrons, and the State in Early Modern France* (2011)

Charles Walton, ed., *Into Print: Limits and Legacies of the Enlightenment, Essays in Honor of Robert Darnton* (2011)

James L. W. West III, *Making the Archives Talk: New and Selected Essays in Bibliography, Editing, and Book History* (2012)

John Hruschka, *How Books Came to America: The Rise of the American Book Trade* (2012)

A. Franklin Parks, *William Parks: The Colonial Printer in the Transatlantic World of the Eighteenth Century* (2012)

Roger E. Stoddard, comp., and David R. Whitesell, ed., *A Bibliographic Description of Books and Pamphlets of American Verse Printed from 1610 Through 1820* (2012)

Nancy Cervetti, *S. Weir Mitchell: Philadelphia's Literary Physician* (2012)

Karen Nipps, *Lydia Bailey: A Checklist of Her Imprints* (2013)

Paul Eggert, *Biography of a Book: Henry Lawson's "While the Billy Boils"* (2013)

Allan Westphall, *Books and Religious Devotion: The Redemptive Reading of an Irishman in Nineteenth-Century New England* (2014)

Scott Donaldson, *The Impossible Craft: Literary Biography* (2015)

John Bidwell, *Graphic Passion: Matisse and the Book Arts* (2015)